Farewell to the South

Books by Robert Coles

CHILDREN OF CRISIS I: A STUDY OF COURAGE AND FEAR

STILL HUNGRY IN AMERICA

THE IMAGE IS YOU

UPROOTED CHILDREN

WAGES OF NEGLECT
(With Maria Piers)

DRUGS AND YOUTH
(With Joseph Brenner and Dermot Meagher)

ERIK H. ERIKSON:
THE GROWTH OF HIS WORK

THE MIDDLE AMERICANS
(with Jon Erikson)

THE GEOGRAPHY OF FAITH
(with Daniel Berrigan)

MIGRANTS, SHARECROPPERS, MOUNTAINEERS
(Volume II of *Children of Crisis*)

THE SOUTH GOES NORTH
(Volume III of *Children of Crisis*)

FAREWELL TO THE SOUTH

For Children

DEAD END SCHOOL

THE GRASS PIPE

SAVING FACE

Farewell to the South

Robert Coles

An Atlantic Monthly Press Book
Little, Brown and Company
Boston · Toronto

FIRST EDITION

T08/72

Library of Congress Cataloging in Publication Data

Coles, Robert.
    Farewell to the South.

    "An Atlantic Monthly Press book."
    1. Southern States--Addresses, essays, lectures.
    2. Southern States--Race question--Addresses, essays,
    lectures. 3. Discrimination in education--Southern
    States--Addresses, essays, lectures. I. Title.
    F216.2.C58   917.5'03'4   72-638
    ISBN 0-316-15158-0

"The Words and Music of Social Change" and "The Weather of the Years" reprinted by permission of DAEDALUS, Journal of the American Academy of Arts and Sciences, Boston, Mass. (Summer 1969) *The Future of the Humanities,* and (Fall 1971) *Twelve to Sixteen: Early Adolescence.*

"Serpents and Doves" comes from *Youth: Change and Challenge,* edited by Erik H. Erikson, © 1963 by the American Academy of Arts and Sciences, Basic Books, Inc., Publishers, New York.

"Social Struggle and Weariness" reprinted by special permission from *Psychiatry* (1964) 27:305-315. © 1970 by The William Alanson White Psychiatric Foundation, Inc.

"A Psychiatrist Joins 'The Movement'" © January–February, 1966 by Transaction, Inc., New Brunswick, New Jersey.

"The Empty Road," "A Farewell to the Old South" and "To Try Men's Souls" originally appeared in *The New Yorker.*

ATLANTIC—LITTLE, BROWN BOOKS
ARE PUBLISHED BY
LITTLE, BROWN AND COMPANY
IN ASSOCIATION WITH
THE ATLANTIC MONTHLY PRESS

*Published simultaneously in Canada
by Little, Brown & Company (Canada) Limited*

PRINTED IN THE UNITED STATES OF AMERICA

To Jane

Contents

Farewell
to the
South

Introduction

By the time this book appears I will have known certain white and black Southerners almost fifteen years. I began living in the South because I was sent there by the United States Air Force. From 1958 to 1960 I was given charge of an Air Force psychiatric service at Keesler Air Force Base, which stands right near downtown Biloxi, Mississippi. In the first chapter of the first volume of *Children of Crisis: A Study of Courage and Fear* I have described what happened to me while I lived there along the Gulf Coast; my whole life changed — and I began to visit with families. They were, and are, black families and white families; and they have been caught up in the momentum of this nation's growth, its struggle to realize itself as a democracy, its struggle to practice what long ago a number of our "founding fathers" preached and wrote about in documents like the Declaration of Independence and the Constitution of the United States of America.

I just used the phrase "visit with families"; for a long time I was not sure what I was doing or how I might even begin to describe what I was doing — until one day (in May of 1963) I was told this by the mother of a black child I was getting to know: "You're visiting us. You're visiting with families down South. You should go tell the doctors that you come see us and we have some coffee and the children do their drawing and their painting for you, and then we all have a laugh about something, and soon it's time for you to leave. Now, don't ask me what you're 'studying.' I never did learn to study myself, not in the five or six years I more or less tried going to school. So, I don't know what it is to study. My children are trying to study. They're trying to find out what's going on in the world. I tell them they can spend the rest of their lives doing that, and there's a lot they'll never get to know, because like the Bible says, His ways are not our ways. But you have to try, and it's just as well that they start early and learn all they can while they're young. When you get older, I believe you become set in your ways — so it's harder and harder to catch on, it's harder and harder to break out of yourself and find out what's happening next door and across the street. We get locked up in our own house and we hardly even look out the windows. To tell you the truth, I believe I should go visiting with some families myself. I can't go up north, like you've come down south, but I could start with crossing the street and knocking on a door. But who has the minutes in the day to spare?"

If I had nothing else throughout the 1960's I had those "minutes to spare." I spent virtually all the time I have not been with my own family during those years talking with other families: black families and white families; families from the rural South and families from cities like New Orleans or Atlanta; migrant farm families and sharecropper families and tenant farm families; families from the hollows of Appalachia and families in northern cities. I write this after having finished three volumes of *Children of Crisis*. Their purpose was to set down something about the "courage and fear" I encountered among families caught up, as participants or opponents, in various phases of the South's civil rights struggle, to tell something about how "migrants, share-croppers and mountaineers" live, and to describe how a family manages when "the South goes North." During the years I spent doing the work that is described in those books I traveled a good deal and gradually cut down on some visits, so that I could spend more time elsewhere. But I have never stopped visiting the children I first met in Mississippi toward the end of the 1950's and in Louisiana and Georgia at the beginning of the 1960's. Nor have I lost touch with some of the young activists I worked with during the stormy and uncertain days of the freedom rides, the sit-ins, the marches in Selma or Birmingham or the longer efforts, such as the Mississippi Summer Project of 1964. And I have similarly stayed in touch with the "ordinary" white families I first met in Biloxi, Mississippi, in 1958 — as well as certain members of militantly segregationist groups, including the Ku Klux Klan. For six years (from 1958 to 1964) I lived in Mississippi, Louisiana and Georgia, but every year since I have returned, so that a season doesn't go by when I'm not renewing old friendships, learning "how things are going," and getting some sense of the ways children grow up, young people grow older, and parents undergo changes in their lives, all in a region which itself continues under pressure to abandon much of its distinctive "way of life."

While conducting my general research and writing, I have found myself constantly anxious to clarify my thoughts by concentrating on limited aspects of that work. In fact, I know I never could have written those three volumes of *Children of Crisis* had I not, step by step, compelled myself to construct one quite limited essay after another. For several years I wrote nothing, except long and discursive memos and reports meant only for my despairing eyes and my wife's more hopeful scrutiny. We were seeing too much. I could only remember and remember again James Agee's stated frustration in *Let Us Now Praise Famous Men*. And as I kept on telling my wife, Agee and Walker Evans spent only a few weeks in rural Alabama.

By 1962 we had been in the South for four years. I began publishing my observations in various periodicals and "presenting" them at professional meetings. No wonder I felt myself drowning in hundreds and hundreds of "notes," "life-history" reports, children's drawings and paintings, fragments from a diary, and always, those "tape-scripts" that contained the rough exchanges between me and others, awaiting editing, pruning, and analysis. In the spring of 1962 I was called by Margaret Long, a southern novelist and essayist, then editor of *New South*, a publication of the Southern Regional Council. She wanted me to write something for the monthly magazine — and she would not take no as my last word. "You've got to start sometime. You can't just wait and wait and collect more and more of those 'data' of yours." I am not paraphrasing her remarks. I can still hear the sarcasm in her voice, too — as she ended with "those data of yours."

Margaret Long was not one to be awed by social scientists and their wordy phrases. Often when I would talk with her she would tell me to stop qualifying myself so endlessly. "My, but you are hemming and hawing," was her way of putting it. She pushed me for months to "say something, say *anything,* so long as the rest of us can learn how those children you are seeing are getting along." And those words, written in a note of hers to me, at last had their effect. I suddenly realized what I was actually doing; I was trying to comprehend how children and their parents were *getting along,* and how youth of a certain kind were *getting along,* and how the South was *getting along.*

Now, to *get along* is not to be "sick" and in need of "treatment," or to be in psychiatric jeopardy and in need of "support" or "evaluation." To *get along* is to live, to manage from day to day — which means one is not a case-history, but rather has a life-history. To *get along* for the children was to be a new kind of Southerner, a pioneer of sorts, a leader of a region hard pressed by its own poverty and vulnerability as well as by those "damn Yankees" I heard mentioned so often. To *get along,* I was told by one black youth, was like this: "I'm trying to fight for the South. Yes sir, it may seem strange for a Negro to talk like that, but as some of the aristocrats say in a city up North, when you meet them: 'We've been here for a long, long time, you know.' We want work. We want to get on welfare if we can't find work — and not be cussed at, pushed around, and maybe even killed by some sheriff or someone from the White Citizens Council or the Ku Klux Klan for being 'uppity' just because we're not willing to starve to death with smiles on our faces, bowing and scraping until we stop breathing. The South is poor, when compared to the rest of the country. The South is always trying to beg those northern industries to come down here. The South has been cheated and robbed and hoodwinked by northern bankers. So, I think the southern Negro knows what his white brother has gone through. We've been through the same thing. We're everybody's football, that's what — to kick around and throw around and put aside and forget about and then take up now and then for a few minutes of exercise and relaxation. That's how I see it; I do, I really do."

He was perhaps making his point too strongly — maybe, I now realize, because I seemed so confused or unbelieving or both. But Margaret Long had no trouble understanding what the young man (already in 1962 a veteran of several sit-ins) was trying to tell me. She told me again and again that he was a Southerner, a Southerner getting along — and if I knew that, she would insist, I knew more than I seemed to realize at the time. Yes, I patiently said; I was sure she was right. Yes, I

said with barely contained annoyance, I was sure a region
could have its "impact" on an individual. But I was hardly
persuaded. I was still trying to get deeper and deeper — so
"deep" that I would *really* understand those children and
youths and parents and teachers and the activists and the defenders of the status quo. Not for me the superficialities of
something called "the southern way of life." Not for me the
notion that a region can shape the character of its people in
some decisive and utterly significant fashion.

I was looking for "psychopathology" in those early years of
my residence in the South. I was an investigator, a child
psychiatrist doing "research," a doctor who had studied
"stress" in hospitals, among patients afflicted with diseases
like poliomyelitis — and who now was going to show what
"external" stress did to that rock-bottom part of the mind, the
unconscious. To do so I was spending long hours listening
and asking questions and watching. Yet, I was missing a lot,
even though I was indeed picking up fears expressed, anxieties made clear, resentments openly acknowledged or slyly expressed or thoroughly hidden — only to emerge in a dream
told to me, a drawing done for me, a casual remark not at all
meant for my ears, but conveyed to them by someone else "in
passing," as a minister once noted: "I'll tell you in passing
what the child told me. I don't know if it means anything, but
she said she was frightened when she got out of bed in the
morning, because she'd been having bad dreams, she thinks,
but she can never remember what the dreams are, and by the
time she's ready to go to school she hasn't an ounce of fear in
her. That's what her mother says, and the child sure seems to
act like that, as you've seen for yourself. The girl did tell me
that she's sure there was a fight in the dream, and maybe she
was hurt, but a nurse took care of her, and told her she was all
right, and told her the people of the state of Louisiana, all of
them, the whites as well as the blacks, would be applauding

her one day, even if it took a few years to happen. I told her not to try to recall those dreams. It's best to let a nightmare pass and get up and have yourself a good breakfast, that's what I told her. I told her all the other children in Louisiana have bad dreams sometimes, so not to worry. And I told her when she's older, those children *will* be grateful to her, just like she seems to be dreaming they will. Can't a dream be hope? Even a bad dream can mean the child is hoping against hope — right?"

Thus did the state of Louisiana become part of a child's unconscious; thus do regional influences make themselves felt way down, deep down — in the mind's most "private" and idiosyncratic "sector," where dreams are constructed and remembered. Margaret Long had no great interest in psychiatry or psychoanalysis, but she knew, as did that minister, how very personal a thing the South is — no abstraction, no mere geographical or rhetorical term, no handy journalistic device to obscure vision, no historical phenomenon, or at least not *only* those things. The South, she once told me, is children growing up in a certain way, and again, people getting along in a certain way. And eventually I began to learn.

I think I was beginning to learn in the summer of 1962, because it was then that I wrote my first article about the work I was doing. "Separate But Equal Lives" appeared in the September 1962 issue of *New South,* and several weeks later I received a letter from a South Carolina lawyer, a few sentences of which, I believe, belong in this introduction: "The South has always had its Yankee visitors; some of them have been carpetbaggers and some not. I hope you keep writing about us. We need some friendly but critical outsiders. We need to be reminded that we are fighting for something important down here — those of us who are fighting. I myself have to be very careful; there is only so much I dare do or say, because I am a professional man. But I fervently believe that by the time we are in the 1970's, a decade hence, we will have a much better South, which means the white man will at last be liberated from the role of oppressor of his Negro neighbor."

The South is not quite liberated, but now, ten years later, it surely is not the same South that lawyer had known all his life. During those ten years I have written both books and articles about the region, always I suppose as the "Yankee visitor" my correspondent insisted I was. I have written about the young children I know and talk with. I have written about their older brothers and sisters and friends and neighbors, about those who resisted, who did so vehemently and with violence, or who did so almost fatalistically, because they knew in their bones that "the time has come, yes, I fear it has." I have tried to describe the region — its land, rich and fertile and blessed with abundant water. A warm, sunny day or azaleas in bloom or the particular freshness of a city street or a country road after a gentle afternoon rain — what can such "phenomena" have to do with the psychological survival of lonely, hard-pressed black children in a newly desegregated school classroom? The sight of a mule grazing near an old, broken-down sharecropper's cabin, the sight of a cotton gin, the sight of levees along the Mississippi River, and yes, the inevitable Confederate statue in the town square — how can such spectacles move tough, unyielding black student activists to something called (*by them*) "nostalgia"? The sound of a Negro minister and his flock praying and singing, the sound of blacks marching to a funeral, the sound of blacks talking as they walk by — can such events possibly touch the hearts of those whites who talk openly of their "superiority"?

Certainly the South can be seen as a section of this country whose land is still blood-drenched, a section where hate and exploitation, for all the recent changes, still persist. Demagogues have yet to be completely banished from the eleven states of the old Confederacy. The Klan is not quite dead; nor are other vigilante groups altogether gone. "It is a struggle of many lifetimes," Margaret Long emphasized to me in 1962, and she has not so far been proven wrong. Nevertheless, the Old South is dying, and even its most steadfast supporters could be heard saying so in the early 1970's — when I could go back and hear this from a man I wrote about in the first volume of *Children of Crisis*, a man who once belonged to a White Citizens Council and a Klan and a less formal or institutionalized group he occasionally thinks about: "I remember when a bunch of us got together and told one damn nigger-kid to stop being so damn full of himself and get out of the way when a white woman walks by. He was headed for the civil rights people, headed to join them, we knew, and we thought we'd help him out by stopping him cold in his tracks. I love the colored. I hear them working themselves up in a church and my eyes fill up. I can't figure out why. I just can't stop myself. I have to go and hide and have a cry for myself. It's hard to talk about. They're part of us and we're part of them and these civil rights people want to ruin them and ruin us. That's how I see it. And I'll be honest: I think they're succeeding. The South isn't the South anymore. The rest of America has come down here and taken us over — and we're giving up. Between the two there's little a Southerner can do but raise his hands up in the air and surrender."

A black child in New Orleans who went past mobs in order to desegregate a school, and in time (over several years) saw herself increasingly accepted by white schoolmates, doesn't really disagree with that man: "I think it's different, what we have down here in the South; I mean, it's *becoming* different, the way black people and white people live with each other. I hope I never leave Louisiana, because we have the best flowers here, and my grandmother grows them better each year, she says. We have sun and rain, enough of both; and every time I get discouraged I do what my grandmother says, I go look at the azaleas and I sit in her chair under our little palm tree and catch the sun and then move to the shade. My daddy says that we haven't got much, but we have a good backyard, with soil that will grow anything and with weather to match. So, we can keep our place clean and pretty, even if there is trouble outside."

And then there was a moment in the summer of 1964, the summer of the Mississippi Project, when I heard a civil rights worker, a black youth already (at twenty) arrested eleven times, tell me about his native state: "I hate the word Mississippi; every time I cross into Louisiana or Tennessee or Alabama and then come back and see that sign, 'Welcome to Mississippi, the Magnolia State,' I want to tear it down and burn it up. The hate in this state, the racist hate — it's hard to say how much there is, because everywhere you look there is cruelty and brutality. My mother said she dreamed every day of her childhood that she'd get to Chicago, one way or the other. At last she did get there, to visit an aunt; and she sure was glad to come back. She was glad to see my grandfather's cabin, as bad as it is. She was glad to be picking cotton again and laughing while my daddy poked at the mule and tried to get him going. My daddy was a kid she played with for a long time before they both grew up and they married. My daddy used to walk all the way from the plantation to the levee and back and tell my mother about the boats he saw — and they dreamed of going on one and never coming back to Mississippi. But they feared homesickness. Yes, they surely did; and so do I. I go up to New York to raise money for the movement and I'll be walking down those streets, those big-city northern streets, and all of a sudden I find myself missing Greenville and Greenwood and Batesville and all the other towns in the Delta. I tell you! I'll be so full of nostalgia that I even miss the statues of the Confederate soldiers. Now, how's that for being crazy!"

Political alignments, rhetorical postures, polemical positions, even deeply felt convictions that go back in origin to early childhood — none of them are adequate clues to the range of sentiments a particular person, black or white, possesses within his or her mind and heart and soul. As I look back at the various essays on the South I have written since I submitted the first one to Margaret Long, I realize how often I have come back to that realization, just stated. I arrived in the South with prejudices and blind spots and not a small touch of arrogance; years and years had to go by before I could unwind, become less smug and self-righteous and condescending, learn not only what I didn't know, but what I didn't *want* to know, what I am prevented from knowing because of my own life.

I would not want a book published if its contents were only a record of my gradual introduction to the subtleties and mysteries of another region, another way of life. The South has had its fair share of fine novelists and essayists. They certainly don't need me as an ally or would-be compatriot. Nothing I say here will add much to the achievement so many southern writers have wrought. I have, anyway, questioned the common habit writers have of collecting together in book form articles written here and there over a period of years. Even when such books demonstrate a certain thematic continuity there is considerable danger that the writer's position will be stated again and again — while, alas, dozens of nagging uncertainties, complexities and qualifications are postponed for "longer" writings.

How, then, can I justify the appearance of this book? Under no circumstances would the book have been assem-

bled, so to speak, were it not my wish to add a substantial
amount of comment — as a postlude, five years after its publication in 1967, to volume one of *Children of Crisis,* a book in
which I tried to describe how various southern children and
youths and older people of both races became caught up in
the social struggle that engulfed the region throughout the
1960's. Now the sixties are for historians to begin looking at
and sizing up. In this book I tell, as best I can, what I learned
during the sixties about the South, and some Southerners,
and how it has all changed.

What has taken place in all those individual lives that I
have been privileged to touch? If there is one thing my kind
of work offers it is the long, long time that the child psychiatrist is taught to spend with those he "treats," in my case, visits at home. In the somewhat pompous language of the social
sciences: We are especially equipped to do "longitudinal
studies in depth." Later on in these pages (in the section
titled "Changes") I offer new information. To my mind that
section is the primary justification for this book.

Yet, I would also like to call upon Freud's sanction for the
balance of the book. Again and again he warned us in psychiatry and psychoanalysis that what we learn about ourselves
as observers is as important as what we learn about our patients; that it is through our various attitudes, our particular
hopes and fears, our preconceptions and inclinations and
blind spots, that we filter the outside world. The first two sections of this book record my struggle as a physician, a psychiatrist and a social observer to understand a region and a number of young people. All of these essays were written while I
was in the midst of my research. Though the pieces are not
openly autobiographical, they by and large do contain a good
deal of information about my responses to the situations I
found myself in, the people I was meeting during the late

fifties and the sixties and the early seventies, and about myself as I was and as I have become.

Repetitions there are; repetitions which, however, indicate a particular viewpoint as it has developed; and I have decided to let them stand — not, I hope, out of laziness or boredom, or because I had nothing else to say. Certain situations have simply repeated themselves; sometimes my attitude to them has changed, sometimes not. As the reader will see, I have almost desperately tried to maintain my "cool," keep myself able to walk both sides of the exceedingly tense streets that separate blacks and whites in the South.

When I started talking with the college youths who staged some of the South's first sit-ins I was warned by them to "go slow" with my various psychiatric words and concepts. They were not "afraid" or "defensive" or "hostile" to psychiatry as a medical subspecialty; they were themselves trying to get rid of a host of clichés they had picked up as they became educated. For me, knowing such youths was a redemptive experience indeed. There are many forms of oppression and bigotry in this world, and if those youths knew all too much about the South's worst side, they had also begun to know how narrow and self-serving academic theorists can also be. During the first, the very first interview I "conducted" with a black man, in Mississippi, in 1959, I heard this: "I'm glad to be in college, but I'm also sad I'm here. All I hear is that the Negro is one thing and the Negro is another thing — until I get sick when I open up those books. They kill us, some of those writers do. They do us in with their words about us. I look at myself in the mirror after I've read their books, and I say: you're *you,* not the object of pity they make of you. I'd rather be hated outright by the Klan than be given all those names you people figure out for us."

I have in general not altered the articles I have chosen to

appear in this book. I have had to correct some misprints which appeared in the original pieces — and occasionally I have cut out introductory paragraphs in which I explain the work I am doing. (I am certainly not arguing that *all* repetitions are valuable or revealing.) But on the whole the various pieces stand as they did when they first came to print — so what I said and how I said it are not changed to fit the convenience of afterthought. I have chosen those articles I believe important — the ones which still mean something to me, the ones in which I said what I strongly believed at the particular time I was writing. I leave it to the reader to decide whether the hopefulness I found in other people and felt in myself has been justifiably replaced by the cautiousness and uncertainty, the tentativeness, which I have later described in Part Three.

I don't know how to acknowledge the obligations I feel toward so many Southerners; I have done so, within limits, in three volumes of *Children of Crisis*. But in a volume like this one wants to list names and names, to summon a whole region for gratitude. I am saying a good-bye in this book, just the way that many who speak in it seem to feel that the Old South is dead, replaced not by a New South but an America which has finally assimilated (politically, economically, culturally) its most defiantly "separate" region. By saying good-bye or "farewell" I mean to say this: In the early 1970's I began to stop visiting certain families "regularly." I began to drop by from time to time when I passed through, or came near, but did so as a distant visitor does rather than one "really on the watch" (the phrase a black mother once used to describe my "approach"). The South is saying farewell now to many of its traditions and customs, and I am ending the most absorbing work I have ever done. Still, I hope I never stop going South, visiting there for stretches of time, feeling so very close to its rhythms — its struggles and controversies and challenges. I also hope I never forget what I have learned from talks with Lillian Smith, Ralph McGill, Medgar Evers and Dr. Martin Luther King, Jr. — each of whom has already said another kind of farewell to the South. And I especially wish to acknowledge my indebtedness to the Southern Regional Council for its kindness to me when I first started to work in the region.

The work I have done this past decade and more has been supported by the New World Foundation, the Field Foundation and the Ford Foundation. Again my thanks to Vernon Eagle, Leslie Dunbar, Paul Anthony, Pat Watters, Margaret Long and Edward Meade. To Paul and Isabelle Johnston of Birmingham, Alabama, and their family; to Alvin Neely, Jr., of Waynesboro, Georgia; and to Wesley and Lee Pittman of Atlanta, Georgia, I extend a special hand of friendship and appreciation. I also want to thank the editors of the many magazines I have in recent years written for — thank many of them for letting me use the articles in this book, and thank all of them for looking sharply but with care at what I have wanted to say. Once more I say thank you to Peter Davison, whose editorial help and friendship I have been privileged to have since I first started my work in the South. And thanks, also, to Beth Garber and Martha Stearns for their help with this manuscript.

I mean the dedication of this book to be a public acknowledgment, at last, of what my wife has enabled me to do, day after day. I have dedicated the books that describe the work itself (the three volumes of *Children of Crisis*) to the children themselves, and to others like them in the South, in Appalachia, in the North. But all along, as I wrote for myself and then for others, my wife, Jane, has been there in a very special way that I believe the children themselves have sensed

— and even from time to time stated better than I ever could: "She keeps you smiling. She keeps you going. She's a real good woman. I feel it's different when you come here without her. It's empty here when she's not there, sitting beside you." Yes, indeed.

PART ONE

The Region

The essays that appear in this first section are of several kinds — though I have arranged them in the order in which they were written. There are essays that deal with the social and political issues I saw developing in the South over the years. There are literary pieces and book reviews — all in one way or another tied to my work as a Yankee who lived for a time in the South and still constantly goes there for visits. (For example, the discussion of James Baldwin's books, or the essays on Southern writers like W. J. Cash, Shirley Ann Grau or Alice Walker.) There are muck-raking pieces, such as those on South Carolina, Mississippi and Texas written in 1968 and 1969 for the *New Republic*. (The "we" that occasionally comes up in those pieces refers to my friend Harry Huge, a dedicated Washington lawyer who was in those instances a coauthor, as well as a tireless and enormously helpful co-worker.) And finally, there are television reviews of documentaries made about southern problems ("Natchez, Lovely Natchez" and "Mississippi Frontier").

Though my focus may differ in these pieces, I believe my purposes were constant. Throughout these articles I seem to be trying hard to make sense of the many paradoxes I kept encountering in southern state after southern state. But novelists know better than to try and make sense of paradoxes; they want to describe, even savor and enjoy, those paradoxes. Over the years during which the essays that follow were written I refer more and more often to Flannery O'Connor or William Faulkner or Ralph Ellison or Robert Penn Warren.

The novel gives a hardworking writer at least a chance at modesty; a plot, after all, is thoroughly limiting and concrete, even as it can be almost infinitely suggestive. I fear we in psychiatry and psychoanalysis are not so lucky — have no such form to fall back on and try to master, unless it be the "life-histories" we write up. So it is well for us to keep in mind the wry William Faulkner or the sharp-eyed and impatient Flannery O'Connor.

Who's Blocking Desegregation?

A Louisiana jailor, curious about my psychiatric interview with one of his prisoners — a twenty-year-old Negro lad charged by that state with the criminal anarchy of encouraging his kind to vote — remarked to me in taunting complacency: "We're just sitting here and waiting. Y'all could stop a lot of segregation if y'all wanted, but I don't think y'all really mean it. . . . Why should we move if we can sit tight and call your bluff?" His challenge may be deserved.

For two years, I worked as a psychiatrist at a large Air Force base in Biloxi, Mississippi. Helping me were corpsmen from Mississippi and Alabama, Negro and white, eating together, sleeping in the same barracks, sitting beside one another in the base theater. When they left federal property, they were fierce in defense of town habits; but when they returned, they yielded to national ones most casually.

We largely know such facts, still we ignore them. Speaking words of apparent concern for the Southerner, we insist that his traditions surrender only very slowly to time. We tell ourselves of the psychological problems at issue, mindful that if we force distasteful feedings of civil rights legislation down an unwilling region's gullet, reflexic refusal (nerves, again) will be the result. Such concern may be as convenient for us as it is patronizing and deeply unfair to the Southerner. Particularly so when many southern segregationists, angered by the Supreme Court's rejection of segregated schools, were nevertheless surprised at the gentleness of the law's enforcement, or, better, nonenforcement. ("We expected it to come right off, and then we realized we were going to be able to dodge it a long time," a Mississippi lawyer recalled to me.) Particularly so when many Southerners feel they are seen and measured by their worst elements. (Northerners forget that the majority of the South is composed of voteless Negroes and silently well-intentioned whites, not to mention a large number of fearlessly outspoken supporters of respect for federal laws or equal civil rights for the Negro. The noisy racists not only exercise minority rule, but are often respected outside the South as its only voice. Whom the North hears and heeds may be *its* measure.)

Historians (psychiatrists are, among other things, historians, collecting information about the past and trying to make some sense of it) may explain our guilty, our tender view of the fragile if strongly hate-saddled Southerner. From the early slave trade to the Reconstruction era, the North has taken a heavy hand in the very evil it has denounced. Even the liberalism of both Roosevelts and Wilson in this century touched Negroes as part of our poor, rather than as a devastatingly bound and exploited race. Only very recently has the Negro's special exile become the target of legal scrutiny, and even more recently have we begun to hear expressions of this cautious regard for the limits of human adaptation under social change. Indeed, we have reached a new refinement in our life: the hard power of northern commerce, the riches of white cotton picked by black hands, the moral outrage of abolitionists or the subtle political separatism of generations of agile southern lawyers and politicians, these all give way to the modern question of human emotions and their frail confines.

Not that I for a moment question the mind's capacity for self-deception, a Southerner's, a Northerner's too. Examples accumulate fast in my work. Even the kindliest teachers in Atlanta or New Orleans, highly favorable, some of them, to integration, believe that their Negro students have been selected and rewarded by the NAACP. Not only have they not been so chosen and paid, but the truth of this organization in the South, its fragmented, hunted, impoverished condition, is an ironic, a tragic example of fears being realized as facts.

We may wonder why intelligent, cultivated people will not, or cannot — have it either way — comprehend the Negro's anger or his more abased and apathetic surrender to his forced destiny. We see from many wise people little concern for the psychological effects of wasted, wanton living in what is for so many a very hell of dusky skin, sometimes painfully caricatured in a guarded black middle class which represents a travesty of accomplishment in its educated but disenfranchised state. That all this could escape at least the acknowledged notice of so many people, reminds me of some patients stricken with polio whom I saw in my medical training. In iron lungs, facing profound illness and likely death, they blandly denied the presence of one or a chance of the other. "I'm fine," or "I'll be up and around in a day or two," we'd hear. What soldier charging a machine-gun nest easily contemplates the likelihood of his death? Yet, doctors and generals must see painful truths even when others don't, and in a democracy we assume every man's vision a king's.

The South, ten-odd states among fifty, about twenty senators among 100, has no corner on tricky mental mechanisms. Above the Mason-Dixon line and beyond the Mississippi, people quickly seize upon the riots and mobs, the fearful violence and the shrill voices. We cannot escape the picture of lonely Negro children walking to school, or students arrested trying to vote or be served in a restaurant. Jolted by these incidents, we conclude that there is a chilling hate in those white hecklers, and a terrible strain and horror for those Negroes. After a while, these become the two situations most familiar and most associated with the South.

Yet, when we announce our civilized shock at the indecencies hurled at a little Negro girl in New Orleans, or an older Negro man in Oxford, when we wonder at their survival under such abuse, we forget the long truth of their lives. I have studied these children and seen remarkably little psychiatric illness among them, despite their trials. Facing a jeering mob for a purpose might seem relatively easy and more sensible to a Negro who has arbitrarily been kept from theaters or sections of a bus, whose parents cannot vote. They are millions in number, these hurts, and they occur daily, most often unnoticed. Kindled perhaps by some particular disaster, our collective knowledge of injustice makes some of us vigorous advocates of change, while others, decrying violence, worry strangely about altering its breeding grounds. Interesting are the discriminations of our sympathy and revealing are those we choose to "understand."

The segregationist, like the Negro who knows his white man so well, understands his Northerner, his American outside the South. He senses their indifference, their ambivalence, their fears and dislikes, similar to his. Waiting, watching closely, taking his neighbor's pulse, he smiles at northern segregation, laughs as Northerners lament southern congressional power but either quietly ally themselves with it or refrain from legislation which would really test its power. Urgency is reserved for liberating the Teamsters or the

Katangese, both of whom seem less curbed than Negroes of the South.

The southern politician, were he certain of no alternative, would survive desegregation. He is a stout, plucky fellow who has recently shown in some parts of the South small embarrassment at his new espousal of "law and order," even integration under the banner of "too busy (with new business) to hate." He, and his voters, will change their customs, as people always do, for compelling reasons: legal ones, such as those which obtain on the military bases which dapple the region, social and economic ones, like less poverty and ignorance, the lure of a better life, the sure knowledge of a worse one without change.

Clearly, then, this stalwart but not crazed southern segregationist, be he citizen or officeholder, needs several pushes to move him to modify an historic relationship with the Negro. He needs to be told that he must. He also needs to lose his need for the Negro, who was once the specific need of a rich cotton economy, later the wayward need of a poor, rural economy for menial work and a target upon which to vent its frustrated sense of inadequacy.

If any region in America needs planned infusions of capital, it is the South. It craves more and better schools and colleges, help as its people move from faltering, insolvent farms to cities, assistance for its sharecroppers, migrant workers, hillbillies. It requires better medical facilities and more decent housing. It needs good jobs for its people, at good wages, not flimsy wages from the sediment of American capitalism in flight from its own marginal existence. Finally, with such better livelihood, it needs, and is beginning to achieve, a political maturity wherein citizens are fed enough, read enough, to want to vote intelligently rather than be whipped or reduced into a babbling, stupefying frenzy.

Some changes are obviously coming, from the Supreme
Court with its 1954 school decison and 1962 reapportion-
ment decision, from first-class private capital as it moves into
the Carolinas and Atlanta. Congress has budged the tiniest bit
on voting rights for millions of Americans, and the Kennedys
are sometimes both firm and inventive in their pressures
upon southern governors or sheriffs. Meanwhile, much of the
Deep South is controlled by the votes of not quite penniless
rural folk, insecure small-town people, or unorganized,
underpaid workers. Consumed by race hatred which dissolves,
like cheap booze, hunger pangs and worries about mounting
bills, they are corralled yearly to elect in fear politicians who
respect not their wants but the desires of the few utilities, the
banks and railroads which dominate the area like no other
part of America. These elected leaders, make no mistake
about it, are not wild Klan types, are not like the New Orleans excommunicatees I have seen. Now ironically holding
hands with the heirs of Lincoln's party, they tell America that
segregation is a psychological problem, one of emotions long
and deeply held, hard to approach, difficult to handle and
change. Slowly, very slowly, we must go, as if through a mined
field, as if hunting a deer, like political bird watchers.
Whether they believe their own words or not, many pay them
attention. Why, when we know that racial hatred is not inher-
ited? Why, when we know that, given reasons to change, motivation to change, human beings are enormously adaptive?
Why, when any southern schoolteacher can tell about the
changes which occur in themselves, in their children, under
daily contact with Negro children?

There may be several answers. Some posture hypocritically
for civil rights, but favor nationally the kinds of political and
economic oligarchies which many of these southern spokesmen
represent. Others, simply pragmatic in all matters, respect

the bargaining power of the region in a nation of competing interests. Then, there is always international *realpoli-
tik,* and its regard for the external threat which demands at
least a semblance of internal cohesion, underneath which remain festering hate, cropping up in race riots, and a waste of
human resources in the illiterate lives of slum children and
farmhands.

Whatever their motives, the southern segregationists know
they have allies all over the country, hidden advocates, or
guilty, if practical-minded, partisans. The jailor was right, it
is not a beleaguered minority against an insistent majority,
but a canny, artful one against a deeply divided and uncertain
one. Recently I watched my junior senator, Mr. Talmadge of
Georgia, gently tease his fellows on the Senate floor by reminding them that no legislation genuinely wanted by about
seventy senators could be prevented yearly and forever by the
South's handful. He seemed confident, and there were, anyway, present to hear him one Republican and two other
southern senators. .

Incidentally, Senator Talmadge recently entertained a
newly elected Negro state senator in his rural Georgia home.
Anyone who knows the segregationist heritage of the Tal-
madges can only marvel at such capacity for change of attitude (or do we have here simply a deep-rooted psychological
need to survive?). If a southern "segregationist" senator can
come along so far, perhaps many Northerners will oblige with
noticing it and drawing the appropriate conclusions: the
South is no more like it was in 1860 or even 1945 than the rest
of our country; and if the North acts as though it were, perhaps it does so for its own selfish reasons. Segregationists from
Dixie, desirous of keeping their society as it is, fighting for their
crust because for them it is cake, have the protection of others
elsewhere in America, but only in exchange for one interest-

ing burden. When the harvest of segregation becomes embarrassing, when the shame of riots becomes brimful and the
scandal in the world's richest democracy of its entwined poverty and violence emerges beyond disguise, he, the southern
race-baiter, stands prepared for our collective need. Upon
him fall our faults and compromises, evasions and duplicities.
Glaring at him we dismiss the herded, inert masses of our
northern Negro slums, or the cynical sectional barters which
ignore human rights, or our many niggardly responses to
needy fellow citizens, hungry, persecuted, or merely in pursuit of a nearby home or school. Off this strange scapegoat
goes, comfortably away from all of us.

I write this having just returned from some unsettling days
in Alabama and North Carolina, the worst of which were
prison visits with the white and Negro youths who tried to
follow William Moore's steps into Alabama, and the best of
which were talks with those "children" who aroused so much
alarm nationally by their participation in demonstrations.

The more I see and hear, the more I think these convul-
sions can only respond to a fundamental assault upon the
ambiguity of our laws, the ambiguity of our stated goals and
intentions as expressed in our Congress. The time is now, because even white segregationists in the South are frightened.
As a matter of fact segregationists in Birmingham talk as they
never have before, because the reality of the Negro's determination, the truth of his feelings, has been made known to
them, as well as the certainty that forceful resistance is not
only futile and costly, but perhaps even a help to the Negro
(rallying him and the country into even greater impatience
and alarm).

Recently I heard a conservative lawyer talk to the Birmingham Council on Human Relations, a group of Negroes and
whites who for years have met in a Negro church, harassed by
police and ignored by everyone but themselves. The lawyer

told me he had formerly supported "Bull" Connor and Governor Wallace. Yet there he was, to present his views — that change was necessary, but that it must be gradual.

These demonstrations are testing not the segregationist power of Alabama but the very strength and value of our political institutions. What is the worth of the President's domestic program if it is enacted for a divided, increasingly unstable country? The genie of rampant nuclear testing may not be the only one out of the bottle these days, for we are finally confronted with the Negro's feelings and demands, long unheeded, overlooked, or rationalized away. When a historical moment allows such emotions expression in a society it can either try to repress them, ignore them and endanger their expression in chaotic forms, or attempt to give their vitality structure and real meaning.

What we must do, if we are to survive as a political and social democracy, is settle this problem of minority rights formally and fully, by changing our laws to guarantee them unequivocally. The very nature of our government limits even the best of our courts, the most effective of our Presidents. The real issue is not our ingenuity or timing, is not even the racial problem in itself, but the life and death of our legislative system, its ability to hear and see voices and faces hitherto largely ignored, its ability, so to speak, to rule over all of its body. Standing in its way, we hear, are a few segregationist senators and their peculiar powers. Well, let us see right now if they are all that blocks the possibility of effective action, because the emotions I see about me in the South, and they are hardly confined here, will not shrink from the committee doors of the Senate, and I suspect, from many others, too.

New Republic, 1963

Mood and Revelation
in the South

Just a few weeks ago in Baton Rouge, Louisiana, I was sitting in a courtroom with a young man who had once been charged by the state with the "criminal anarchy" of trying to alert his people to the possibility of the vote — not that those who *do* vote in Louisiana, and other states too, always shun the criminal anarchy of some of their elected officials. Two years of litigation still found this college student facing undaunted segregationist justice — and in this case a kind that had once driven the youth near insane, and could likely do so again.

In such a state Shirley Ann Grau lives, and of such matters she writes — of black and white caught in the tension between their private lives and a society commonly less than just or charitable to all its blacks and enough of its whites who are unimpressed by the validity of its racial conventions.

The story of her latest novel, *Keepers of the House,* is simple: Abigail sets out to tell about her family's long and fairly aristocratic history, including the most recent moments which have resulted in her lonely but defiant position. We learn about her grandfather, Will Howland, a wealthy farmer descended from generations of similarly established and prosperous people. He is the comfortable man in the midst of relative poverty and occasional desperation. As a young man he lived in Atlanta two years studying law, and while there met his wife. They returned home to his town in Alabama, though the town can clearly be located allusively anywhere in the Gulf Coast states, the heart muscle of the Confederacy. His wife bears him two children, but dies shortly after delivering the second one, and that one dies a year later.

Will Howland spends his major energies thereafter at his work, growing crops, developing a dairy farm, sitting on the slow realization that his land is worth a fortune for its wood alone, wood for pulp for paper. His daughter Abigail marries, and shortly afterwards he meets a young Negro woman and takes her as his mistress. They have three children. In the midst of this his daughter Abigail, separated from her husband, returns home with her daughter, also Abigail. The younger Abigail lives and plays with her mother's half brother and two half sisters. All three of these children are eventually sent north to school, to avoid the fate of the southern Negro. Abigail also leaves home for college, and in time marries an ambitious law student who hopes to be governor of the state. They have four children, and he works hard at politics, and soon he has the governorship in his apparent grasp with a victory in the Democratic primary.

During the campaign he had made the required racist remarks and one of them had made its way north to Robert, his wife's mulatto half uncle and Will Howland's only son by his Negro mistress. Robert returns enraged and looking for vengeance. He reveals that his father had secretly married his mother in Cleveland, thus making their children legitimate. A segregationist thus becomes legal kin by his wife to a Negro and, of course, even a Republican is preferable. The book ends darkly: the politician leaves his wife and children, thus clearing himself of the devil's work in the hope that a few years' forgetfulness will allow him another political try. His wife is left to face an angry mob bent on destroying their home, and is only narrowly saved by her own ingenuity and steadfastness. She confronts Robert with his outsider's thoughtless, ill-informed, presumptuous behavior and her town with the penalty they must expect for theirs, economic ruin at her wealthy hands.

Plot aside, it is a southern novel all right, and one often beautifully written: the flowers and trees in all their semi-tropical variety and abundance; the kin that connect and connect until you think everyone is related to everyone else; the swamps and rivers and bayous — much of the region is graced with water enough to make its rich and black or copper-red land seem fresher than the rest of American soil; the birds, grateful in their wide assortments for the temperate climate — herons rising out of a bleak patch of wet, wild grassland and ranging near moss-dripping oaks are an unforgettable sight; the special food and the names for the food; and everywhere the special relationship, grounded in history, buttressed by customs, insisted upon by laws, of Negroes and whites, so close to one another, so dependent upon one another, so mutually frightened.

I read this novel on my way to present a paper on the psychiatric roots of prejudice. I felt like throwing away my "reports" and reading passages from this almost haunting book, stunning passages, descriptions of how a Negro child of mixed blood grows, sees the world, and learns its severe lessons on skin color and human worth. (Most Negro children in the segregated South *are* of mixed blood, and I have seen pictures of their white forebears on flimsy cabin walls, a startling experience for a naïve if earnest "field worker.")

Shirley Ann Grau has been demonstrating her gifts as a

sensitive observer of human development and growth for some time now. With a few words she can establish a mood, mixing man's emotions with appropriate reflections of them in landscape. She knows her heavy, low southern moon, her southern turtles and snakes and herb gardens. She knows the old houses with their long windows and the nodding breezes which come upon thankful, clammy skin. She knows the people, knows the ambiguities of race relations, the devices, pretenses, ironies, absurdities and incredible frustrations, all of them constant reminders of the mind's capacity for illusion, rationalization and even delusion under an irrational but powerfully coercive social and economic system. She knows the Negro as an emotional alternative for the white man's personal loneliness or isolation. She knows the white man as an awesome, enviable attraction for many Negroes. She knows how a Negro mistress must silently and discreetly grieve at her white man's death; and she knows the rising warmth and fear which struggle in a white man when he begins to respect a Negro rather than use one.

Most significantly, she writes at a time when she can know some answers, too. For this is a novel which in its own sudden and firm way has a statement to make. Robert is, after all, the composite Northerner, the outsider, black and white, and the South has its reasons to fear and hate him. The author does not shirk the complicated nature of the problem. Her segregationist is no demon, but any region's ambitious, aggressive politician. He can be tender with Negroes, affectionate with his family, can even disbelieve his own racist talk. How many Americans can really get very smug with him or about his adjustment to his society? And who can deny his wife her anger at what this "outside agitator" has done?

The South's Negroes and liberal whites have a real need for national help in their struggle for freedom. Yet I have seen dedicated Negro and white students of the sit-in movement horrified by some of the ignorance, recklessness, and self-righteousness displayed by certain distant or only passingly nearby "supporters." Some of them have had to be asked for silence or a return north, leaving the hard battle to those tough and wise enough, and especially flexible enough to know the power of the enemy, the supple strength of his social and economic institutions and the many chances, as well, of undermining them as well as assaulting them.

Still, the author does not back and fill between a story crying out for change in the ways Negroes and whites get along with one another and justifiable criticism of those whose efforts at change merely lead to worsened strife in the future. She gathers herself together and ends her story by insisting that deceptions exposed are ultimately if painfully better than compromises and falsehoods endured. Robert may have been gratuitous and ignorant in his intervention but his action reveals to the white community and to the wife of its segregationist politician the reality they have so long dodged. The town learns that economic ruin follows violence. A wife learns what she had really sensed all along, her husband's faulty, compromised nature.

It is said that people are tired of the South and the southern novel. Yet, I wonder where else in this country past history and present social conflict conspire to bring forth so much of the evil in people, so much of the dignity possible in people, so much of the "pity and terror" in the human condition. Looking at people living elsewhere, in bureaucratized passivity and efficiency, in faceless bustle, in cliché-riddled "progressive" comfort or sophisticated but paralyzed bewilderment, we can turn to the South in horror and fascination, and on those counts alone, in some hope.

Baldwin's Burden

Less and less today are the lives of *individuals* developed and explored by novelists. Many writers might be called "literary" social scientists, spending their major energies on descriptions of social struggle, cultural change, or clinical psychopathology. Their novels reflect this kind of categorical thinking as much as their essays. Characters are not explored with a compassionate eye for how extraordinarily complex — marvelously so, terrifyingly so — human beings are. Characters tend to be merely illustrative of the emerging Jewish middle class in America, of the Negro struggle for survival, of the problem of identity in college students, the nature of the unconscious in children or adults. Character portrayal by way of *appreciating* the particular has given way to the meticulous study and representation of various groups and "problems."

Ironically (should I say unselfishly?) even the individual author's private life, let alone his characters', submits to this new and imperative fashion. James Baldwin, in *The Fire Next Time,* isn't satisfied with a letter from a region in his mind. He can't be satisfied simply with relating a critical time in his early manhood to the tragedies of our country. He is impelled to expand his feelings, make them into the feelings of all Negroes, make his struggle theirs, his conclusions their demands, his frustrations their accusation, his anger their threat. He is determined to offer a general truth out of the sphere of his own life, and has a grandiose remedy for our social ills. For Baldwin — a sharp critic of America's vulgar piety — it is love, love, love.

Baldwin translates his own adolescent agony into the hate in all Negroes for whites and then predicts the white man's inevitable doom unless he learns a radically new way of getting along with the Negro. In this painful, alternately hopeless and hopeful trek, with its mingled overtones of augury and fierce accusation, we pass through one man's encounter with a fearful and senselessly oppressive world to his final recognition: power is the heart of the problem of the races, the Negroes have suffered from the lack of it, the whites have it, though not for long, and it is power alone that Negroes want from their persecutors. He does not specify how history or political action will reverse the present power balance, though his confidence is high that a reversal is at hand. Baldwin's sense of history is old-fashioned. He talks of America as if it were Rome, as if our internal corruptions will slowly cause our defeat, our loss of world power. But the relationship between corruption and power in a nuclear age is not so direct. It is not, after all, the issue of power on the wane but of the uses of incredibly multiplied power which must concern us.

I would imagine that what Baldwin means is that the Negro himself would like all that power, the implication being that he would exercise it more sanely and justly. Baldwin is not very much interested in tying such implications to the constant paradoxes in man's nature or condition — victims hate themselves too; hate blinds as well as illuminates; suffering can both stunt and inspire; power corrupts as well as enlivens. These paradoxes make generalizations about human nature a risky business. Baldwin, however, is not afraid of the risks: he tells us not only that all Negroes hate whites, but also that they know whites better than whites know themselves. More than that, Baldwin's white man suffers, burdened by a corrupted Christianity and a falling West, while the blacks, from suffering which Baldwin strikingly illustrates, emerge with the strength that allows Negro children to face mobs.

Approaching these little Negro children who walked past fearful, foul-mouthed crowds before two schools in New Orleans, Baldwin describes himself as apprehensive. In his fear of sentimentality he resorts to a kind of dogmatic firmness of statement that is merely another form of sentimentality: "Life here so briefly and inadequately sketched has been the experience of generations of Negroes, and it helps explain how they have been able to produce children of kindergarten age who can walk through mobs to get to school. . . . The Negro boys and girls who are facing mobs today come out of a long line of improbable aristocrats, the *only* genuine aristocrats this country has produced." (The italics are mine.)

Baldwin was right in being apprehensive about describing those children who attended two elementary schools in the fall of 1960 and the ugly spring of 1961. They do not require unearned emotion from us, not even the kind of extravagance that emerges from Baldwin's description of them. Who are these children — these so-called "aristocrats"? Precisely what happened to them, and why? During the worst of it they were a handful, four little Negro girls and about six white boys and girls. The streetwalkers, mouthing threats and acting out some of them, wanted a boycott by a united white population. A Negro mother's words on one of my tapes will be sufficient to describe what happened: "We had it bad all right, but those white kids got it worse than us because they were after them more than us."

These aristocratic children were white and Negro alike,

and that they managed so well is a mystery that has nothing to do with color. During the Second World War Anna Freud noticed that under severe bombings, even with separation from or loss of parents, children survived quite handily, given certain conditions. These conditions were not always very apparent but they were very real and important to the child. The National Academy of Sciences in Washington has published studies of children in a vivid assortment of disasters or crises such as tornadoes, floods and fires. All these investigations reveal that successful survival (there are, sadly, other kinds) may be discriminatingly indiscriminate, oftentimes ignoring social, cultural or economic categories — and racial ones, too — in order to draw upon certain nuances of family life, of an internal, private, seemingly trivial nature. These psychological factors, here so significant, may, of course, be largely irrelevant in other crises of survival (in concentration camps for instance) demanding physical strength or what might be most properly called "ethical" strength.

Is it heartless to deny the special claims to aristocracy of these Negro girls in New Orleans? On the contrary, such claims are more likely to be unfair to them, to be a way actually of segregating them. We can be proud of them without turning them into martyrs. A martyr "wins" by losing. These girls have not lost. Others have — millions of Negroes over several centuries of time. Baldwin's case is strongest when he emphasizes how many people — they include in my experience Negroes as well as whites — still refuse to recognize even the conditions which he exposes. Moral decadence, a devious network of rationalizations and denials, obscure the blunt horror of what it means for one race to brutalize another.

If these Negro children and others like them throughout the South are not to be stripped of their humanity the highest honor we can grant them is the truth of their lives. Anger for past hurts is inevitable, nor can we completely avoid fresh outbursts of fury caused by new sins inflaming past sins. We can, however, try to spare these children by giving them this measure of freedom — to be themselves: not the white man's nigger or the Negro's lash. If Baldwin's whites need to be flogged, as a race, for their historical crimes, whether by Negroes or at their own behest, when will racism stop?

"Man, worse than the cops in Mississippi, is finding what's happened to us after all these years. They've made those people so scared, and they keep them so scared that I get more discouraged with my own people than the local whites." For me it might just have been an interview, but for him, a young Negro college student, a freedom rider, a veteran of an appalling number of arrests after countless sit-ins, these were the hard facts of life: that large numbers of Negroes in the South, as a result of the very bondage and daily terror described by Baldwin, are dispirited, worn people, and, from a doctor's viewpoint, very often sick; sick with vitamin deficiencies and their sequelae; sick with a high incidence of venereal disease, hypertension, alcoholism, paranoid schizophrenia, tuberculosis, undiagnosed or wrongly treated fungal diseases, parasitic diseases, bacterial diseases — diseases of the poor, the ignorant, of the wayward and backward. Failing to register to vote in cities and towns is for many of them less a considered policy than merely a consequence of their being deadened, apathetic, almost silly and senseless, so far have fear and hunger and misery overtaken them and generations before them. "They've been killed, that's what," to quote my student friend again. Not fear always, certainly not everywhere, and fear that is often reversed by glimmers of hope and of new possibilities. But hope comes rarely to these grim settlements of shanties with littered yards along frowzy, unpaved streets, the inhabitants barely literate, really illiterate, with ragged, unsightly, outlandish clothes and ill-made, tasteless furniture. The people in these settlements can be among Baldwin's aristocrats only if suffering is his criterion, but for most of them whom I know life is instead an endless matter of merely automatic or sometimes wanton twitches and exertions.

Nor is this the end of the chronicle of disaster which in one way or another the entire nation, *all* its people, must overcome. The problem is not merely that of crushed and forlorn people in rural or urban slums eating fatback, though this is a millstone enough. The cumulative ravages of oppression affect even the apparently comfortable, if numerically skimpy, Negro middle class, persisting in the psychological structure of many Negroes of all classes and regions. It is true the young child can survive a mob for reasons that have nothing to do with race or ideology. However, his older, more self-conscious racial brothers, facing similar threats, are ironically susceptible to maneuvers of the mind by which the oppressed, in their self-contempt, look at themselves just as their oppressors do.

I am thinking, in this connection, of a young man, tall, quite thin, with straplike muscles and a supple body. His mother approached me one day with a confidence. She was a poor woman from a sharecropper farm in South Carolina, and her son had recently led his race into a white high school of the deep South. The situation was still a little incredible to her: the ugly, incessant telephone calls that went on for three months before the start of desegregation, the police visits and the police escort for her son when the opening day arrived, the press, the television, and her son's stories, over the following weeks, of harsh words and quiet, puzzled faces from silent white adolescent classmates who didn't know what to think or say or do. Like him, they were confused, because what they had learned when they were younger was in conflict with what they were experiencing. Yet most of them were determined to study, just as he was determined to stay with them and study. It was this common, very simple determination, rather than any ideological enlightenment, that carried them together through the year. The youth was in a school where he met much less scorn than others had met in his city or in other cities. Nów well past his initiation, her son had gone to a football game between two Negro high schools, one of them formerly his, and had seen a razor pulled, a fight develop, a person hurt. "Mother, they're animals," he said, "they're animals, and you know it when you go to a white school and see how civilized people behave." She was a heavy woman who never could resist starches, and she finished the last of a doughnut and told me: "If that's integration, for my boy to talk like that, I want to go back to our farm."

I had seen worse than this. In a southern college, recently desegregated, social and economic distinctions and snobberies appeared among the three Negroes pioneering desegregation. In the midst of the agony of public outcry, of heckling and jeering shared by all three, one poor Negro was "cut" by the others, finding himself slighted by his two Negro classmates.

I recall all the mixed motives, all the ambivalence of the white and Negro parents alike in New Orleans, and all the usual range of hesitation and suspicion, trust and kindness I saw among the Negro students in Atlanta and elsewhere. Do these people need to be sanctified by converting them into aristocrats? I have not heard too many claims from them to special worth or insight. On the contrary, they are anxious to be quite realistic about themselves, even willing to say as one did to me, "I get a kick out of the people who make a big thing out of what we do. . . . I know it's important, but I'm getting a lot out of it too, and I'm not so pure as some of those speeches say. . . ." (He was a shrewd young man indeed, bright and forthright, nobody's coward.)

To solve our national problem of racial tensions we must think clearly and plan soundly because we are in a delicate moment, when the anger of many Negroes is naked and the sorrows and guilts of whites more exposed. For Mr. Baldwin, regardless of *what* we say or try to do, Western civilization seems suspect and faltering. He allows the Negro scant susceptibility to the many problems which afflict whites — of identity, of religion, of survival, of intimacy and sexuality. The Negro is an outcast, plundered so long that his fate becomes a historical judgment upon the white, Western world, a world which, according to Mr. Baldwin, knows very little about itself, because as he points out, it cannot understand the Negro. Yet, apparently the Negro can understand the white man, and can save him from his impending doom. The Negro, according to Mr. Baldwin, having given love to inadequate whites, is the crucial factor in finally enabling the white man to solve his problems of identity. There is a cynical medical and psychiatric core in me which must reject such an argument. The problems of identity and sexuality are simply too complicated for rhetoric of Baldwin's kind.

In short, Mr. Baldwin may have cornered himself into a dilemma not unprecedented. He tends strongly at times toward portraying the Negro as a kind of "natural man," an outsider, persecuted and untainted by the white marketplace. He alone, or perhaps with the gallant help of Mr. Norman Mailer's "white Negro," can save us from its commercial toxins. But it is for this same "natural man" that Mr. Baldwin wants civil rights. We are told he went to Oxford, Mississippi, at Robert Kennedy's urging, to persuade James Meredith to stay in the very kind of situation which he has deplored as a mockery. If the Negro joins the American dream, will he not also suffer its nightmares?

This dilemma — of demanding acceptance by a country simultaneously denounced as almost worthless — is more of Baldwin's fancy than fact, a result of romanticized notions which in themselves are part of the problem of racial unreason as it plagues the educated and the gifted. We hear sweeping, categorical and conflicting generalizations, based upon partial visions or deliberately unqualified ones. Then we are given further generalizations, now remedial ones, in hasty conclusion: love is the answer, though hate is everywhere, and power the only real objective in a barely acknowledged war. After such talk where are we, who are we, and in heaven's name, what do we do?

We might begin by remembering how difficult it is even for people who know one another well to love and trust one another. Understanding, as defined and required by Baldwin, is at such a rare premium anywhere that we must ask where he locates it positively in the areas of life that concern him. It isn't necessary to defend psychoanalytic observations on child development, or the observations of generations of artists, to say that hates and loves, variable and unique, mixtures of both, are in all of us. We all struggle to achieve that elusive "identity" which often defies the most dedicated descriptions. Yes, love is the remedy, but how cheaply and above all, how easily, some prescribe it these days. And Mr. Baldwin, who has exposed the tawdry in us and helped, more than most, to make us question our facile slogans, should know this.

And so, we have come, at long last perhaps, to the rather self-evident truth that the problems of racism, white, black, or any kind, are not fairly treated in this injunctive or sentimental fashion. Indeed one of the chief lessons we can learn is how enticing some of the irrational snares of racist polemic can become. As I was debating in my mind whether I would sit down to write, in some clarification for myself, just what Mr. Baldwin said, and meant to say, I came upon the following comments from my senior senator, Mr. Russell of Georgia, expressing his reaction to a rather modest civil rights legislative program sent to the Congress by the late President Kennedy: "People of good will can agree on most of the President's objectives. The trouble with the government's undertaking to solve by force some of the problems suggested arises from the collision of politically established rights of one citizen with the rights which have always been claimed by other citizens. . . ." In view of this honest, "realistic" appraisal of power politics, I wondered what need there was for a writer like Baldwin to engage in more eloquent reaffirmations of the same message.

Yes, the lot of the Negro is tied with power, and so, in one sense, who can disagree with Baldwin? By his ability to convey his feelings, Baldwin has contributed to public discussion and information (I suspect Baldwin touched on the guilt of many, to judge by his critics). And, finally, it must be obvious that the very appearance of this kind of article indicates that we are moving into that important time when the Negro and white people of this country are not simply politically or economically more nearly equal or "free," but socially, personally, humanly face to face.

A Negro youth in Birmingham who had read Baldwin had this to say to me: "Baldwin jumps all over the white man, and sometimes I feel like doing nothing else. . . . But you can't win if you're white. I mean no matter what you try to do, you're wrong. . . . If I felt like Baldwin, I wouldn't try another sit-in. I'd be too depressed . . . if I were white I'd get annoyed with him after a while, because he goes overboard . . . you know, talks like a seggie in reverse. . . ."

At times Mr. Baldwin comes very close to this man and his world. He also leaves him far behind to enter other territories, to engage in angry exhortation or theoretical speculation The sad fact is that our country needs to know this youth better — and others, white and black, like him. It needs to know itself.

Is There a Mind
of the South?

When in 1940 W. J. Cash gave his book the title *The Mind
of the South* he was making a statement, perhaps the last and
most forceful one of the southern agrarian tradition. Not only
did he argue for a southern history, distinct and burdensome,
a history that shaped the geographic South into a "region," in
some respects a nation within a nation, but he insisted upon
the existence of a southern "mind," too, one that very much
has its own style or character. Today Cash's thinking is not
very influential. While his book is still a "classic" — that is,
often enough, a book ignored through reverence — its willingness to emphasize the relevance of history, daily customs,
even climate to the life of the mind causes it to be branded,
I am sure, by many as quaint or, most damning of all, "superficial." Ours is, after all, an age of "depth" psychology and
"hard" economic analysis.

Yet I am not so sure that in the long run Cash the writer —
like Agee and Evans whose *Let Us Now Praise Famous Men*
described and pictured southern yeomen — will be shown
more profound than all the social scientists whose "tech-

niques" and "methods" are so fashionable today. What Cash saw, what Agee and Evans saw, what Faulkner saw, what Lillian Smith still sees and speaks of, is the astonishing power that history and everyday life exert upon our emotions, not to mention our voting or working habits. Though there is nothing very extraordinary about such a vision, the categorical minds that collect people and subsume their souls, not to mention their every word and intention, under labels like "The Southern School of Writers" or "The Southern Romantics" have long ago decided that those who hold that vision have missed the main point of life. Sums of money and childhood experiences — especially the early ones — are what really count, what really distinguish people. Even social institutions are not granted too much these days. They, too, are derivative — masks for the brute power of the stock exchange or for this or that "instinct." As for writers, they are in serious trouble. They think they can understand people, even that abstraction "society," by looking around and putting to word what they see and feel, when it is obvious that only an experienced onion-peeler stands a chance at knowing the "real" truth, covered as it is by layers of illusion, deception, guile and bluff.

When I left New England in 1958 to take up residence in Mississippi I was filled to the brim with such thinking. I knew that, really, people were very much alike, that at some "basic" level it is for all of them, in the words of the song, "the same old story, a fight for love and glory." Yes, there are differences, all kinds of "superficial" differences, of talk or clothing, of preference for food or religion or entertainment; but "deep down" is where the real, blinding gold lies, in those elusive dreams and in the baffling entity "the power structure."

I can't get rid of that kind of thinking, and to some extent I don't want to do so. I do, however, owe to my years in the South whatever subtlety, and plain common sense, my mind has achieved. No other part of America lives so intimately with its past, or struggles so hard to survive its ruinous contra-. dictions. As a result, I submit, there *is* a "mind of the South," and it is as powerful and devious as any other "force" people must face on this planet.

What I came to see in Mississippi and Louisiana, and later in Georgia, was how utterly relevant it was for a psychiatrist to know more about people than what ails them and brings them to his office. For one thing, when I studied Negro and white children going into desegregated schools in New Orleans and Atlanta, I failed to find psychiatric symptoms in children facing terrible stresses, far more dangerous ones, obviously, than those confronting the middle-class children I had treated in Boston. For another, I saw to my surprise and confusion hate and intimacy between the races so interlaced as to demand from any psychological appraisal of the "prejudice" of the South a far more complicated starting point than "self-hate" and its social expression. Finally, I came to feel what I later heard a ten-year-old girl from McComb, Mississippi, express after an "exchange" stay of two weeks in Harlem was over: "It's different up North. They don't have the room we do, and they don't talk to anyone no matter what his color be . . . and I think the colored and white, they're spinning in different grooves. Back home, we all go around together. We may not be very equal together, but we're around each other, and we know things about the other race. . . . Me, I don't think I could live up North. It makes me nervous. The streets and the people do, and you get so cold, you just pull yourself into your scarf and forget everyone."

It is not simply that this rural girl had found the big city too much to bear. That is part of it, but only part. The South is indeed "rural," though less so than the West. The South is self-conscious, though, in a way that the West is not, or the North either. It is self-consciousness that I think ties the

white and Negro Southerner together, and sets both of them
off psychologically from the rest of us. I refer not to the self-
consciousness of the poor or the "outsider," also prevalent in
a region long compelled to deal with Yankee money and
sophistication. I am thinking of that developmental self-
consciousness known by the growing child, and somehow pre-
served — more or less so — in the grown-up.

Child psychiatrists know that self-consciousness is more
than self-awareness, that it is linked with the child's gradual
sense of right and wrong, his capacity to feel shame — and the
retaliatory anger which sometimes follows shame. In my experience, which has included interviews with committed segregationists as well as civil rights workers, "the Southerner" is
more than a resident in the South. He exists psychologically;
and in at least that respect he exists across the barriers of race
and class. He is the one American — hater or hated, owner or
piece of chattel — whose ancestors, generation after generation, lived at cross-purposes to every political principle of this
nation. He is the one American who really knows history because he lives constantly in its vengeful presence. He is the
one American who cannot take this country's democratic institutions for granted, or proclaim them with easy pride or
modest conviction.

If he is a white Southerner he may be nervously prone to
nostalgia, or angrily prone to self-pity, all out of shame at
what seems an impossible state of affairs, distantly arrived at
and even then by accidents and avarice rather than willful
planning or faith, they to come later. If he is a Negro Southerner he may be terrified and struck with horror, acquiescent
out of despair, or almost numb with rage, all out of a terrible,
galling sense of shame: that it could have happened at all,
that it could have happened in this country, that it could have
happened without exception for three centuries to a race of

people living in a nation that considers itself Christian and democratic.

"I'll tell you when I feel ashamed," said a Negro youth from Mississippi shortly after the Freedom House that he called his home (for me it was a place to visit, hence I have my own cause for shame) had been nearly destroyed by dynamite: "I feel ashamed every time I think of how long we've had to take it, take it, take it. I almost wish we had all been killed a long time ago, standing up for our rights, even if it meant death for every one of us."

A year before I heard a white woman half crazy with segregationist passion tell me, in the curious, ambiguous rhetoric of the repeated question: "Do you know what it is to feel ashamed? Do you know how it is to see everything that's right falling to pieces, and the worst things taking over? Isn't it somehow our fault that this is all happening here? I mean, if the white man lets it happen, doesn't he deserve it?"

Now, I am not trying to develop the Southerner into a new and grandiose psychiatric type — Lord knows we have enough of them, too many of them, already. I am simply trying to say that the pain and torture of the South's history has been shared by all its people, even as the region's beauty, despite the ugliness of the past, is yet appreciated by more of its people — more of its Negroes — than a few apologists for "the old and dying order" would ever dream or care to know. That Negro girl from Mississippi I heard talking in Harlem was a Southerner, even as Faulkner was, or Ralph Ellison in many ways still is. Their minds have all taken in the region's hurt and bad blood, but lived also in company with the region's warmth, openness, and really splendid countryside. Most of all they have all shared the pitiable self-consciousness that allows neither exploiter nor exploited whatever sanctuary the one thinks the other has. Shame and self-consciousness may not be emotions that seem likely to generate the best beginning for a happier and more honorable people (or a more honorable region,) but in the face of the gluttonous apathy our social critics describe elsewhere in America, and even western Europe, those emotions may offer real and binding hope where it is most needed and deserved.

New South, 1966

Natchez, Lovely Natchez

I recently saw a film that is a valuable historical document. In one hour, years of argument and rhetoric are neatly and quietly compressed, but also brought to life. The film is *Black Natchez*, and it was made by Edward Pincus, a graduate student in philosophy, and David Neuman, recently out of college. I suppose they would be called "amateurs" by those who like to know exactly who is who and why. On their own, with meager money and rented equipment they went to Mississippi in 1965, determined to stay for many months, not to "do" a movie, but to live and learn, to find out whether their presence could eventually become irrelevant enough to enable the kind of film footage they wanted.

They chose Natchez, "lovely Natchez" we used to call it in the fifties and early sixties when I lived in the state. We had no civil rights problem then, only "peace and tranquility," as our distinguished governor, Ross Barnett, used to remind us when "violence" broke out elsewhere. The city is in the southwestern part of the state and stands on bluffs more than 200 feet above the Mississippi River. During steamboat days its port was busy, not only with cotton but people, slaves being transported or fine families stopping off for food, rest and gambling, which flourished there. The *Natchez Free Trader* kept its readers up to date on river news, and just before the Civil War Frederick Olmstead was able to say that the city had "the best hedges and screens of evergreen shrubs . . . in America." To this day thousands go there every year to see handsome antebellum homes, about two scores of them as I recall, enough to keep the serious visitor several days.

In 1963, George Greene moved to Natchez, and because he was a SNCC field secretary he found it inconvenient to visit those homes. He even found it inconvenient to do the kind of work most civil rights workers do in the South, because along with those homes Natchez can claim many Klansmen. The terror in Natchez and adjoining Adams County in a sense turned even Greene and one or two others into social scientists; for a year they did nothing but document incidents of violence reported to them by a few Negroes bold enough to do so.

I well remember what historic, scenic Natchez did to the mind and spirit of George Greene in one year. I also recall the hours of debate when the Mississippi Summer Project of 1964 was being planned. How could anyone do anything in that fortress of racial "stability"?

By 1965 no part of Mississippi was safe from "agitation." Negro children, some of them twelve or thirteen years old, had the nerve to picket stores, demanding better jobs for their parents. They wanted other things, too, like access to the town's library or auditorium, not to mention its voting booths and the "other" school system. In retaliation George Metcalfe, president of the Natchez NAACP, was critically hurt by a bomb attached to his car. The town was upset. The *Natchez Democrat* reported the mayor's words: "Natchez is a peaceful, law-abiding community whose citizens deeply resent violence in any form." A reward was offered to help capture the would-be murderer — and Negroes were arrested by the carload for picketing, then shipped in chartered Trailways buses to the infamous Parchman State Penitentiary. Eventually the National Guard took over the city, in the face of continuing marches and protests by an aroused Negro community. In the end (after stalled negotiations, resumed talks and new federal laws) an almost standard southern solution occurred: a few Negro police were hired, a few Negro faces appeared here and there in the white world. It is safe to say that the following (1960) statistics for Natchez and the rest of Adams County still hold: The population is half and half, but the median family income for whites is $5,600, and for Negroes, $1,994; school expenditures per pupil for whites come to $162.81, and for Negroes, $99.05; the number of whites making under $2,000 per year is 369, and the number of Negroes, 1,944; the number of whites making over $9,000 per year is 996, and Negroes, 24. Over a quarter of a century ago that situation was described in a matter-of-fact way by the authors of *Deep South:* they used the words "white power."

The two young men who made *Black Natchez* came there well before the NAACP official was hurt, before the city faced a major crisis. They did not arrive on scene because "news" was being made, nor did they try to make news, or a "story" by arranging and rearranging people or situations. They lived in the town, the black side of the town, and over the months became familiar with it, and known to its people. They knew how to keep their equipment under wraps, how to live and observe. They were no "camera crew," nor did they have any deadline — or cause to fight. When they started filming they did so around the clock, to learn.

Eventually Natchez settled down, and eventually the two filmmakers retired to do their work, edit over ninety thousand feet of synchronous sound film. (The result will be shown on National Educational Television this spring.)

What have they produced? *Cinema verité* (direct cinema) it is called; everything "from life," with no "reconstructions," no "interviews." Yet, a movie is more than the technique its makers used — though today that may be an old-fashioned assumption. In this case the city of Natchez provided the two observers a bonus they never dreamed possible, a drama with rising and falling action. A situation of "ordinary," stagnant injustice suddenly exploded into a noisy, stirring emergency, with its aftermath of bitter fatigue and resignation.

The film does without interpretive narration. It opens with some Negroes talking about forming an organization like the Deacons to defend themselves. They are ordinary men, not leaders and not civil rights workers. They are afraid — afraid of whites, afraid of their own weakness, their own useless, necessarily subdued anger. Above all they are afraid to do anything, even to arm themselves, because they have no conviction that anything they try will make the slightest difference in their everyday lives. The camera moves from face to face, then moves outside, to the town, to black Natchez, whose houses command no tourists, whose people are lucky to eat, sleep, and love unmolested by white intrusions of one sort or another.

From the sight of Natchez as a representative southern town, we slowly move to the experience of a particular moment of political conflict. Children are picketing and trying to get more for their parents, for themselves as future parents; and a white organizer tries to inspire Negroes to follow suit, out of shame if not pride. "She don't understand," though. We see exactly what she doesn't understand — how they feel, what they see, and what a request from her of all people means. Ironically, once again the white man reduces the Negro to fear, to excuses and to the further calculated display of apathy.

Then the bombing, the almost successful assassination takes place, and Natchez is a different city. A thousand psychological and sociological truths are shattered, turned into splinters by the fact that violence can sometimes generate a new relationship between victim and oppressor. Crowds of Negroes assemble, full of anger and determination. The press arrives and television cameras, so that one camera can show other cameras at work, influencing by their very presence the people whose actions are making news. That vague abstraction "the community" suddenly becomes tangible, visible. Charles Evers is on hand to exhort people, to give them direction. Others are there, too — young men and women from the Mississippi Freedom Democratic Party. The battle is joined, between ministers, businessmen and teachers on the one hand, and young "activists" on the other. A committee that is to bargain with the mayor has no members that had been picketing, none that are poor, or young or women. The struggle is by now a familiar one, but the experience of seeing it unfold at close quarters in a movie house is altogether new.

Events conspired to furnish additional drama for the film. A curfew was called, followed by the entrance of the National Guard, with its helicopters, jeeps and drawn guns, showing once and for all the force and power that keep voteless, impoverished people respectful indeed of what sounds so right and good to the rest of us when it is urged — "law and order." There were night meetings, and day meetings, with increasing tension and increasing despair. The committee of Negroes was rebuffed by the mayor, and of course had to save face with the crowd, temporize, strive to keep pressure on white Natchez and the momentum for change alive in black Natchez. All this the film captures unforgettably: the leader's eyes, both wary and confident; the mixed faces before him, impassive, tentatively hopeful, disbelieving, full of zeal, ready to die, unwilling for a moment to lift a finger; and the guile, bluff and make-believe that all sides practice, part of what politics is, I suppose. The moderates of Black Natchez show their corrupt, pompous side, but more than a touch of arrogance and cruel insensitivity appears among the radical youth — including one scene that finds a white, northern civil rights worker trying to sell Ivy League logic ("You've just contradicted yourself") and Robert's *Rules of Order* ("That's right, the majority decides") to legitimately confused and agitated people.

The end comes swiftly and is true-to-life. Fervor subsides; weariness and a sense of futility return; the decisions will be made by negotiators, who will determine what those who have must give to keep those who have not more or less "quiet." People scold one another, or scratch their heads in bewilderment. How did it happen, so fast? What made a promising moment die? How is it that people can change overnight, abandon their lethargy, become willful, then put back on their old masks? Who speaks for Black Natchez, for Harlem or Watts?

I know of nothing in print that can match what *Black Natchez* offers: a direct look at a community, and one seized by a crisis, as well as an honest look at all sorts of things that social scientists study and study and study. If I were applying for one of those "research grants" to "evaluate" *Black Natchez*, I would say the film deals with real big things — like crowd behavior, social change, ideology in action, the ethnic politician, the generational gap, Negro nationalism, black power, class structure as it determines individual behavior, and all the rest of it, the deadening phrases and lifeless terms that are guaranteed to make the eyelids become heavy.

In any event, for an hour I could look and not read, and see people I have known all along in other cities brought to life. I am told that films like this are rare, and not encouraged.

There is no money for them. They are a "risk" and not very "useful," though millions are available today for every kind of incomprehensible and absurd venture by the most incredible assortment of "investigators." I suppose there is a reason why. Pounds of wordy reports can help us dally forever over nothing.

A film that records what is actually happening leaves us only one clear-cut alternative, to remember or to forget very, very hard. Things being the way they are, we perhaps find it cheaper emotionally to forego an inexpensive *Black Natchez* and invest in costly, evasive language.

New Republic, 1967

Mississippi Frontier

"The reason we went on strike, I was tired of working for $6 a day, and I was tired of my wife and kids working for $3 a day." Those are the words that open the documentary *Strike City,* and they are spoken by a Negro sharecropper who had the nerve to leave a plantation in Mississippi because he was not getting enough money. Of course others have left plantations; by the thousands families have slipped away, and in a few hours felt the exhilaration that goes with seeing those signs that say "Magnolia State" recede into the horizon. Months later, in Chicago or New York, they begin to wonder — not whether they had good cause to move, but whether the new and different misery of the ghetto justifies the ironically sad good-bye to the land (exploitation or not, the rural South has been home) and the long trip into a strange city where (at last, but to no avail) the Negro can vote, and not be denied a welfare check for doing so.

Yet some Negroes in Mississippi know what is in store for them "up North there," and refuse to go. They are not all tired, or lethargic or worn out, or without imagination; on the contrary, as *Strike City* shows, they have yet to surrender their minds or their hearts to the sheriffs and landowners who

run things in Tribbett, Mississippi, where the film was made.
Two other first-rate documentaries — *Black Natchez* and
Lay My Burden Down — have recorded the despair and fear
and resignation that southern Negroes feel. *Strike City*
catches a different "truth." It is about an act of sustained defiance and protest by the so-called "hopeless."

Two young men went down to Mississippi to work alongside the rural poor of the state. They were not filmmakers
bent on "doing" a documentary, nor were they out to "study"
something and then write a paper. They taught in a Head
Start program and eventually they watched a few bold sharecroppers think of ways to earn a living off the farm. They
were on hand when the incredible happened: field hands, Negroes living in Mississippi and on a large cotton plantation,
decided to leave their "jobs" and their "homes," to risk both
everything and nothing for higher wages.

I doubt many of us take on the brute force they did, with so
little chance of victory. They gave up the shacks their bosses
supplied, and they gave up the few dollars they earned when
there was work to do. (For many weeks they are without any
money at all.) They took on "law and order" in the Black
Belt, and did so at a time when their bosses were just about
through with them anyway. (Machines now harvest cotton,
and chemicals protect it from weeds.) They set up tents, right
out in the open of that small and special world of the Delta,
and they were joined by veteran civil rights workers, like
Frank and Jean Smith and by Tom Griffin and John Douglas,
who still wanted to be with them, and advance their cause. So
the Negro sharecroppers became strikers, and the white
youths became filmmakers.

A trickle of money and food came in. Churches and college students helped. The tents stayed, and their occupants
planned for the future. They met and talked. They decided

to stay, to build homes with their own hands, to grow food for themselves, to find work, if possible. They built a Head Start center. They appealed to outsiders for technical help and of course they appealed to the government of the United States, "their" government. They had become a "community," and they wanted action. In the film their determination to get that action comes across.

In April of 1966 they went to Washington, pitched their tents in Lafayette Square, opposite the White House, and embarrassed the strongest, richest nation that ever was with their presence. Naïve, demanding, unwilling to wait and wait (perhaps for fifty years, perhaps for a century), they had the nerve to think that the federal government could be of help to its very poorest citizens. They soon found out that there was nothing for them to do but go back to the rural South, and survive however they could. Washington had other things on its mind — and other wars to fight. No historian a few centuries hence will be able to say that this great nation turned inward on itself and worried selfishly about its own hungry people. Like the English before us, and the French before them, we have eyes that scan the entire planet, and leaders with a global sense of destiny. Destiny may not fill up the stomachs of children in Strike City, but national sacrifice is the price of being first.

In Strike City there aren't many belts to be tightened; the men mostly wear overalls, and the women loose-fitting dresses. The children are lucky to have clothes at all, particularly such irrelevant items as shoes and socks. Still, the film that documents their kind of life does not have them *only* in rags, *only* poor and fearful. In thirty minutes we see a far more unsettling spectacle: dispossessed sharecroppers who really want to work, who have energy and intelligence and vitality and crave some way of building a better life for themselves. In their film, Mr. Douglas and Mr. Griffin are making no claims, political or social or anthropological. They want to show what they saw, and lived beside in order to see. They don't intrude at all — even by announcing at the beginning or the end that they made it. I suppose an explanatory statement at the start, in the fashion of Robert Flaherty's documentaries, would help "orient" the viewer, but it really doesn't take long for the people and the routines and struggles of their lives to get across — and placate the viewer's need for order and "context."

The first few sequences are unforgettable. For a moment one feels in the presence of Hiroshima; a shot of the Delta reveals desolate, muddy land, with timber and steel and tin strewn about, reminders that some form of civilization once existed there or nearby. To the right is a tank of bottled gas, to reassure us that we are in the twentieth century. A "tent city" is in the making. The neighboring land may be beautiful, with cotton and pines and grazing cattle; but freedom is where you find it, even in America, and for these families it was to be found in a littered stretch of land near Tribbett, Mississippi.

From the land the camera moves to the people, to the eyes of a child, to hands fingering black-eyed peas, to bodies huddled near an old stove, to faces looking at one another with whatever affection and reassurance is possible. They are not going to flee the state, not going north for anything. For what, really? For a lousy welfare check and a ghetto tenement building, that's what. They know it and say it: "Once you run, you always run. It's not better up there."

They have decided not to run, but what can they do but sit still, be idle, go hungry? The camera lingers on soda pop, old cans, signs urging Dr Pepper and L&M cigarettes, and in a country store the inevitable jukebox. America's ironies are before us. Machines, slogans from advertising agencies, songs on the hit-parade, all in the middle of a community of hungry and cold people who have no money and no jobs.

Yes, winter comes to Mississippi also, and can bring snow on occasion. In winter the tents look curiously alone; except for them everything is white and indistinct. "It ain't too good living in a tent," a man says, "it ain't too bad and it ain't too good. But I don't care how tough it gets here at Strike City, I ain't going back to no plantation, and that's for sure." They look at the nearby shacks of those other sharecroppers who do not dare to go on strike and they feel the reassurance of the beleaguered fighter: things are bad, but at least a fight is under way. With warmer weather they work the land, start building "permanent" homes, and eventually leave — their destination Washington, their purpose an appeal to the White House, to Congress, and to something called "the public conscience."

Their decision to make the journey, their departure, and their encampment in the capital are strikingly conveyed, but the scenes in the Rayburn Building — *their* building — are almost too much to bear. They are there to ask redress of grievances, and before them spreads the congressional "scene," the corridors and offices, the hearing room with the Great Seal on its wall, the duly elected representatives and their aides, all of them embarrassed and a bit confused by this literal-minded exercise in democracy on the part of "innocent," illiterate field hands. What can any self-respecting congressman do with people like that?

"We need houses in Mississippi, and work," they told the reporters and television commentators who, like our congressmen, were embarrassed, and who dutifully and sympathetically told the public what they heard and saw. The *Washington Post* ran an editorial; The *New York Times* covered the story; and on Friday, April 8, 1966, on page one of the *Post*'s section called "City Life in Greater Washington" there was the merciful headline: "Camp-out in Park Ended, Mississippi Negroes to Quit City." They were going home for Easter — utterly disappointed.

Well, they are still there, still trying to make Strike City a going thing. They are still doing what the film shows them doing — listening to songs like "I'm Falling in Love Again," washing floors, planting seeds so as to grow grain and vegetables and flowers. There are a few, desperate efforts under way to bring work to them and other rural people — who will otherwise have to go to Chicago or Detroit, whether they want to or not. The "projects" go by names that are all too true and ironic — "The Poor People's Corporation," "Crafts of Freedom," "Liberty House." They are cooperatives, "small-scale" ones, and they are working well, in view of the limited resources they can muster. Recently the Vice President and the Secretary of Agriculture have said that our rural areas are neglected, and that the price of that neglect is riots in those large cities that every year absorb thousands of indigent and bewildered people who might otherwise be learning and working in the villages and towns they leave only in desperation. However, as *Strike City* shows, the desperate problems of southern sharecroppers simply cannot make a dent on this nation's capital today. We are, I fear, a nation that still lives most fully and wholeheartedly on the frontier; and tents or no tents, in 1967 that frontier is not in Tribbett, Mississippi, but in Saigon.

New Republic, 1967

Maddox of Georgia

The term "Southern Demagogue" should be recognized for what it is, a political epithet. It does not contribute anything to our understanding of the men to whom it is applied. I hold no brief for men of this type, nor for Tom Watson in so far as he was representative of them. I do not believe it is accurate to blame Watson for the "sinister forces" already mentioned. To do so would be to assign him far too important a role, a role that belongs to the vastly more impersonal forces of economics and race and historical heritage.
— C. Vann Woodward in *Tom Watson: Agrarian Rebel*

Lester Garfield Maddox, seventy-fifth governor of Georgia, walks by a statue of Tom Watson every day. Watson stands in front of Georgia's capitol building, his right hand forward, his left hand raised high, the South's Demosthenes in action. Below him one reads of his many achievements — he was an editor, a lawyer, a historian, an author, and in Washington, Georgia's representative and senator — and one also reads these words of his: "Give us the fortune which, through the cloud and gloom and sorrow of apparent failure, can see the instant pinnacles upon which the everlasting sunlight rests."

Governor Maddox knows about those "instant pinnacles," and if thousands of Georgians who live in what they now call "Maddox Country" have any further say, he will know about "the everlasting sunlight" of political power, perhaps one day like Tom Watson as a United States Senator. When I lived in Atlanta a few years ago Maddox was not quite, or not only, the loser and eccentric he is often described as once being. He was, in fact, a successful businessman, and an exceedingly well-known man who in 1961 had shown his strong hold on Atlanta's white vote in a mayoralty race with Ivan Allen, the present incumbent. If a successful politician is among other things a man who knows how to command and keep the attention and sympathy of his potential voters, the Maddox I used to see in the early sixties knew the people he was after, and knew how to reach them and stay in touch with them.

Sometimes I went to his restaurant, the Pickrick. The food was good and inexpensive. The owner was right there, friendly and willing to talk to anyone, as if his store were his home, and his customer his guest. The Pickrick's chicken was always being advertised in the very Atlanta papers Maddox considered so infamous and radical, but did not hesitate to use. He bought space to urge his food on the public, but he also wanted them to know they were victims. Washington, Communists, outsiders, a coalition of sinister and unpatriotic forces were not only at work, but in power; they controlled Atlanta through its "moderates," who step-by-step were selling out every conceivable principle for the almighty dollar.

"He's honest," I kept hearing from the white students, and even from the Negro students, who found the open, direct outrage that he directed at their cause easier to comprehend and fight against than slogans like "too busy to hate," the more or less official slogan that Atlanta used — and used successfully — to help avoid the riots that had plagued Little Rock and New Orleans when they yielded to the court-ordered desegregation of their schools. When the Civil Rights Law of 1964 was passed, so that Maddox was required to serve Negroes, he consolidated himself in the minds of millions all

over the country as the beleaguered idealist, the odd businessman who in the clinch would sacrifice a going concern, an
established moneymaking enterprise, for the sake of his
strongly held feelings. He would not be evasive, and raise his
prices to keep Negroes out, or try to get around the law by
calling his restaurant a club. He would not let them in while
under scrutiny or "attack," then do everything possible to ignore or insult them later — when, anyway, few of them
would want to come. He would stand and defend his turf with
a gun and a hatchet, and eventually he would surrender and
fold his tent and walk away.

To the white upper-class people of Atlanta — a number of
whom in 1961 had sent their children to private schools in
order to avoid the "tension" and "disturbance" that school
desegregation might bring — he was a fool, a nuisance and an
embarrassment. They had no desire to take on once again —
a hundred years after Appomattox — the money and power
of the North. They wanted their share of what New York or
New England have; they were beginning to get it; and they
were glad.

"Lester, he's a nut," one heard again and again. Lester
went on to open a furniture store, and to sell souvenir axes,
reminders of his last stand. Lester also was "crazy" enough,
"grandiose" enough to feel that his resentment, his sense of
galling defeat, his desire to strike out, strike back, get revenge, was shared by others — others in Georgia's countryside, its backwoods and small towns. He kept talking and
running — in 1966 for governor.

The rest now has to be called "history," rather than one
man's fate. The campaign was a fascinating one, with a prominent millionaire, Howard ("Bo") Callaway, the owner of
textile mills and a graduate of West Point, trying to lead the
Republican party to a victory over what seemed like the
fatally divided Democrats. Everyone expected the Democrats

to nominate Ellis Arnall, a liberal former governor, and everyone expected the segregationist conservative Republican to take after the Democrat as a dangerous radical, who would bring in more "federal controls," that is, further changes in Georgia's racial climate.

All the while Lester Maddox was going about and saying that he would be governor, and those in the know wouldn't even take the trouble to laugh anymore. The real thing to watch was the Republican resurgence. Georgia had gone for Goldwater. The state was prospering, with a lot of new business and a rising middle class. Callaway offered respectability and clear-cut power to the lawyers and doctors and bankers and engineers and managers. At long last they could join company with their counterparts elsewhere. The Southern Democrats could become the Republicans so many of them in essence are. As an avowed opponent of John F. Kennedy and Lyndon Johnson and the Civil Rights Bill of 1964, Callaway was a Republican who could defend the Southern Way of Life, but not at the cost of an economic recession. He was an industrialist, and he would bring in more industrialists; and the nervous poor whites, they'd vote for him too — because it was the Democrats who were the race-mixers, not only in Washington, but Atlanta. With Callaway in office Brooks Brothers might be persuaded to open a store in Atlanta, and there wouldn't be a lot of Negroes wanting to buy — or even sell — the clothes.

Well, Lester kept on visiting what Faulkner called the "hamlets" and the nearby towns, one after another; and down in Waycross, and over in Tallapoosa, and up around Jasper, white people stood around and said: "that man Arnall, he's one of the Atlanta boys, northern-bought, who's trying to slip the nigger over on us, so that they can keep on making their money. And Callaway, he's a rich boy with lots of airs, and a Republican. Hell, what choice have we got?" But then, there was Lester, tacking up his homemade signs and reminding anyone who came near that he was still going strong, despite the laughs and the jeers and the indifference of the wealthy people and the college types and their Negro friends, who are voting all over now. (It had come to that!)

When Primary Day came Lester Maddox became the nominee of the Democratic Party of Georgia. Callaway had to go out and tell people he was better, more stable, more reliable. He kept on pushing his conservative, segregationist views and he had a lot of money to help him do so; but Lester Maddox had some capital that the richest man in America couldn't equal. He had his life, all the words he'd spoken and the deeds he'd done — and let his fellow Georgians know about. No one's credentials as a conservative and a segregationist could possibly equal his; so he was free to take his reputation for granted and indeed build on it in a way that put Callaway on the run. He was Lester the loner, the little man who was self-made, not rich but with some savings from hard work. He had no big eastern money to fall back on, and he didn't have the railroads and the utilities behind him, and he wasn't going to be a front man for the *Atlanta Constitution* and its connections in Washington, D.C., and New York and God knows where else.

Callaway realized he was being boxed in, and grew desperate. The liberals said they weren't going to support him and they never could stomach Maddox. Lester kept pointing to himself as the honest white underdog and convinced a lot of people to vote for him. He didn't get a majority, but neither did Callaway, because thousands of liberals begged the issue by writing in Ellis Arnall's name. The Democratic legislature had to make the choice, and Maddox was a Democrat.

As governor, Maddox has been something of a surprise, so far. He made a temperate inaugural speech, and ever since has rather consistently toned down his language and stopped emphasizing his horror at the course of recent southern history. Since his election was considered first unbelievable and then the worst possible disaster by hundreds of thousands of Negroes and white liberals, his behavior to date puzzles them. "What happened to Lester?" I hear from some whites in Atlanta. When I asked a Negro youth I know to evaluate the governor's few months in office he put it this way: "It's still the same old Maddox underneath; you can feel it, and every once in a while he forgets, and then you *know* it. But I guess they're all sitting on him up there in the capitol and telling him what to say and he listens to them." I asked him *why* Maddox listens: "I don't know. Now that he's governor he sees he has to play ball with people and keep quiet." Then he asked himself and me the same question: "Sometimes I wonder why he *does* seem to be listening to the 'moderates.' Now that he's governor you'd think he'd really let loose; but no. It's as if he's changed — though you can't really believe it."

One hears he is shrewd; that he knows he has won, and cannot succeed himself; that he *has* the rednecks, and need only toss them an occasional word or act, whereas a restrained administration will gain him the skeptical white middle class, many of whom objected more to his manner than the substance of his ideas. Then, there are the "socioeconomic" interpretations. He was born poor and worked his way up. Now he is there, and dizzy because of the height. He is insecure, or in some "deep" way troubled, and his past rancor can be attributed to that fact. Since hard work and luck have carried him to the very top, his sensitive, uneasy self is at last appeased, and he no longer "needs" to tremble at the prospect of desegregation. Anyway — say those who dismiss all other explanations as superficial and frivolous — there is just so much a governor can do, and Maddox has found that out. A handful of bankers and corporation presidents and those who carry out their orders really run things, and every governor has to make his peace with them. Somehow "they" have "taken care" of Lester.

A short while ago I went to see Governor Maddox. In one sense things hadn't really changed much. In the Pickrick restaurant he had handed out chicken all day long, and now it is pork — favors, jobs and appointments for "the people." His outside office was full of them, the Flem Snopeses of Georgia who want, want, want. The phone calls come in from all over and without letup. I've had some experience with *need;* in the emergency ward of a hospital there always seems to be someone in trouble, day or night. For a moment I made the comparison: citizens have their troubles, and they take them to their governors. Yet the talk in the governor's anterooms and on his phones gradually weakened my analogy. Greed is a very special kind of need, and deserves its own recognition.

Perhaps we are so surprised or puzzled by the "change" in a man like Lester Maddox because we see all men as consistently and inevitably the "products" of what they *were.* They had a particular kind of childhood; they grew up in this neighborhood or that region; they formerly said or did something; and so there they are, fixed and predictable, easy prey for our categorical minds. Yet, at any moment new possibilities and new demands can come upon a person — and make him different; not different from what he *was,* but different because of what *is.*

I asked the governor why he seemed to strike so many people as a different man, an unexpectedly "moderate" one in the political sense of the word. (Personally he is a devoutly moderate man, a Baptist who prays often and hard and avoids liquor or cigarettes.) Ask his friends, he said; they would tell me he was the same person, "the very same one." So I said that if that were true, he was the same person doing different work. And he said yes, that was the case, and he loved his new

job. Then he talked about the job. It was hard and demanding. He was in the middle of things as he never was before,
and subject to pressures he'd never known about, and aware
for the first time of countless problems and people. Moreover,
every day he had to act, or seem to act; say something, or
sound as if he was saying something; take sides, or claim himself neutral and from that position use his weight here or
there.

Faced with the difficulties and ambiguities of a kind of
"power" that is always apparent but not quite as immediate,
tangible and unequivocal as its trappings suggest, Maddox is
doing what many political leaders always do. In that sense he
has not "changed," but come to terms with his position in a
particular way. In his own words he is "going to the people"
rather than trying to be a lawgiver. ("New legislation isn't as
important as being the best example, being for Georgia an
honest governor.") He wants to sell the state, "unite the people and stand for sensible government." As if Georgia were a
Beauty Queen, he has mastered all of her vital statistics, and
he will advertise them and defend them — every day, in every
way, and all over. He is up to the job, to the travel, to the
begging and coaxing, to the flattery that he must give as well
as get, to the reporters and the television cameras, to the various people and groups who want from him the *act* of a statement, the *move* of patronage, rather than any sustained and
coherent social policy or initiative. Gestures of course can become so much sham, but here I think Lester Maddox will not
fail. He conveys sincerity and he is also tireless. No aura of
cynicism or pragmatism will surround his administration.

Polite, methodical, persistent, able to tell every stranger
how good it is to see him (and make it sound believable) he
has seized upon the Truth of Enterprise; beside it issues of
race or reform seem unimportant. Did I know that "tourist
expansion" is way up in Georgia? Did I know that he is wel-

coming more visitors, more business leaders to the state than any of his predecessors? Did I know that for the first time *any-one* can come into his office, on the first and third Wednesday of each month? "They come in, all the people, wealthy or barefoot." He hasn't asked for new taxes from his rich visitors, and I didn't see any shoes around for the barefoot ones, though I spotted a book called *Praying Can Change Your Life.*

In a flash he can surprise his listener with the use of the expression "power structure." He was elected governor "without the help of the power structure." To spell it out, "not one big paper, not one railroad, not one magazine, not one courthouse" supported him. But "the power structure" he once fought at a distance is now nearby, and ready to be of help. He told me that he wants "to prove his critics wrong." He already has. He has learned how to deal with them — and with himself. If you pick him up on the term "power struc-ture" and ask him about "it," he can reply with all the indi-rection that the rest of us learn: "People in office tend to get isolated. They stick with the power structure too much and they're not close to the people anymore." The literal danger then is guilt by association. Maddox has always worried about the company he keeps, and he realizes that not only Negroes, but well-to-do whites refused to vote for him.

In essence he will avoid a fight and run to the voters. The "power structure" will meet up with no angry populist — at last in power, at last ready to get revenge. A man who has been called every psychiatric epithet emerges as "sane and sensible." What is more, he will use as well as be used, and thus show how "creative" and "adaptive" he is. The poor and the hungry can enter his office. They may not get food or cash from it, but they will see it, and not picture its owner a traitor who spends all his time currying favor with high society.

Maddox is hardly a Tom Watson, but he does manage to take up where Watson left off. The brilliant "agrarian rebel" found turn-of-the-century southern politics so frustrating, so dishonest, and so devious that he just about lost his senses, and surrendered his mind to the region's terrible historical ironies. First he kept his populism, but cut it off from the Negro; and then he became so obsessed with the Negro (and additional "others," like the Jews and the Catholics) that he even lost interest in the poor white man. Having fought "the power structure" and lost to it, he learned to escape noticing it through the rhetoric of blind hate.

I do not know whether "they" in rural Georgia "really" believe Lester can make a difference in their lives, but I think the governor has indicated that he understands their feelings. He knows what in sophisticated Atlanta inspires their awe, and he knows that awe is a mixture of fear and desire. Through them he has "made good," but if he wants to stay in power he'd better not forget that.

It all works out well for "the power structure," too. The governor who says he's for "the little man" has to speak and act like one. All the pieties of America and the South will be his to mix adroitly: the democratic ones with the racist ones, the ones that urge "equality" with those that glorify competition and the lonely winner. The "little man" like everyone needs someone to trust, someone who speaks for him regularly and "naturally." Because he will concentrate his energies on keeping that trust alive, Maddox will threaten no one important, and in fact be a very handy man for many of those who fought him to have in power. He will "keep them happy down on the farm" or in the towns by doing his share to make certain that the real workings of Paris never come to anyone's attention — even his own.

New Republic, 1967

More on Southern Politics

Of books about the South, there is no end. Nor will there be so long as the South remains the region with the most distinctive character and tradition.

— V. O. Key, Jr. in *Southern Politics*

It is as if the terrible curse upon states like Mississippi, Georgia and Virginia has driven more than the usual number of men and women to the word, printed or spoken. In the nineteenth century the South claimed its famous orators and its clever historians or ministers — who had to justify the unjustifiable and presumably felt that continuous talk would conceal the brazen dishonesty of any argument. Then, there were those diaries written before, during and after *the* war. A book like *Diary From Dixie* tells the reader more than what happened to Mary Boykin Chesnut, and even more than what "life" was like under the Confederacy. She could not quite deceive herself, or stop trying to do so — and in either case she had to write. Nor is it an accident that the South has produced some of our finest newspapers, journalists — and incidentally, social scientists.

Climbing Jacob's Ladder is another of those "books about the South" that V. O. Key described; and it is, I believe, a worthy successor to his own *Southern Politics*. It is something more, though, because it was written by two Southerners who not only want to educate and inform their readers, but "speak" to them in the emotional and religious senses of that word. The result is a scholarly text, crammed full of facts, documents and statistics that will be indispensable to future historians and political scientists. Yet even more valuable is something else that comes across on every page: a "feel" for what makes social change, for what can happen between individuals and their government, given the "right" moment. In other words, Pat Watters and Reese Cleghorn not only want to record what happened, they want to tell how it all happened, and how it felt as it was happening. Theirs is, I suppose, an "interdisciplinary approach" that uses the skills of the political scientist, the social historian, the anthropologist, the psychologist and not the least, the writer. Since they are "only" journalists, and have no great "training," no "credentials," one can only admire their achievement all the more. Or could it be that they are warm, vivid writers, and shrewd students of that "interdisciplinary" phenomenon called "life," *because* — among other reasons — their minds and hearts were not squeezed dry and buried in some academic graveyard?

In any event they have written a beautiful book: beautiful in its blend of documentation and passion; beautiful in its clear direct language; beautiful in its persistent fairness to what *really* happened, no matter how tempting a little bit of retrospective distortion can be; and finally, beautiful in its stubborn refusal to make flashy, appealing generalizations about a region that has always been prey to the global and partisan conclusions of its observers.

Watters and Cleghorn wrote their book to record a significant turn in American history, "the arrival of Negroes in southern politics." In 1960 the sit-in movement began when four Negro youths asked for some coffee from a reluctant waitress in Greensboro, North Carolina. Those youths might then have traveled all over the South in vain pursuit of the vote as well as food and drink. In point of fact, members of the sit-in movement did just that for several years; they planted themselves in Mississippi and Alabama, in Georgia and Louisiana, and they tried to "organize" rural Negroes, persuade them against every instinct to go seek the vote. Yes, there were forays into restaurants, libraries and (under court order) schools or colleges; but the major thrust of the civil rights movement in the early sixties was political. Then, as now, Negro activists wanted more "power" for their people. In those days the rallying phrase sounded more conventional — "the power of the ballot" rather than "black power." Yet, the revolutionary implications of the civil rights struggle eventually had to emerge. Negroes for all practical purposes had lived outside the South's economic and political system. The time had come to enter, to make demands, to upset things as they are, to make things different, and inevitably to confront and challenge "law and order" — the kind that for generations kept voteless American citizens miserably poor and legally removed from every one of our significant social and cultural institutions. Put differently, the time had come for Negroes to start running their own lives, clearly an unacceptable idea to white people, who desire cheap and compliant labor, and a fearful idea to rural Negroes, who know all too well what a sheriff can do, let alone a mob or any old bossman.

So against white power and Negro fear a relatively small number of people started out making the "rounds," living in the "community," going out in the "field," and ultimately attempting to persuade grown men and women that — of all things in twentieth-century America — they should try to register as voters. The heart of this book tells what happened to the activists and leaders, to the masses of Negro people, to this nation.

The authors are Georgians, and in the period covered by the book (1961 to 1965, when a voting rights bill was finally passed) they both worked in Atlanta as reporters. Their story opens with a haunting description of a meeting in Terrell County, Georgia. The year is 1962, and Pat Watters was there. Charles Sherrod led the men and women in prayer. They were assembled in a Baptist church and a painting of Jesus hung over the pulpit. On another wall a picture of President Kennedy was prominently displayed. I suppose Sherrod could be called a "youth," a "civil rights worker." He was also a minister, and those were the days when the most "radical" of Negro and white students still quoted from the Bible. "If God be for us, who will be against us?" Sherrod asked and intoned in prayer. The sheriff was there, ready and willing to answer the question. They sang and they sang:

Voices that were weak at first gained strength as they moved up the scale with the old, familiar words: *We are climbing Jacob's Ladder | Every round goes higher, higher | We are climbing Jacob's Ladder.* Sherrod spoke again, softly, almost singing the words. "All we want our white brothers to understand is that Thou who made us, made us all." Another voice spoke: "Everybody is welcome. This is a voter registration meeting." . . .

A few nights later that church, the Mount Olive Baptist Church, and two others nearby were burned to the ground. Presumably the pictures of both Jesus Christ and an American President were burned to ashes. The authors remind us of much more than the events that took place in southwestern Georgia. They begin with a historical account of southern political life in the nineteenth and early twentieth centuries. They offer a detailed and fair account of the "movement" — its forerunners, its uncertain beginnings, its gradual rise to a position of real significance. They describe the old Negro leadership, in cities like Atlanta and in rural areas. Then comes the climax, like Act III in one of Shakespeare's plays: "The Struggle — Fear and Apathy," followed by "The Struggle — Jacob's Ladder," and then "Field Report — Telling It Like It Was." Those 100 pages document some of the most stirring and heartbreaking moments in American history. One "field report" follows another — from John O'Neal, from Bob Moses, from Frank Smith, from Jack Chatfield, from Reginald Robinson, from Elizabeth Wyckoff and Prathia Hall. Those of us who lived in the South then, and in one way or another worked beside such incredibly determined men and women, will find it hard to deal with long stretches of *Climbing Jacob's Ladder.* I felt in myself a curious mixture of sorrow, indignation — and yes, nostalgia, because those were days of hope and trust.

They were days of action, too. The Voter Education Project of the Southern Regional Council was set up by foundations with the "advice and consent" of the Kennedy Administration. The purpose was simple: Find out why thousands and thousands of American citizens are afraid to register to vote, and "educate" them to be — well, what politicians call "loyal and responsible citizens."

I fear no one was fooled. Southern politicians, like all politicians, know when patriotic or "high-minded" talk ends and a threat to the "realities" of our social system begins. A public official in Louisiana put it all very directly to me a few years back: "Why are they quoting all that Constitution stuff, and the Declaration of Independence? Don't they know who runs things down here, and how we're going to keep it that way? And if it takes a few bullets, I think that will happen, too."

He and his kind did fire bullets. They used bombs and they burned buildings down to the ground. They terrorized and continue to terrorize thousands of American citizens. The Voter Education Project was in fact an attempt to get those

American citizens the vote without the help of new federal laws; and it both succeeded and failed. In some areas voters were enrolled; in others there was the kind of fanatic and murderous resistance that ultimately led to the Mississippi Summer Project of 1964, the Selma March, a host of murders (this book is dedicated to thirteen known killed from 1962 to 1967) and eventually a bill passed by a Senate finally able to cloture itself.

The authors can only be cautiously hopeful. Reese Cleghorn is an editor of the *Atlanta Journal*, whose office is a reasonably short walk from Lester Maddox's office in the state capitol. Pat Watters is the director of information for the Southern Regional Council; every day he has to deal with the awful news that comes into the office of that unique and fascinating organization. As a matter of fact, *Climbing Jacob's Ladder* is one effort (among many) of the Council's to make sense of what happened, is happening, is likely to happen in the region. This book is, of course, unusually significant, but from month to month the Council's "special reports" and its quarterly, the *New South,* continue to press upon us the somber and shameful conditions that still exist in a very prominent section of America: hunger, malnutrition, overwhelmingly segregated schools — yes, and counties where Negroes do not yet dare vote. In his bluntly worded introduction, Leslie Dunbar, who until recently headed the Southern Regional Council, has this to say: "For every victory has demonstrated to Negroes how deeply and firmly embedded in our social system are the causes of their disadvantage, and many have grown weary of victories, purchased by turmoil and yielding too little to requite all that went into their gaining."

Here we are then, in 1967. All sorts of changes are occurring in the South, but all sorts of terrible inequalities persist. Men like the ones who wrote this book and wrote its introduction continue to do what they can. What is needed, though, is money, lots of it, and all that goes with money — plans, ideas, jobs, a break with the stale past. Billions go into another nation's South, in the form of guns and bombs. But even if we were not at war, would our own South ever get that kind of money? Will the South's old Bourbons give way to a new breed of wily or simpleminded segregationists — governors from Jackson, Montgomery and Atlanta who want to give Washington's "living" a try? Does this nation have to permit hundreds of thousands of its citizens to live as people do in the rural South, or Appalachia, or our northern ghettos? Those are tired questions today. They've been asked again and again, and there were moments a few years ago when it seemed that they just might be decisively answered by a President, a Congress and a nation that were "going someplace." But in a flash our destination was changed, and who right now knows where we'll end up?

New Republic, 1967

The Way It Is
in South Carolina

No southern state can match South Carolina's ability to resist the claims of black people without becoming the object of
national scorn. Since 1954, cities like Little Rock and New
Orleans, or small towns like Clinton, Tennessee, have become
discredited as riots and mobs formed and did their ugly work.
It was in relatively progressive North Carolina that the sit-in
movement began. It was in proud, sophisticated (and boss-
dominated) Virginia that a county closed its entire school system to prevent "race mixing" among the vulnerable young.
It was in Jacksonville and St. Augustine, Florida, that bloody
racial fights took place over and over again. Mississippi's
notoriety needs no mention, nor do Alabama's Selma and
Birmingham. In Albany, Georgia, one of the decisive battles
of the early civil rights movement was fought. Through it all
South Carolina remained relatively untouched and unnoticed, an island of unyielding segregationist defiance — managed and run, though, by exceptionally clever and cool political leaders who long ago learned how to dress up the rankest
kind of hate and exploitation in those lovely, old, "fine-

appearing" clothes that go under the name of "southern gentility."

Things were not always so shrewdly done in the state. Early in this century "Pitchfork Ben" Tillman and Cole Blease and "Cotton Ed" Smith went up to Washington from South Carolina and effortlessly set the standard for any young, aspiring southern politician who wanted to know the ins and outs of racist demagoguery. Back home, the state until recently was caught in a series of vicious and stormy feuds: between "city folk" and the farmers; between the highland, the industrial piedmont section and the low counties along the coast; between mill workers and millowners; between proud, haughty, lovely, more than faintly decadent Charleston and the rest of the state, thought to be so boorish by the old seaport's self-conscious aristocrats, who have always known that a taste for azaleas, palmetto trees and antique furniture can keep the mind off those touchy political issues; and most of all, between the races, the whites and the many hundred thousand blacks who until around 1930 made up a majority of South Carolina's population.

It used to be that, in Rupert B. Vance's succinct words, "the ability to make a class appeal without offering a class program" took a skilled and loudmouthed politician to the governor's chair in Columbia and then up north, where the floor of the United States Senate had to be turned into the cheapest of backwoods stumps so that the "good white people" back home would feel racially redeemed if not well fed. Now a senator or congressman from South Carolina can take the home front for granted and keep his eyes on much larger things — in the case of Representative Mendel Rivers, the whole military establishment, and in the case of Senator Strom Thurmond, the men Republicans nominate for President and Vice President.

Recently, and by no means for the first time, we traveled

through Mr. Thurmond's state, and went through a sadden-
ing, yes a gruesome series of experiences in Mr. Mendel
Rivers's congressional district. To be exact, we visited Jasper
and Beaufort counties, both south of Charleston; and just off
the mainland, we spent time on Hilton Head Island, one of a
number of colorfully named islands — St. Helena, St. Simon,
Jekyll, Racoon, and most important, Parris — that hover over
the coasts of Georgia and South Carolina. Once pirates escaped to Hilton Head and Parris islands; now marines by the
thousands are there, and also rich tourists, who come to places
like the Sea Pines Plantation for golf and sun and swimming,
and often enough remain there forever in attractive homes
purchased from the Plantation, which is both a resort and a
company that among other things develops land, builds
houses, plans whole communities. We had lunch at Sea Pines,
but we also went to other parts of Beaufort County, to the
homes of white and black people who live near the Plantation
or the famous marine base on Parris Island, or a naval hospital at Port Royal, three miles away. With us was Dr. Milton J.
E. Senn, a distinguished pediatrician, Sterling Professor of
Pediatrics at Yale, and for a long time, head of Yale's Child
Study Center. Also with us was Dr. Donald Gatch, a hard-
pressed general practitioner, a white man who works among
the poor of both races — alone, day and night, often for nothing.

What did we see among those poor? More to the point, how
can we possibly convey the truth of what Dr. Gatch sees every
day, convey it in such a way that a rich, powerful nation will
pay even a token of attention? In fact, the nation is paying a
kind of attention — to Dr. Gatch if not to his patients. Mr.
Jamie L. Whitten represents Mississippi in the Congress and
is chairman of the House Appropriations Subcommittee on
Agriculture. In the past few weeks he has sent investigators all

over the country to ask men like Dr. Gatch exactly why they have the gall to say that thousands of Americans are hungry, malnourished and disease-ridden. Dr. Gatch was closely questioned, as was Al Clayton, a first-rate photographer from Nashville, whose 200 or so photographs, taken all over the South and in Appalachia, recently shocked the Senate Subcommittee on Manpower, Poverty and Unemployment.

"I told those investigators to go look at my patients, dozens and dozens of them," Dr. Gatch told us. "I told them that it's a disgrace that investigators are sent down by the government to bother me — I work about eighteen hours a day with those people and I don't live in a big, fancy house — rather than look at the conditions here, the way these people have to live. There's a lot wrong here, but there must be a lot wrong in Washington, too."

In 1968, as Lyndon Johnson's Great Society comes to an end, as Richard Nixon's Presidency, dedicated to so-called "forgotten Americans," gets ready to begin, we saw "a lot wrong" all right, and we saw "forgotten Americans" all right: "Well, no sir, there just isn't no work for me. There isn't. So, I don't have any money coming in, none. I have my neighbors and my brothers and they help. And I hope maybe soon I can get some work. Now my wife, she's sick, real bad sick, and I don't know what I can do. What can you do if you don't have a dollar and your woman, she's bleeding, and your kids they seem sickly a lot of the time?" He is white, a white South Carolinian, a member of Mendel Rivers's constituency. Mr. Rivers makes sure that billions of dollars go to arm this nation, but he certainly isn't going to do all that, only to let communistic schemes develop in Beaufort County — schemes that would provide that proud white Southerner with food and medical care and the work he craves.

Down the road we visited another family in Mr. Rivers's district. The home stands on cement blocks, a wood and tarpaper shack, with newspapers stuffed in cracks here and there. There is no running water, no central heating, no electricity, not even an outdoor privy. Water is toted from afar, and it is bad water, pumped from a well that does not go deep enough, and is contaminated. The fields nearby take human waste; and flies and mosquitoes are everywhere. The house has no screens. In winter a small coal stove provides all the heat that eight American citizens will get. Beaufort County has a food stamp program — unlike some other counties in the state — and here is how that works: "You've got to have money to buy the food stamps, and if you don't have any, you can just go and starve to death. My husband is with me, and so we can't get any welfare, not a penny of it. He can't get work, and we don't know what to do. I guess you go north or you starve. If it wasn't for the little we grow and the fact we all try to look after each other, we'd be dead right now; yes sir, most of us would just be dead and gone."

Beaufort and Jasper counties are full of disease and hunger and extreme poverty. "We need a hundred Dr. Gatches," the woman in that cabin went on to tell us. "When you're born, you haven't much of a chance here. Chances are you'll die before you should. I can't believe God meant for us to bring children into the world, only for them to go hungry all the time, and be sick every last day of their life." Her doctor agrees with her. Dr. Gatch describes the conditions in the county so grimly and sadly that he can easily be dismissed as hysterical or overworked and fatigued — until his listeners become his companions as he makes his medical rounds: "They're born in those shacks, hundreds and hundreds of children every year. If I don't deliver them, no one does — except the husband or a relative or a woman who calls herself a midwife, but has no training whatsoever, and keeps on shouting 'push, push' at the poor woman. Then from the day they're born they know trouble, the kind of trouble I once would never have dreamed existed in this country. Their mothers are poorly nourished. If they have a good milk flow, that's lucky; but you don't see bottles here, or many bottles of milk in these homes. The infant gets sick and there's no one to see him, no hospital for him to visit, no doctor or nurse — unless they get to me. Pretty soon the baby becomes hungry, then undernourished, then malnourished. His body doesn't have enough protein, or vitamins or minerals. His bones don't develop as they should. His muscles become weak and flabby. His joints are swollen. His skin is covered with sores and infections. He may get a cold — and die, die in a matter of hours; or they live on, but with all kinds of things wrong with them. You wonder how they *do* manage to live on."

We saw many of those children, and we saw the things wrong with them. We saw the food they eat: old, stale bread and grits and more grits and gravy over the grits. We saw sick children, sick with not one or two but a whole series of diseases. Dr. Gatch claims that every day he sees diseases like rickets, scurvy, beriberi and pellagra. Medical students are taught that those diseases no longer exist in America; and upon our arrival Dr. Senn questioned Dr. Gatch very carefully about his patients, about their problems and symptoms. Then we all went to see them, the men and women and children we had talked about in a doctor's office; and we did indeed see what those medical textbooks describe: weak, lethargic children, with swollen legs and swollen bellies; children whose skin was dry and rough and infected and discolored and ulcerated and excoriated; children whose muscles were wasted, whose bones were quite obviously deformed; children who were no longer hungry, because they were too ill to desire food. Later, we discussed the blood tests that had to be taken to clinch a diagnosis of this or that vitamin-deficiency disease — in contrast, that is, to such "routine" diseases as anemia or pneumonia or the worm infestations. But tests or no tests. Dr. Senn could only say, "Yes, the clinical picture is not only one of malnutrition, but vitamin-deficiency diseases — which really aren't supposed to exist in this country."

Not that we need any new and fancy medical or sociological studies of Beaufort County or dozens of counties like it in South Carolina and elsewhere. The facts are all there: 17,536 people in that one county have an income under $3,000 a year; 11,064 see less than $2,000 a year; 1,145 families get less than $1,000 per year; only 898 people receive public assistance; in 1965 the infant mortality rate, among the very highest in America, was 62.4 per 1,000 births, the kind of figure one expects to see beside the name of an underdeveloped nation in South America, Asia or Africa; about four percent of Beaufort's people have health insurance; about half the county's people have less than eight years of education and 20.4 percent have been declared "functional illiterates"; over a third live in houses called "substandard"; and among blacks about four-fifths of the population has not gone beyond elementary school, and many have never had any schooling at all. "One-third of a nation is ill-housed, ill-fed, ill-clothed," said Franklin Delano Roosevelt in 1933. The white people of Beaufort County still have reason to say amen, and as for the black people, they must insist that the figure be doubled at the very least.

We doubt that Senator Thurmond or Representative Rivers will be much troubled by all those facts — obtainable from federal agencies located virtually next door to their offices — or by reports that thousands of their constituents are hungry, sick, jobless and penniless. But neither of those two honorable men can afford to ignore the implications of another set of medical statistics. In 1962, an article appeared in *Public Health Reports* called "Study of Intestinal Helminth

Infections in a Coastal South Carolina Area." Hundreds of people were tested for worms, tested in order to determine the prevalence of parasitic infections in Beaufort County. Over 70 percent of the people examined carried worms inside them, and over 80 percent of the children were so infected. Dr. Gatch can show his visitors X-rays in which long worms are seen happily and snugly rooted in the intestinal walls of both young and old, black and white American citizens. He estimates that over 90 percent of his patients suffer from round worms. Naturally the parasites have to live, so they feed off their hosts, who develop anemia, lassitude, weakness — and worse, because the eggs of some worms are carried through the blood to the lungs, where they incubate and frequently cause pneumonia. Of course, children in Beaufort County are always getting pneumonia, or so the "socialistic" Dr. Gatch says: "They'll be weak, anemic, underfed, and living in those shacks. A freezing spell comes, and they've had it; a baby dies here, another one there, next door. And the worms, they go all over the body — to the eyes, the lungs, the stomach, the liver. The other doctors here never see any of these people; and then when I describe conditions like these, they turn on me and call me every name in the book."

He has indeed been called every name in the book, and threatened with death again and again. For testifying before the Citizens Board of Inquiry into Hunger and Malnutrition in the United States, at hearings held in Columbia, South Carolina, in November of 1967, he earned the additional contempt of his colleagues, who can't see why he "bad mouths" his neighborhood. If he is shunned by other doctors, he has a devoted following among poor people of both races. A number of those people have been singled out for an educational and medical program whose ultimate purpose is to determine how the county can essentially be freed of the worms that plague its people. The rich and powerful (and rather lib-

eral) owners of the Plantation know that medicines alone cannot solve the problems. So long as houses lack decent sanitation and clean water the eggs and worms will reappear,
however successfully eradicated (for a while) by a program of
chemotherapy for everyone. Poor, badly educated people can
be taught better habits, but they also need better homes if
they are to stay well — and keep working. At Sea Pines em-
ployees are examined every six months for worms, which in
Beaufort County can only be considered a tentative and ineffective effort at medical surveillance, all of which the men
who run Sea Pines know very well. They also know that the
tourists who come to their lovely and even spectacular resort
would not take kindly to the news that worms are all over
Hilton Head Island and Parris Island and Bluffton and other
places in Beaufort County. Nor do the thousands of American
soldiers and sailors stationed in the county deserve exposure
to worms — which a nonmilitary employee can always bring
in. We have heard a lot these days about the role of private
enterprise — and the Department of Defense — in the war
against poverty. Perhaps the people who run Sea Pines Plantation and our marine base on Parris Island will persuade
their congressman and senator that a lot has to be done
nearby — not to further communism, but protect a lot of free
enterprise in their state.

Certainly the poor people of Beaufort County, for all their
sadness and weariness, would respond to any help that came
along. In the midst of a very gloomy stay we happened to notice a sign that announced "Hilton Head Fishing Coopera-
tive, Inc." Perhaps we were looking for something, anything
to distract us, to divert us from the overwhelming misery —
so much of it, and present everywhere, in shack after shack
after shack, without letup. We drove down a long, dusty road
and met a strong, well-spoken man who is one of the Coopera-

tive's officers. "It's bad here," he started out, but he also had a little hope for us: "A lot of people here they're gone. They're as good as dead. A lot of others, they go north — and then white people down here laugh, because they've got rid of us. And in the North, they get angry with *us*, and they forget it was down here that they treated us like this, and drove us so hard that we're half-dead, more than half-dead, by the time we get up there. I know, because I see people leaving here all the time. They carry South Carolina up to New York, and down here, the white people say 'good, good we got rid of them,' and up there, the white people don't get angry at the white people down here, no sir. They take it out on us. Yes sir, that's the way.

"A few of us, we figured we'd stay. We figured we'd build a few shrimp boats and try to get together; you know, work side-by-side and pitch in for one another. Then we heard we might get some help from the government, an FHA loan, so we could build a dock and a little railway to unload in, and carry the fish, and a place to work and store what we catch."

Eventually they got their FHA loan, and now the dock is built and a processing house is half done. We walked on the dock and on a beautiful southern midafternoon we could see those shrimp boats coming out of the Atlantic into the nicely protected cove. One boat had already docked and been emptied. Its crew worked busily on deck; the head of each shrimp had to be separated from its meaty tail, the part we eat. The men took the shrimp between thumb and forefinger and in a flash the head was gone, and the rest of the shrimp at rest in a growing pile. Later the cargo would be washed, weighed, put on ice — and inspected by visiting buyers, from Charleston and as far away as Tampa. Yes, the sea was refreshing, and its quiet, uninterrupted blue, its gentle wind, and its sandy edges offered a brief respite from all we had seen and were to see.

But we had other reasons to feel good. The black shrimpers appeared vital, confident, proud and industrious. They talked easily with the white buyers, and with some white shrimpers who were asking to join them. They also were showing some tourists around, guests at the Hilton Head Hotel, which is part of Sea Pines Plantation. For a moment, in front of the sea, all the barriers of race and class and region meant nothing. For a moment poor black men could help poor white men and even teach a few things to rich white men.

Yet up there in Charleston, that same day, the *News and Courier,* which seems to look upon the twentieth century as one giant conspiracy, had other things to shout about than Beaufort County and its problems: "For twenty years, ever since Nixon exposed Alger Hiss, the master Communist spy, the Communists have hated and feared Richard Nixon. Hanoi would do anything to block Nixon's election. The Communists know that with Nixon in the White House they would be in serious trouble." Now that Mr. Nixon will be going to the White House perhaps the *News and Courier* and Senator Thurmond and Congressman Rivers will be able to relax, sure at last that the Republic is no longer about to go Communist. Perhaps they will look at other threats — at the death that stalks their state: death of infants; death of bones; death of muscles and skin; death of the mind and heart and spirit of thousands and thousands of American citizens. The day after his victory, before he headed south, Richard Nixon said he wanted to bridge various "gaps," between the young and the old, between the races, between his supporters and his critics. If he is interested, if he means what he says, he will find no wider gaps than the ones that prevail in his friend Strom Thurmond's South Carolina. At last South Carolina's distinguished senator will have influence in the White House, because at last Mr. Nixon has got there. We have been promised real leadership from a man who aims to forget the political deals and maneuvers of the past and turn his eyes to the history books. The people of Beaufort County, who have their own history to live with, every single day, can only sit and wait.

New Republic, 1968

A Message from Mississippi: "We Need Help"

In May of 1967 six physicians — I was one of them — spent time in Mississippi's Delta. Dozens of homes were visited; children and their parents were given medical examinations; and the conditions of life that thousands of American citizens still must take for granted were observed and described. In July of 1967 a committee of the United States Senate heard it all — the hard-to-believe medical facts that again and again had to be insisted upon: Americans go hungry every day, become malnourished, die because they didn't get enough food and the right kind of food and fall sick and never, never at all see a doctor; American children possess bloated bellies and swollen ankles, even suffer from kwashiorkor and marasmus, diseases that mark the very last stages of starvation and that are associated with countries like Biafra or cities like Calcutta.

Mississippi's two senators were given a chance to cross-examine the doctors, but declined to do so. Mississippi's governor, Paul Johnson, sent out doctors of his own, well-established and conservative ones, to make the same rounds the other doctors had, to find out whether their charges had any substance. Eventually they, too, submitted a report to the Senate, and in essence said the same thing:

"In summary, the situation as observed in Humphreys County does not appear to be markedly different from that in Leflore County. Here, also, there are persons who are under-housed, underfed, undereducated and underemployed. Some of them lack sufficient medical care and hospital facilities, and many are virtually unemployable."

Senator John Stennis responded with a bill aimed at feeding the nation's hungry and providing the Senate with more scientific information about who is hungry, where, and to what extent. His bill easily went through the Senate, but somehow became stalled for months in the House of Representatives where other Mississippians also wield great power, among them Mr. Jamie L. Whitten, who ranks third among the fifty-one members of the House Appropriations Committee and is a member of the Appropriations subcommittee for National Defense, for Public Works and most important, for Agriculture.

For fifteen years Mr. Whitten has been chairman of that Agriculture subcommittee, a position that has given him a decisive say in everything the government does and does not do with and about our farms, our enormous surpluses of food and our hungry citizens. The testimony of the six physicians before the Senate and their report "Hungry Children," issued by the Southern Regional Council, may have brought national attention to conditions in Mississippi and may even have moved the state's senators, but from the very beginning those doctors had been warned of the congressional facts of life. After their survey was finished they left Mississippi for Washington, where they were told by a high official of the Agriculture Department that they, and all the hungry children they had examined, and all other hungry Americans, thousands and thousands of them, would have to reckon with

Mr. Jamie L. Whitten, as indeed must the Secretary of Agriculture — whose funds come to him through the kindness of that same Mr. Whitten.

Since then Jamie L. Whitten has given some ground, but not all that much, to critics of the government's various efforts to get food to extremely poor families. True, the price of food stamps went down somewhat, and the government pressured reluctant counties in various states to accept the food stamp program, all of which came about because of the Senate's hearings in 1967 and 1968, strongly pushed by Senators Clark and Robert Kennedy, and because of the forceful, comprehensive and unnerving publication, *Hunger, USA,* put out by the Citizen's Board of Inquiry into Hunger and Malnutrition in America — the board's members were drawn from business, labor, the churches and the various professions — and finally because of the CBS commentary, "Hunger in America," which for an hour without letup presented an almost unbearable spectacle of extreme want and distress among many different people (of all races and creeds) in many regions of the nation. Yet, Mr. Whitten has made it amply clear that it is just so far that he will be pushed without fighting back cleverly, tenaciously and with an interesting assortment of weapons: strong pressure on the Agriculture Department to defend inadequate programs that simply are not reaching thousands of needy people; strong interference with the workings of the Department of Health, Education, and Welfare, whose nutritionist, Arnold Schaefer, for some reason stayed out of Mississippi in the course of his research on the incidence of hunger in the nation's rural and urban areas; and in the clutch, resort to agents of the FBI, who contacted poor and frightened people all over the country, but to round out their investigative picture also contacted men like Dr. Schaefer and the doctors who went to Mississippi two years ago, as well as other physicians at work with the poor.

In fact, Arnold Schaefer's report — he is chief of nutrition at the government's Center for Control of Chronic Diseases — gives scrupulous and statistically precise confirmation to the clinical impressions that many doctors have had and on occasion asserted in public. "We had certainly hoped to go to Mississippi," Dr. Schaefer said to reporters after he testified on January 22. He wouldn't say why he never got there, though he did say "Yeah!" to the question, "Was it politics?" A few weeks earlier, when asked about the use of FBI agents by his Agriculture committee, Mr. Whitten made it quite clear that he did not believe the charges that widespread hunger and worse, severe malnutrition, exist in America; nor was he willing to let those charges be asserted again and again: "If what's said is true [about hunger, for example], we need to correct it. If not, we need to stop folks from making wild charges."

We recently visited Mr. Whitten's congressional district with his admonition in mind. We had no interest in once again taking note of the state's difficulties, so often in the past used by self-righteous critics to divert themselves from some of their own problems, far nearer at hand than the Delta's. But Jamie Whitten and his good friend Congressman Tom Abernathy — their districts adjoin one another — have repeatedly demonstrated that they have every intention of ignoring needs and demands of thousands of people who live far away from Mississippi. Hungry men, women and children in Appalachia or in Texas or on Indian reservations in Arizona or in the poor sections of our large northern cities are denied food they need because a congressman like Jamie L. Whitten can frighten federal officials and prevent the Congress from acting quickly in the face of a medical emergency, a social disaster, and not the least in this powerful and wealthy nation, a moral outrage.

Mr. Whitten's district is made up of several tiers of Mississippi's northern counties. The district's eastern section contains some foothills of the Appalachians, including Woodall Mountain, at 806 feet altitude, the highest point in the state. Nearby is the fine, relatively progressive city of Tupelo and, about forty miles westward, Oxford with Faulkner's lovely home and the University of Mississippi. Further westward the Delta begins and with it mile after mile of farmland and, of late, pastureland. Day after day we went through that territory, accompanied by white and black people who were born and have lived all their lives in Mr. Whitten's Second Congressional District. We went to Savage, Mississippi. We went all through Tunica County and Tallahatchie County, where Mr. Whitten was born (in the little town of Cascilla), and where he still lives (in the county seat of Charleston). We talked with children and parents in Panola County and Yalobusha County where school districts under orders to desegregate or lose federal support have earned a possible reprieve from the Nixon Administration. Later we left Mr. Whitten's district for Mr. Abernathy's — and we revisited some of the families visited two years ago by the team of doctors who told the Senate that severe hunger and malnutrition (and associated diseases) are to be found in the state. Though we spent much of our time with poor black families, we also managed to see a number of white people in Mr. Whitten's district: schoolteachers, students and businessmen. In Mr. Abernathy's district we went to Mrs. Fannie Lou Hamer's house, but we also went to the Sunflower County courthouse — where we heard that if only there were more money, from Washington or any other place, "we'd be able to do better things for our colored folks . . . build new homes for them in Indianola."

Yet Mr. Whitten feels those "folks" don't even need better food, let alone such other "better things" as decent homes or jobs. From his various votes these past years one can gather his constituents don't need the Office of Economic Opportunity and food stamps for free and surplus food and community action programs and clinics that provide medical care and dental care and medicine. They don't need the Job Corps or Vista, or for that matter the right to vote explicitly spelled out by the federal government. Most of all, they don't need outsiders coming down and stirring things up — poking into their homes, shouting about their nutritional status, calling them sick, and trying to "get them going" as we heard it put in Jamie Whitten's hometown of Charleston.

Whatever Mr. Whitten's ideas about the desires of the people he supposedly represents, thousands of them don't quite see it his way. Just outside of Savage, Mississippi, and just inside Tunica County we spent an afternoon with a family who see, maybe, three or four hundred dollars in the course of an entire year. They live off the road in a broken-down shack of wood on the sides with a slanted, rusty tin roof on top. They have a coal stove for heat and cooking. They have no electricity, which means no refrigerator as well as no lights. They lack running water. They use a shallow, contaminated well, which is "just a mile or two off." They lack even an outhouse. Several relatives have gone north, but the word has come back that it's much better there in some ways, but no great paradise in others. What is life like for them in Tunica County? What do they eat? How is their health? "Oh, we're getting along," we are told for a start by a tall, large-boned mother of five who speaks much too softly at first, but several hours later almost like an old-fashioned orator, at last with an audience of countrymen to address. Then came the qualifications about "getting along," and an afternoon of them could have been a week of them, a year of them:

"Every morning the first thing I think about is what I can do to feed the kids. I don't have no money coming in. My husband, he works for him, and you know the bossmen around here, they'll give you some things and they won't give you others. We can use this house, it's his. He told us last year that as long as we didn't get any smart-alecky ideas in our heads, we'd be all right here; but if we did, we could go on up to Chicago where the niggers belong, and the mayor up there, he'd be taking care of us just like they do down here in Mississippi. The bossman don't give us much money, but there'll be ten dollars one week, and maybe five the next, and he gave us twenty for Christmas, I'll say that for him. He don't want us trying to vote and like that — and first I'd like to feed my kids, before I go trying to vote. For breakfast there isn't much, but they know it's not until the middle of the day they can eat. I give them some soup I make — I boil up a bone and some beans and there's the water and I salt it real good. I put some of the milk flakes [powdered milk] in the children's coffee, and that's good for them, I know. They gets their energy from the candy bars, of course. And I gives them grits. His wife — the bossman's — she'll come over here sometimes and give us some extra grits and once or twice in the year some good bacon. She tells me we get along fine down here and I says yes to her. What else would I be saying, I ask you?

"But it's no good. The kids aren't eating enough, and you'd have to be wrong in the head, pure crazy, to say they are. Sometimes we talk of leaving; but you know it's just no good up there either, we hear. They eat better, but they have had things up there I hear, rats as big as raccoons I hear, and they bit my sister's kid real bad. It's no kind of country to be proud of, with all this going on — the colored people still having it so bad, and the kids being sick and there's nothing you can do about it and like that. No sir, there's no doctor hereabouts for them or me or anyone like us. My kids, they were born right here, with my sister by my side and my aunt — she knows what to do. The white lady says if anything real bad ever

comes up, she'll take care of us, with her doctor, and I've
taken one or the other of my kids to her in the past, and she
tells me they're going to be all right, and you know, she gives
me something for them and tells me to rest them and not let
them be so wild out in the woods and like that. Well, I gets
what she's saying all right. You people talk about the vote. To
me what counts is if I could be able to feed us better and we'd
see a little money each Saturday or even the beginning of
each month, or so. My girl come home and told me we
haven't been slaves since way back, according to her teacher.
And I said, yes, that sounds real good. But when it gets cold,
she can't go to school, because there's no shoes for her and we
have to stay close to the stove. Do you think that man — Mr.
Whitten? — do you think he'd ever come here? I doubts it.
He's probably with the bossman's side, don't you know. He's
with them. No one's with us but ourselves, and no matter how
many of us there are, we don't have what they have. What do
they have? Oh, isn't it just about everything?"

It is possible to find out who has everything and who has
nothing in Tunica County where that woman lives and which
Mr. Whitten represents. Out of a population of 16,826, 79.1
percent of it black, no less than 13,500 make less than $3,000,
and 11,370 see less than $2,000 in a year. Only 1,506 people
receive public assistance, though — and only 6,307 have been
allowed to participate in the food stamp program. The median income in the county is $1,260 per year and the infant
mortality rate per 1,000 live births is 64.5, some three times
the national average and utterly in keeping with figures that
come out of the world's poorest, most "underdeveloped" nations. In Mr. Whitten's home county, Tallahatchie, the figures are similar: out of 24,081 residents 18,800 make less than
$3,000 a year, 15,197 make less than $2,000 a year, but only
6,710 get food stamps. Blacks make up 64 percent of the population and 74.4 percent of the population is poor. Median

income for the county is $1,588. Yet only 2,367 people are on public assistance.

Counties such as those Jamie Whitten represents have sent thousands of hurt, sad, bewildered, hungry and frightened people north and west; but those counties also continue to present us with a surprisingly large number of our poor people. By and large we tend to equate "poverty" with our urban ghettos, but one government estimate has our urban poor (some 18 million) making up 55 percent of all the nation's poor with the rural poor (over 15 million) about 45 percent of the total. It is one thing to be poor in a big city, and another thing to be poor in, say, Mr. Whitten's congressional district. The mayors of our cities and the men those cities send to Congress by and large acknowledge the ghettos they represent and struggle to govern — and plead over and over again for help, help of all kinds. Every day in the papers, in books and articles and on television the "urban crisis" is frankly acknowledged as the serious and threatening matter that it obviously is. Meanwhile, the Tunica counties of this nation go relatively unnoticed, *and* even more significantly, more tragically, their sheriffs and congressmen fight with all their considerable power to make sure that state of affairs continues. Meanwhile some of the hungry children seen two years ago in Leflore and Humphries counties continue to go hungry, continue to demonstrate clinical signs of malnutrition. Meanwhile an integrated and beautifully run preschool nursery we visited in Oklahoma has been denied further funds by HEW's Children's Bureau, in the words of one federal official, "because of Congressman Abernathy." Meanwhile several farm cooperatives we visited — they are designed to feed the hungry — get not a cent from Washington. Meanwhile the mother of a child in one of those two school districts fighting to keep federal money but not comply with federal laws told us: "I'm afraid of their cracking down from Washington — because you know what they'll do around here, they'll just close our schools altogether. One of the big-shot white people, he said to us the other day, that he didn't think we really cared much about our school the way we were acting."

We asked a friendly professor at the University of Mississippi whether we had any right to come in as outsiders, do our work, then leave and have our say. A reply was instantly forthcoming:

"These people, the people you've seen these past days, desperately need people to speak for them. Their congressmen don't; in fact, their congressmen have worked day and night to kill dozens of programs that are aimed at the poor. Anyone with half a brain in his head knows that the only way we've come as far as we have in this state is because all those 'outside agitators' have bothered us and bothered us and bothered us, at least they did for a while. To be honest, I'm worried that they've forgotten us of late; and they've forgotten what a man like Whitten does, not only to keep *our* people 'in their place' but other people all over. Isn't *he* an outside agitator? Isn't *he* interfering in the lives of others, in their struggle for a decent life? But we don't hear it put that way, I'm sorry to say. And people don't know what's going on in the backyard of the most powerful men in the Congress of the United States, the men who keep on saying that everything is just fine, and we don't need any new laws, any changes in our society. We have wonderful people here, white people who have been fighting this fight for years; and they — I'll say *we* — need help from outside. We can't bear it, personally, to fight alone all the time, not when the odds are so heavy against us, and when we *also* love this state."

Yes, as we drove through Mr. Whitten's district we once again saw what the professor loves: the rich, alluvial earth;

the quiet of a rural state; the flaming sunsets and the full moons that are a rich orange-red rather than a pale yellow, and that hang unnervingly low enough for a sharecropper to have asked us, "Why do they say it's so far to get to the moon, when it seems as though you could touch it if you went and climbed up that tree over there?" We had to leave the road to find that sharecropper, drive along those unpaved, dusty pathways that bring the visitor out of one world and into another. The grazing cattle, the silos, the fine ranch houses, the quaint and nicely kept-up churches, the endless stretches of open land, the cotton gins and cotton wagons, the colorfully decorated grain elevators and tractor companies give way to — well, all that the statistics we have mentioned imply. It is awful, and for all the efforts of our writers, for all the studies and reportage and photographs and documentaries, there is something indescribable about the sadness and pain and stubborn willfulness and slyness and cynicism and resignation and resourcefulness and hope and bitterness that exist side by side in such people whose ambiguities and inconsistencies are more than matched by those to be found elsewhere in America.

New Republic, 1969

Thorns on the
Yellow Rose of Texas

About as much cotton is grown in Texas as in India, which is the world's second-largest producer. Texas sends the most beef to our markets. It offers up our chief supply of oil (about half the country's yearly supply). A huge chemical industry flourishes near Houston. Wheat production is very substantial; the same goes for corn, rice and peanuts. Texas is a large turkey-raising state; its land is grazed by thousands and thousands of sheep and goats; it yields enormous amounts of magnesium, sulfur, natural gas and bromine. In large cities like Dallas and Houston, the state has institutions that accompany all that wealth: well-run banks and insurance companies, well-known theaters and private museums, well-supported medical centers and private secondary schools, prosperous department stores whose buyers travel to London, Paris.

There's an unusual richness of social and cultural traditions as well. Counties along the Rio Grande are heavily Mexican and Catholic. The southeastern section is very much a part of the South. A quarter of the nation's rice is grown there. Near Corpus Christi millions of waterfowl from all over North America choose to winter. The people on the Gulf Coast and to the north, in the so-called "piney woods" section, are also southern: Protestant, tied to one another the way rural people are, but also deeply divided racially. Further north and to the west, white, Anglo-Saxon Protestant fundamentalism loses whatever softening a warm and wet climate provides. The land becomes dry, the countryside more austere, and the people sternly, insistently Baptist. In Waco, right in the center of the state, sixty-six Baptist churches are needed by a population of about 100,000.

W. R. Poage, Chairman of the House Agriculture Committee, proudly calls Waco his home. The eleven-county district that he has represented in Washington since 1936 is doing just fine. His counties and dozens of others in Texas don't need a lot of newfangled social legislation meant to feed the hungry and give them money and work. In Poage's words: "From my limited knowledge of nutrition I would assume that it was true that many Americans suffer from an improper diet, but the problem there is one of education and of personal decisions. It differs greatly from the inability of citizens to secure either through gainful employment or public relief enough nutrients."

William Robert Poage wrote those words in a letter to county health officers all over the nation. He asked whether those health officers have "any personal knowledge of any serious hunger" in their counties, the kind of hunger that is "occasioned by inability of the individual to either buy food or receive public assistance." The replies came back from all over, and in a chorus they said no, there isn't any serious hunger or malnutrition among Americans. One doctor in Texas didn't mince words: "I am very sorry that the poor have become a political football, because the kicking around does them more harm than good. I am persuaded that it is only by learning and working that people can better themselves. Giv-

Farewell to the South

ing them 'things' and doing things for them can only make them weak." In Limestone County, part of Poage's district, the health officer shunned such long, philosophical discussions. His reply was the shortest one received: "I have had no cases of starvation or malnutrition reported to my office." The health officer of Milam County, also in Poage's district, insisted that "the general health of the people in the county is good and that in my private practice I have not had the opportunity to treat any patient with any of these conditions." He had earlier said: "Not a single death [in the county] was *ascribed* [italics ours] to malnutrition or any disease caused by any dietary deficiency."

Recently we traveled around Poage's district. We went to Milam County and Limestone County and Robertson County (which connects them). We went to Waco, in McLennan County, and to small towns nearby or not-so-nearby — Sunrise, Hearne. We started in San Antonio, which is only a few hours' drive from Mr. Poage's territory. Located midway between the Atlantic and Pacific, San Antonio is the first large city north of the Rio Grande, and in 1960 its some 700,-000 people were about half "anglo" and half of Mexican descent (41.7 percent) or black (7 percent). There's an excellent system of freeways, a fine new library, a new convention center, new office buildings and hotels, a river that works its way through the heart of the business district and is lined with cafés, restaurants, stores and even an outdoor theater, all very European in atmosphere; and not the least, a few old and graceful buildings in the Spanish missions (San Jose, Espada) whose arches, courtyards, aqueducts and beautifully wrought façades remind us that not all "culture" comes from England by way of New England.

There is another San Antonio, much of it on the city's West Side, which is predominantly Mexican-American. No outsiders like us have to come there and make a lot of mean, wild, reckless charges; the office of San Antonio's city manager has bluntly and extensively described the *barrios* in an application to the Department of Housing and Urban Development "for a grant to plan a comprehensive city demonstration program." The city officials acknowledge that there is a "San Antonio where 28 percent of the families have incomes of less than $3,000 a year, and where over 6 percent of the families have annual incomes of less than $1,000" — the latter figure almost incredible for an urban center. "The need for physical improvements . . . may best be described as total," the city manager says. "The environmental deficiencies have their effect on every aspect of the residents' lives."

What San Antonio's officials spell out we saw: unpaved, undrained streets; homes without water; homes with outdoor privies; homes that are nothing but rural shacks packed together in an urban ghetto that comprises only 8 percent of San Antonio's land area but whose residents must put up with far higher percentages of suffering — 32.3 percent of the city's infant deaths, 44.6 percent of its tuberculosis and well over half of its midwife deliveries. After we had gone from home to home on one street we began to realize that in almost every way thousands of people are walled off — as in the ghettos once present in Europe. The white people we met, rarely go "over there," as one lawyer put it, and the Mexican-Americans rarely leave except to seek out work, which often enough they don't find: "Yes, we came up here to San Antonio because we thought surely in a city we could find work, but we can't. My husband looks all over but finds work nowhere. He is sad, very sad, and sometimes he says life is not worth living. We would all starve to death if I didn't go wash the floors, in the bank, and thank God for my mother, that she is here to care for my children. You ask how much money we have for ourselves every week. I'm afraid not enough: sometimes it is $25, and sometimes less and sometimes up to

$40, when my husband and me both can find something to do. My sister, she's here, too; and she is very sick with her lungs and can't work. If the priests didn't help her and her children, they would all starve to death. Her husband can't find work, and they told him to go home, the welfare people did, and keep looking for a job. Maybe if our men left us, we could get relief, but they won't leave. I pray every day that it will all get better, but I'll be honest and tell you, I don't believe there is much hope, no sir, not until the Next World. I've lost three of my children, and when I cry about it, I quickly remind myself that they must be happier where they are. No, a midwife helped me out, right here. I don't think I've ever seen a doctor for more than a minute. I haven't the money, and they're not around here to see; and the hospital is way away, and how can we get there; and if it's life-or-death, like with my babies it was, each time, because they were sick — well the priest, he got us there, but it was too late, and the nurse, she said we should take better care of ourselves, and go get some help someplace, though she didn't know where."

Albert Pena is one of Bexar County's four commissioners (San Antonio is in Bexar County) and was born in those barrios and still lives there. We asked him where this woman could go for help. "There's nothing the poor here can do," he said, "except try to make their voices heard, and it's not easy by any stretch. They've gerrymandered the city so that the Mexican-Americans have one congressman and the rest of the city shares two others. They won't let our children speak Spanish in school; instead they tell them right away, in the first grade, they have to learn English and be graded by the way they speak it — mind you, the children are six or seven and have been speaking Spanish all their lives. The children are scared and confused; soon they drop out, by the thousands they do. As for welfare and public assistance, it's almost unbelievable. Over 100,000 people in the county make below

$2,000 a year, but only about 20,000 people get public assistance, and *less* than that have been allowed to take part in the Agriculture Department's food program."

We went to see Joe Bernal, the only Mexican-American in the state's senate. (There are a million and a half Mexican-Americans in Texas.) An active, outspoken, basically joyful man, he gave us a stern and somber lecture. He reminded us that Texas, unlike any other state, sets a constitutional limit on the amount of funds that can be spent for public assistance. Despite the natural population growth, despite inflationary pressures that have reduced the value of the dollar, there is no way to increase welfare payments or even hold payments to their present levels without excluding all new applicants — unless the voters agree to raise the ceiling on welfare funds, which in 1968 the voters refused to do. As a result grants to the poor are going down and will be going down further — the latest cut to go into effect May 1. Estimates of what is to come have a family of four or more children getting under $100 a month. Since rents are fixed and often half or more of that figure, the amount available for food is obvious. Families get no supplemental allowances — no money to travel to a hospital, no money for drugs, no clothing issues, bus tokens, shelter provisions.

Senator Bernal told us about another one of his state's laws. Section 288 of the Texas Penal Code, passed in 1933, makes it illegal for teachers, principals and superintendents to teach or conduct school business in any language except English, except when they are teaching a foreign language to English-speaking students. All textbooks must be in English. The state's two voices of enlightenment in Washington, D.C., Senator Ralph Yarborough, who authored the first bilingual education legislation introduced in the Congress, and Representative Bob Eckhardt of Houston, recently cosponsored and helped become law the Bilingual Education Bill. It aims to help schools in, say, Texas or California teach Mexican-American children how to read and write English as well as Spanish. Next to California, the various school districts of Texas have sent in more requests for funds under this new Bilingual Education Law than districts in any other state — but all to no avail unless the state legislature acts.

Men like Commissioner Pena and Senator Bernal are intelligent, tough and lonely. Few of their people have risen high in office; every day there is a new indignity, a new outrage to fight: the Texas Rangers, a virtual law unto themselves, and the way they intimidate and manhandle farmhands trying to follow the lead of Cesar Chavez; the absurd welfare laws; the severe unemployment among Mexican-Americans; the insulting educational practices that lead to almost unbelievable statistics — for example, 52 percent of all Mexican-Americans in Texas over twenty-five finished only four years of school, and a mere 11 percent went to high school. The city manager of San Antonio admits that 44.3 percent of the Mexican-Americans under his jurisdiction are "functionally illiterate." The 1960 census showed that 20 percent of adult Mexican-Americans in Bexar County "have not completed any years of school at all."

Things are changing, though. We met a number of young men who intend to follow the lead of Albert Pena and Joe Bernal, who speak of *La Raza* (roughly, a prideful way to signify the Mexican-American "people") and insist upon the rights and power that must be won for some 5 million citizens who live mainly in the Southwest. One youth put it this way: "We've been quiet. A lot of us have been afraid to speak up. We've been content to go to church and pray, and be happy we have our family together, as bad as it is. Some people here, if you talk with them, you find they're afraid they'll be sent to Mexico, or something like that, if they start protesting like the black man has been doing. But something is happening, I can tell you. If you look into it, you'll see that our people are organizing — in Los Angeles and New Mexico and here in Texas, too. They're breaking loose from the anglos, and from our own bosses, who work with them and are just as bad as the anglos are. It won't take as long as some people think before we're really on the march."

North of San Antonio one sees gently rolling hills, small but full rivers, scrub oaks. Austin rises out of the prairie, but a few moments later the countryside is once again quiet, even desolate except for cows and chickens and an occasional scarecrow. We approached Congressman Poage's territory from the south and west. In Hearne we interviewed some of the congressman's constituents: Mexican-Americans, blacks, whites. "Up here we're white, not anglo," a grocer told us. "You know why? The Mexicans are thinning out, and the Negroes, they're getting thicker. I've been through Alabama and Mississippi, because I was stationed there during the war, in Montgomery, and I'll tell you, around here it's like there — not completely, but a lot so. To tell the truth, I prefer it like that — rather than like you find it up in New York and Philadelphia. I've also been to both of those places, and the colored there, they're fat and sassy. They think they own the world, that everything's coming to them for free. You see it on television all the time, the way they're pushing on us, pushing all the time. I'll say this about our colored folks down here, they're a lot better. They'll only do what they *have* to, of course — but at least they're not marching down our streets asking for this and that and everything."

Actually, the blacks and Mexican-Americans of Hearne have a hard enough time walking down their own streets, which are unpaved and on occasion hard to drive through, let alone march down. Near the 79 Hi Café we crossed the railroad tracks and entered the city's black section. The inevitable shacks were there — mounted on cement blocks, full of cracks, lucky if tin roofs covered them and if a somewhat decent privy stood nearby and if a boardwalk made the last steps into or out of the house a halfway easy job. An earlier rain had settled into muddy ditches, which were everywhere. We asked a number of people how things go for them, and from one man heard the following: "We don't have heat here, except for the stove; and no water running, not inside the house, only in the streets. Plenty runs there though — yes it does. So, I guess it's hard, but isn't it always? The first thing I remember my mother told me, it must have been thirty-five years ago or so, was never to expect much, just be glad if you stay alive. That's what I tell my kids. No sir, we don't have food stamps, but there's commodities, if you're good and lucky and they says it's OK, the welfare people. I don't get welfare, and I don't want it if I can help it. I try to get by through the small jobs I get, one this week, then maybe one the next. If it's a good week I'll get $50, but most of the time, I confess, it's half that. You don't get rich that way, I guess; but there's no use complaining. There's no one to complain to, anyway. You go downtown and they'll throw you in jail fast as can be if you do that."

Downtown, the town of Hearne has railroad tracks and railroad cars and a bank called The Planters and Merchants State Bank and a moviehouse which featured *Night of the Living Dead* and a black business section in which one sees Pentecostal churches and men walking the streets in overalls and cowboy hats. Not far away is the large Hearne Cotton Compress Company, which receives cotton from gins in Robertson County and presses the bales and ships them out.

It is all very interesting and educational for people like us, but not so good for thousands of people whose way of life does perhaps explain why Representative W. R. Poage of Texas and Representative Jamie Whitten of Mississippi think and vote so much alike and become similarly enraged when those bleeding-heart liberals from the North start talking so emotionally about "hunger" and "malnutrition" and all the rest. In Robertson County, just outside Hearne, and again in Limestone County, we asked several members of the middle class who should know (because each runs a grocery store) whether children go hungry and become malnourished because their parents cannot afford the right amount and kind of food. "Well sir," replied one grocer, "I don't think they're really hungry. No, they get a lot of Coke and they love Kool-Aid. They take to starches, too. I'm not sure which is the cart and which is the horse, though. The cheapest things are your soft drinks and your starches — bread and things like that. It *is* expensive to buy meat and fresh vegetables, especially in the wintertime. We don't have food stamps here, just the commodities, and I'll admit, I couldn't get my family to eat that stuff day after day, all that flour and cornmeal. I think a lot of those people are just lazy, but if you ask me where they can find good jobs here, I'd have to admit it's not so easy. I know, because my kid brother came back from Vietnam and he didn't just find work ready and waiting, and he's — well, he's not a nigra and not a Mexican. I'll admit it's easier for us, but in this country if a man really wants to work, he'll go and do it. He'll sacrifice and pray hard and somehow he'll get ahead. I believe that. Of course, if a child is hungry, and he's not getting the right food, then he should be fed. But his parents owe it to him to get off their rear ends and work, and if they can't find any, they should go some place else and get a job there. My father, he came here from Louisiana. Yes sir, there wasn't work there, so he came here, that's right."

We found him kind, helpful, even generous with us. He wanted to tell us about the town, his county, even show it all to us — the rich land, the flowers just beginning to appear, the open, courteous quality of the people he brought us to meet. Meet them we did — and found them sturdy, stubborn, God-fearing, possessed of a curious and almost uncanny mixture of pride, aloofness and friendliness. They all fought as hard with themselves, with their conflicted sensibilities, as we did with the logic of their various assertions. Yes, children are innocent and need to be fed; but no, we cannot coddle people. Yes, there is plenty of misery around; but no, special "favors" (we heard that word over and over again) simply cannot be granted. Yes, some people really do need help; but no, the only help we ought to get has to come from God and our own exertions.

So we left and drove on, past signs that urge each and every driver to "Get Right with God," signs that straddle twenty centuries, like "Christ Is the Answer — Wrecking Service." In Waco and the rest of McLennan County, Congressman Poage's home county, it is the same story — prosperity and misery. ("Waco is in trouble . . . Almost 30 percent of Waco's buildings are substandard," says the city's chief official in his Model Cities application to the federal government.) Once again the blacks are found living near the railroad tracks, on unpaved Harlem Avenue. Once again the effort is made to speak with reasonably prosperous white people, and once again they reach out for understanding and compassion, but suddenly stop and with a remark or two summarize this nation's ambiguities: "Why can't we get rid of our slums, here in Waco and every other place? I believe in justice, and so does everyone I know. You'd think a lot of our poor folk, they'd be doing better by now, with all the prosperity we've had since the Depression. Maybe they just don't care, don't really *want* to better themselves."

The masked lady of justice — scales in hand — stands on top of the McLennan County courthouse in Waco, there to be seen for miles around. Nearby the Baptist churches fight it out with Sophia Loren, one of whose movies is in town for the weekend. Nearby, people live decently and comfortably, and live lives that eventually get to make up a bundle of dry statistics: in Limestone County almost half the population makes less than $3,000 a year, and a quarter makes less than $2,000, but only 1,681 people get public assistance and 1,947 get commodity foods — and the infant mortality rate is 42.4, double the nation's rate. In Robertson County the same figures hold. In McLennan County — because of Waco it is called 80 percent urban — nearly a third of the population makes less than $3,000 a year, 7 percent less than $1,000, but only one-sixth of those who make less than $2,000 are permitted to take part in the commodity food program.

There are other statistics, more encouraging ones. The *Texas Almanac* declares that the same Limestone County has been found to have one of the state's major oil fields, with an estimated volume of over 100 million barrels. All that oil makes money, of course, and the Securities and Exchange Commission has on file the earnings of some oil companies that operate in Texas. Texaco had a net income of $754,386,000 in 1967; Gulf managed to reap $578,287,000 that year and Sinclair Oil Company a modest $95,322,000. At the same time, as of November 1968, Texas — whose large cities and industrial wealth make it comparable to Michigan and Pennsylvania — ranks forty-seventh among states in welfare payments per recipient, ahead of only South Carolina, Alabama and Mississippi, which have no such wealth. As for Mr. Poage's congressional district, during 1966, $244,000 in food assistance money came into the eleven counties from the Agriculture Department, but one-tenth of one percent of the people in the district — a handful of rich farmers — managed to get $5,318,892 in various benefits from that same Agriculture Department. Still, as the grocer insisted, "oil and crops are our big, important businesses here, and you've got to support them. You can't interfere with them, because then you're down the road to socialism."

We have traveled hundreds of miles down the roads of that grocer's native state, and it turns out he has nothing to worry about. The miserable, wretched roads and the first-rate, well-paved ones cover different territory, and few people in Texas are interfering with anything very big or important.

The Empty Road

Loneliness can seize anyone, but some of us are peculiarly susceptible, because we live almost alone, in out-of-the-way places — places whose very appearance suggests mystery, grief, and suffering. In parts of the South, the trees weep with moss, and a bayou can be wholly the property of a single heron at the water's edge, unconscious of time, its long neck arched and motionless, its long bill pointing to something miles away, its long, fragile legs planted in sand or muck, or seemingly on the water's surface. North of moss and bayous come the foothills of the Appalachians — and fear. The roads wind dangerously. The driver feels dizzy; the trees hover; and rocks can come tumbling down at any moment upon the highway. Finally, one catches sight of the Cumberlands — high, misty, many a mountain still untouched. "Hereabouts, it's just you and what you're doing each day, and you don't have much time for talk and visits and like that. In the morning you hope you'll be here to go to bed, and at night you're glad you're still around up here. So you close your eyes and look at one of the hills and say, thank you, God, for sparing me this far. Tomorrow He might not be so kind." As I read Cormac McCarthy's second novel, *Outer Dark,* I kept thinking of the man who said this to me. He lives in Needmore, a North Carolina town near the Great Smoky Mountains. McCarthy's people could be from Needmore. They talk and act like Appalachian highlanders or yeoman farmers, but they seem meant to represent something else, something that stretches beyond the limits of space and time. What matters is not the where and when of McCarthy's story, for all the intricate and lyrical descriptions of rural life, but the feeling that he wants to make his stories suggestive, allegorical, apocalyptic. Plot means little, even this mixture of the sublime and the grotesque, the religious, the rude, and the barbaric. The ground rules are clear: we will be told a story that will frighten and alarm us, but, as in a nightmare, the mood evoked will matter more than details — the mood of darkness and hopelessness that no technological progress, no refinement of psychological analysis, can explain away or (that cool, slippery word of our times) resolve.

Cormac McCarthy's "outer dark" is not that by now cozy unconscious whose wild and irreverent and banal tricks continue to amuse our fashionable novelists. Nor is he interested in becoming a gilded version of the American social scientist, who has a name or a label for everything and wants at all costs to be *concerned* and *involved*. McCarthy's "dark" is not the mind's interior or the world's exterior; it does not deal with the conceits and deceits that are always at work everywhere — even, say, in the White House and the Kremlin. One begins by wondering what McCarthy's psychological and political purposes are. (Everyone, we have discovered, must have such purposes, and be knowingly or unwittingly at their mercy.) Soon, though, we are asked by the author to stay in the presence of this "outer darkness" and suffer what Conrad called "the horror, the horror" or else to dismiss his novel as dense and out-of-date and so muddled with biblical and Attic overtones that it is the worst of all possible things today — *irrelevant.*

Culla and Rinthy Holme, brother and sister, are lovers, and the parents of a son. Culla delivers his son in a shack no visitor has entered in months, and immediately abandons him to the woods. A tinker whom Culla, shamed, has rebuffed outside the cabin, because Rinthy, inside, is obviously pregnant, discovers the child, gives it to a wet nurse, and goes his way. Rinthy sets out to find her child, because she does not believe Culla's assertion that he is dead. She senses that the tinker may have come upon her child; she may have heard his wagon pass by. Then Culla sets out to find Rinthy. So they pick their way through woods and hills and across swamps and rivers, resting under trees, in houses, in towns that seem deserted. Mostly, because they are wary and haunted, they stalk the land. Who are they and what do they intend, the country folk along the way ask. "I'm a-huntin this here tinker." And why the tinker? Did he steal something? "Well. Somethin belonged to me." What? "It was just somethin." Culla is often assumed to be an outlaw, a rascal on the run, and therefore easily exploited by law-abiding citizens, who can have it both ways — the profit from a desperate man's plight, the pride and power that go with hospitality. Hungry, frightened, driven, Culla and Rinthy never stop anywhere for long. They meet all sorts of obstacles, human and natural, as they move relentlessly on:

She slept through the first wan auguries of dawn, gently washed with river fog while martins came and went among the arches. Slept into the first heat of the day and woke to see toy birds with sesame eyes regarding her from their clay nests overhead. She rose and went to the river and washed her face and dried it with her hair. When she had gathered up the bundle of her belongings she emerged from beneath the bridge and set forth along the road again. Emaciate and blinking and with the wind

among her rags she looked like something replevied by grim miracle
from the ground and sent with tattered windings and halt corporeality
into the agony of sunlight.

It is a hard book to read — a book written with fervor and
intensity and concentration, an urgent and at times an inscru-
table book. As if to assert timelessness and universality, Mc-
Carthy moves from the clear, concrete words of the moun-
taineer to a soaring, Faulknerian rhetoric of old, stately
words, unused words, medieval words. Here is the baby, left
to die: "It howled execration upon the dim camarine world
of its nativity wail on wail while he lay there gibbering with
palsied jawhasps, his hands putting back the night like some
witless paraclete beleaguered with all limbo's clamor." Yet, a
few pages later, the mother, on a road that will never end, can
stop at a store and ask for water and remark simply that it's
"been a little warmer" and say "I thank ye" and comment
that she "ain't eat two pones of lightbread in my life." The
brother and sister are forever alone: "They ain't a soul in this
world but what is a stranger to me." The author uses nature
to establish an ironic tone, to comment indirectly on mankind, and to entrance his readers with his flowing and at
times stunning descriptions of rats and turtles and spiders
and snakes and birds and trees and flowers:

When he came out on the creek a colony of small boys erupted from a
limestone ledge like basking seals alarmed and pitched white and naked
into the water. They watched him with wide eyes, heads bobbing. He
crossed at the shallows above them with undiminished speed, enclosed
in a huge fan of water, and plunged into a canebrake on the far side.
Crakes, plovers, small birds clattered up out of the dusty bracken into
the heat of the day and cane rats fled away before him with thin squeals.
He crashed on blindly.

That he does — crashes on blind to his fate, blind the way
fugitives and vagabonds become, blind the way Cain was
when God said to him, "Now art thou cursed from the earth."

Cormac McCarthy's first novel, *The Orchard Keeper,* won him the William Faulkner Foundation Award and a grant from the Rockefeller Foundation. *Light in August* comes to mind as *Outer Dark* unfolds: the poor white people, the harsh puritanism, the disastrous collision of Instinct with Piety and Custom, and the imagery — of the exiles, the wanderers, the outcasts, all dressed up, though, in rural American habit. "I et polite . . . like a lady I et. Like a lady traveling," says Faulkner's Lena Grove, and then, "So she seems to muse upon the mounting road while the slowspitting and squatting men watch her covertly." In *Outer Dark,* as in Faulkner, we are required to pay close attention. But McCarthy directs our attention to very few people, nor are we allowed to sit back and relax and just laugh, though there are lovely, tender moments and a few eerily comic scenes. McCarthy's handful of characters move from place to place, always going downhill. Their curse is explicit, and the futility of their lives is spelled out: Rinthy finds the bones of the tinker and her child, and Culla meets a blind man on a road toward a swamp, "a spectral waste out of which reared only the naked trees in attitudes of agony and dimly hominoid like figures in a landscape of the damned." In *Outer Dark,* characters touch, collide, then go on, rather than get to "know" one another; they hurt and are hurt in accordance with unfathomable necessities. They don't analyze themselves or others. They don't have to earn their distinction, their significance. Their origins don't have to be expressed and related to society or "the culture." They are immediately presented as people larger than life, important for reasons everyone can sense. The "action" — again there is the contrast with Faulkner — is swift and unequivocal. One person commits a crime against the gods, then others are drawn into a series of accidents, misfortunes and, finally, disasters, all of which make for a tragedy whose meaning every reader had better comprehend.

Not for a long time has an American writer — a young one, at that — attempted to struggle with the Fates and with what Plato called their mother: Ananke, or Necessity. On our way to another planet or layer of the unconscious or new "social structure," we of this century don't worry about the dread every man is heir to, nor do we consider envy, passion and hate things that will always plague man, however lovingly and scientifically he is reared, and in whatever social, political or economic system. Always it is the next bit of progress, the next device, the next body of knowledge, the next deal or plan that will — what? Make man superman? Free man of himself, of his nature as someone who is born, lives, and dies, and in between, for a second of eternity, tries to flex his muscles, clench his fists, and say "It is me, me amid the outer dark"? Necessarily, said Plato, the Fates can never be thwarted, and they cannot be thwarted today, even by a million computers and consulting rooms. Necessarily, says McCarthy, the dark is out there, waiting for each of us. Necessarily, our lot is assigned; we have to contend with our flaws, live with them, and all too often be destroyed by them.

We do not learn what Rinthy and Culla Holme were like when they were young and perhaps smiled and laughed from time to time. We meet them in Hell, and we keep wondering what they could have done to earn their desperation. At worst, they are a little too stubborn — thickheaded, and unwilling to share themselves with others, to share their vision, their secrets, their temptations, their humanity. Questioned, they demur, they flee. A touch of self-righteousness comes through — brilliantly and subtly arranged by a writer who can bring about emotions in both his characters and his readers without making a whole showy business out of the effort. Then all is scrambling and grumbling; the road turns and one desperately makes the turn, and no fire, no roof, no blanket will work. McCarthy's "outer dark" is austere and bleak and blue and cold and ultimately impassable; his mountains open up only to reveal a foul swamp, a wild river, and yet another mountain. If exiles and fugitives have fascinated writers — who themselves often keep their distance — so have men like McCarthy's tinker. V. K. Ratliff, Faulkner's sewing-machine agent, is a reminder that we the readers are there, with advice and ideas and *our* stories to tell. *Outer Dark*'s tinker, who not only sells or repairs kettles and pots but offers everything from food and soap and liquor to gadgets of all kinds, is something else. It is a measure of McCarthy's seriousness that we are allowed no letup. The tinker provides us no alternative, no vision of a better world. What hope and encouragement we do get can come only from a rural landscape that is rich with life, variety, spontaneity, endless possibilities and an unself-consciousness that Culla and Rinthy Holme will never possess.

The only diversion granted us is in the best sense unintentional; it is the commanding diversion a writer's skill provides. McCarthy works hard to write well and ingeniously, but there are moments in this sad, bitter, literally awesome book when only an exceptionally gifted and lyrical writer could take his audience's continuing attention for granted. To say that a book is hard to put down is no compliment these days, when books pour upon us from all quarters, and when the reader impatiently wants to hold on simply because he wants to be done, to go on to the next "experience." *Outer Dark* is arresting and puzzling enough to drive one to distraction, but always to the next surge of reading. It is as if the reader, too, becomes a traveler, and for doing so is rewarded with an astonishing range of language — slow-paced and heavy or delightfully light, relaxed or intense, perfectly plain or thoroughly intricate. Eternal principles mix company with the details of everyday, pastoral life — always under some apocalyptic cloud, though. Errors will be punished, retribution exacted. The blind lead the blind, though some think of themselves as seekers rather than driven, as knowing rather than compelled. And we all must face that final reckoning. Three horsemen ride through *Outer Dark,* looking for someone, covering the brooding countryside with their dark and fierce presence. Cormac McCarthy knows the Revelation of St. John the Divine, who announced that he would set down "all things that he saw" and the "bare record of the word of God." I suppose good writers also come dangerously close to doing that, seeing so much and putting so much down on paper that the universe itself is spread out before us, and the words come near to being the Word — to haunt us and make us pause and wonder for a moment, even though, alas, we keep moving on our particular roads.

New Yorker, 1969

A Farewell to the Old South

The South has been and still is many things, as Pat Watters, in *The South and the Nation,* wants us to know, but no longer is it a really serviceable scapegoat, for it has by now given up enough of its particular habits and customs to become more like the rest of America. In Watters's words, at the end of his exceptionally clearheaded book, "the South was not just of America; America was of it, their destinies inseparable." Any way of life can be justified as everything that is exemplary and sensible; if the South has been scorned by self-righteous outsiders, it has also had its apologists. Pat Watters might easily have become one. He is not black. He is from Georgia and unashamedly loves the state and its neighbors. He has not left his birthplace for California or New York or New England; he works for the Southern Regional Council, a group of proud white and black men who will not let Northerners be their moral guardians. Nostalgic sentiment is an old (and inadequate) refuge that could be particularly attractive to anyone who writes about the South, and Pat Watters is a kind and decent and sensitive man who quite possibly might not wish to dwell on the meanness and brutality and injustice those who live there know all about. Being good with words, he might have rubbed things in a little at a time when the North's ghettos are in such trouble and its "progressive" universities are so filled with bitterness and suspicion and confusion. And he might have pointed out how unspoiled, by comparison, the South is, how much of its land and water and air are still clean, how lovely and inviting its hills and farms and forests are, how moderate and enjoyable its weather is; he might have emphasized that as things go in the United States today, many parts of the region are quiet indeed: no mobs, no demonstrations, no violence, no youths full of back talk and insolence. But smug regional pride, twisted apologetics, rationalizations of the arbitrary and the irrational, cleverly contrived justifications of the outrageous, resorts to metaphor and allegory and, in the clutch, outright mystification employed in the hope of distracting if not conning the reader (and maybe the writer, too) — all these are missing from *The South and the Nation.* What comes forth is a sense of relief — that the worst in the region is something an entire nation now has to fight against, and that the best in the region is what we had better fight for. To Pat Watters, the worst in the South is not only the racial hatred and exploitation but the success with which the region's "leaders" have been able to take advantage of the fears and insecurities of emotional, vocal, unsatisfied, plain-talking white yeomen, who would be a political majority there even were every black man to vote. Decades ago, C. Vann Woodward, in *Tom Watson: Agrarian Rebel,* showed how insidiously and systematically the legitimate aspirations of those people (today they are called "the lower middle class" or part of "the backlash") have been ignored or betrayed — not by demagogues, not by the Ku Klux Klan, not by ignorant and vulgar politicians, but by sober, respectable, quiet, high-sounding men, individuals who have disliked lynchings, become embarrassed by the franker kinds of racial slurs, and urge upon the South such pieties as patience, restraint, dignity, even tolerance of a kind.

Those who want to understand why Lester Maddox is governor of Georgia and why George Wallace is so popular in Alabama (among other places) will find Pat Watters, like C. Vann Woodward, helpful indeed. There comes a time, Mr. Watters says, when certain voters will respond hungrily to "populism," as long as it is delivered in a palatable form, and, for a number of social and historical reasons, only the "right-wing" form is politically possible in the South at the moment. The problem is the white fear of the black man as a rising competitor, and worry about "outside agitators," but the problem is also that "the taxicab driver, the textile worker, the barber, the beautician" — a foursome Mr. Wallace often summons — all feel looked down upon, and therefore not much different from those "colored people" the Alabama politicians sometimes call "good, God-fearing, and law-abiding." Pat Watters convincingly shows that Martin Luther King and George Wallace addressed themselves to the very same thing — the shared self-doubt of their listeners. "You're good," Dr. King said to his tired and dubious and worried and brave and stubborn audience. "I came over here to tell you [that] you are somebody. You may not know the difference between 'you does' and 'you don't,' but you are as good as any white person in this country." And across town was George Wallace, addressing his proud and uncertain and apprehensive audience: "They look down their noses at us and call us red-necks. But I'll tell you, when they write against us, and say those things, that's just one person writing that. And you're one person, too, just as good as he is."

If the South has denied so very many people of both races the self-respect Dr. King and Mr. Wallace spoke of, the South has some pleasing sides to it — sides Mr. Watters presents in great detail. More significantly, he shows what it is that enables the eleven states of the old Confederacy to exert such a forceful and unyielding influence on the rest of us — regardless, it seems, of which party is in control of the White House or the Congress. The region has an intactness all its own; no other group of states has ever banded together, tried to separate itself from the rest of us and to become another country. The South's "way of life" goes back far in time. For as long as we have been the United States, the South has been there, its men among our first Presidents, its plantations and its commerce a means by which the country grew. In recent decades, millions of blacks have brought the region north, and whites from the South have gone west. With them have gone disease, despair, hate, ignorance — but also energy and hope and determination and memories and values and interests and tastes. They preferred certain foods. They had listened all their lives to jazz and spirituals and country music, long before the rest of us took up Bessie Smith and Johnny Cash. They came from parents who called themselves believers, who wanted to be saved, who feared damnation, who feared (maybe as the devil) man-made complexities, of either the intellectual or the institutional kind. Moreover, black and white alike, they had known the defeat that persisted for decades after Appomattox, the defeat that goes with poverty, the defeat of slavery and peonage, the defeat that a collapsing agricultural economy brought to many thousands of "small farmers."

Mr. Watters is "only" a journalist. He has done no "study," no "research." But he knows his people. He writes understandable sentences and, at times, touching, spirited, eloquent prose. He has no bundle of concepts to impress us. He speaks to readers who want something more than definitions and italicized conclusions. I suppose it can be said that he speaks in an older tradition of social science, and a southern one. In the twenties and thirties, men like Rupert Vance and Howard Odum wrote or inspired an assortment of books that compose a "social study series" published by the University of North Carolina. Some of the titles suggest, in their directness and simplicity, what disciplines like sociology and psychology have lost in recent years: *The Negro Workaday Songs, Southern Pioneers in Social Interpretation, Law and Morals, Farm Life Abroad, Roads to Social Peace* — books meant to alert the reader, keep his attention, and (in the southern tradition) describe. Narrative power is what those books have, what C. Vann Woodward's *The Burden of Southern History* and V. O. Key's *Southern Politics in State and Nation* and Wilbur Cash's *Mind of the South* have, too.

The South's torment, its aching racial problem, its vulnerability, its contradictory mixture of violence and calm, its natural beauty in the midst of which brutish men continue to commit ugly crimes against innocent and defenseless neighbors — all this appears to defy being put into words, but it has compelled the effort of words from many a frustrated, aroused, driven novelist. Pat Watters may not be a novelist — he is in essence a historian — but he has a novelist's eyes and ears. He can sense and convey drama and ambiguity. He can give the readers heroes they might not otherwise come to know — men of courage and decency, like Elbert Tuttle and John Minor Wisdom, both federal judges of the Fifth Circuit Court of Appeals, both appointed by Dwight D. Eisenhower. Those two are Southerners and Republicans worthy of the Supreme Court, but there is reason to doubt whether they will ever be nominated. Some southern newspaper editors have also shown themselves able to say no to segregationists, however numerous and influential. The South continues to publish fine newspapers: the *Arkansas Gazette,* the *Miami News,* the *St. Petersburg Times,* the *Chattanooga Times.* And one finds independence of a special sort in thoroughly surprising places; Mississippi, says Pat Watters, is "blessed with a

curious abundance of courageous and intelligent small papers, including the *Tupelo Journal,* the *McComb Enterprise-
Journal,* Hazel Brannon Smith's *Lexington Advertiser,* and
Greenville's *Delta Democrat-Times.*" Anyone who has spent
time in Mississippi knows how profitable and convenient it
would be for the Hazel Brannon Smiths of that state to go
along with things as they are, or keep a discreet editorial silence when that subject of subjects — race — comes up. Why,
for instance, does Mrs. Smith take the stand she has taken?
Throughout his book, Mr. Watters seems to be struggling for
the answer to that haunting question. Equally haunting are
the conditions under which the South's black people live —
conditions that prompt the outsider's indignation at Mrs.
Smith's fellow-whites and the outsider's generous sympathy
for the millions of blacks who, for all the migration north,
continue to live in states like Mississippi. Pat Watters feels
just as indignant and sympathetic, but he asks whether Mrs.
Smith's courage is totally idiosyncratic and whether the black
people of Mississippi (still almost half the state's population)
don't require much more than our alarm and anger.

In the early sixties, when some Northerners and not a few
Southerners took up the cause of rural blacks, irony and contradiction became apparent: persecuted, underprivileged and
impoverished people were declared also to be perceptive,
clever, strong-willed, inventive, imaginative, stubbornly
persevering and — surprising and inappropriate as the words
may seem to some — courtly and genteel. I recall in meeting
after meeting how young civil rights activists denounced the
South's social and political system and then, moments later,
called the region's blacks fine, intelligent and sensitive people. Perhaps some of the praise was well-meaning exaggera-
tion or nervous ingratiation or the romanticism that catches
up even foes of the South's "old order." Nevertheless, something else was noticed by the young protesters — something

Pat Watters wants us to think about and something those who have tried to change things in Mississippi have talked about. That something was summarized by a California civil rights worker: "We came here to the Delta to change the whole setup, and all we had was pity for these 'poor folks,' and we kept telling them that *we'd* do something, leave it to us. Then we got to like them, and we started patting them on the head, like a good master does with his 'help.' Now we're in awe of them, because they seem so smart, and they make us laugh, and they don't miss a trick, and we say they're 'wonderful.' One of the kids in the family I'm staying with heard a few of us talking, and he said we've got it wrong. He said his family isn't wonderful, they're just themselves." One ponders this worker's effort to reconcile his sure knowledge that virtual peonage is the lot of many blacks in the South and his new awareness that out of misery and wretchedness people can fashion a manner of survival, with its own quality and dignity and coherence. One also realizes — as blacks in the Delta have already done — that whites in the South for generations have been betrayed and cheated and exploited by segregationist rhetoric. I knew the ten-year-old child that civil rights worker was speaking of — a child who could say memorable things. When I asked him about the white people of Holmes County, one of whom is Mrs. Hazel Brannon Smith, he said, "There are a few good ones, and a few bad ones, but a lot of them, they're just bad off, I guess, like us."

Books can be written about a remark like that, and Pat Watters has written one — about places like Holmes County, about children who speak like this. In order to do it, he chooses to emphasize riddles and puzzles, to acknowledge life's contrariness. He does not take a particular ideological "line" and then ignore or explain away what his viewpoint, his "position," causes him to find inconvenient. There is in *The South and the Nation* a quality the author describes as "more specific than abstract, more impressionistic than statistical." He aims to give us cause for plenty of anger — not the distant, detached, reflexive anger that the South has always inspired in people up north or out west but an anger qualified by an awareness of "the nation's coming plight in the South's continuing one."

Pat Watters and his book will not have an easy time of it, in either the South or other parts of this country. He has a streak of the proud farmer boy that will not go down easily in cities where big buildings and factories are equated with "progress." He sees the industrialized South a victim of smoke-filled air, poisoned water, ruined land. He sees in "every misbegotten and misguided effort of the South to catch up to something that was essentially sorry and shabby in the rest of America" a reflection of how powerfully influential a particular kind of society can be, and not always for the good. It has been easy to dismiss the southern agrarians, men like John Crowe Ransom and Allen Tate and Robert Penn Warren; they are writers, poets, unpractical men. The South needs industry, we have been insistently told, so that its people can secure the half-decent standard of living they still in such large numbers lack. And yet with industry and all those "northern-bought changes" (to use an expression one often hears from rural white people of Georgia or Alabama or Mississippi) has come not only pollution but the dreary, faceless, grinding life, however well-upholstered, that many of us now think is far more dangerous to America than the shrill, canny segregationists who get elected governor or United States senator. The point is not to glorify a rural countryside litered with hungry, ailing children and jobless, near-illiterate parents; the point is to ask how, without undercutting them, the strengths of such people and their worthiest values can be maintained, and even buttressed, in the presence of what food and family allowances and educational programs — that is, encouragement — this rich nation can offer to its communities.

The once almost religious word "community" is now jargon. Still, throughout history man has struggled for what the word suggests: a sense that amid the masses of men and against the onslaught of time people can come together and know one another and work alongside one another and feel (though it can be only to a certain extent) as one. Christ's disciples were a community, and since His time families have joined on farms, in colonies, in settlements, with the hope of resisting various evils, affirming various virtues. The civil rights worker I have cited had stumbled upon one of those communities in Holmes County. He had seen people down on their luck yet able to depend upon one another, share what little they had, and in their own way — against great odds — keep their self-respect, their sense of worth as human beings: "rebuked and scorned," as they admitted in church to being, but not anonymous, not ciphers, not cogs in someone's machine.

"I give all my children two good names, so they'll be able to know who they are every day of their life," I was told by the mother of the child I have spoken of. Most probably, her efforts are in vain; she and her children seem definitely doomed. And yet, and yet . . . One has to zigzag with one "and yet" after another, just as Pat Watters has to keep saying "yet" and "but" and "nevertheless" and "although" — because his mind willingly faces *real* complexity. "I went once on a cold winter's day," he says, "with a bottle of Jack Daniels sour mash whiskey for sipping among three of us, to a backwoods clearing, the turnoff from the dirt road marked by a dead hawk hung on a tree, to a clandestine gathering of southern country white men who still persist in the illegal sport of cockfighting." He expected "to be sickened, to gaze once more in a new context into the depths of the ugly and demented side of the white South's psyche." Instead, he saw the warmth and tenderness of those men, the restrained, carefully regulated way they permitted their sport to unfold, the pains they took to avoid the very violence they wanted to witness but not let get out of hand. Like their black neighbors, those men are human, full of kindness and generosity and good sense as well as prone to superstition and meanness and worse. And perhaps we might have been expected to know that all along — we who have known *Absalom, Absalom!* and *Invisible Man*. But, in Flannery O'Connor's words, "anything that comes out of the South is going to be called grotesque by the northern reader, unless it is grotesque, in which case it is going to be called realistic." Pat Watters has written a book that will make it a little harder for us to do that; at the same time, his book — a sort of farewell to the old, distorted South — requires us to look at what is both real and grotesque in the rest of America, what threatens not only "the South and the nation" but the whole world.

New Yorker, 1970

To Try Men's Souls

We all know that America's cities are in trouble, especially because blacks have fled to them in mixed hope and fear. We know, because we are constantly told, that the whites don't understand the needs of the blacks, that we will go from bad to worse, that it is too late, because another apocalypse is at hand. But almost no one has tried to tell us about the early lives, the *inner* early lives, of black people, the particular ways that black children in a rural setting grow, only to leave and become the urban poor, the "social dynamite" we hear abstractly described again and again. The tragedy had to be documented, yet social documentation and political prescription can be static and flat and self-defeating when the men, women and children involved become merely part of something called "a history of exploitation and oppression." And books and thinking that carry on in this fashion will not, unfortunately, really be counterbalanced by Alice Walker's *The Third Life of Grange Copeland*. Novelists and poets (Miss Walker is a published poet, too) are not the people we look to for help about "ghetto children" and "racial violence in our cities." Moreover, Miss Walker was born in and has spent most of her life in the southern countryside, and she is now a

writer-in-residence at Tougaloo College, a black Mississippi
school that is not in a city. What can she know of the crime
and violence, the drug addiction and alcoholism and despair
we have been told exist so significantly in our urban ghettos?
What can she volunteer about the "attitudes" of black children or their "problems"?

In her own way, she has supplied some answers, but she has
not written a social novel or a protest novel. Miss Walker is a
storyteller. A black woman from the farmlands of Georgia,
she knows her countryside well — so warm and fertile and
unspoiled, so bleak and isolated and blood-soaked — and especially she knows the cabins, far out of just about everyone's
sight, where one encounters the habits of diet, the idioms of
speech, the styles of clothing, the ways of prayer that contrast
so strikingly with the customs of the rest of us. Fearful and
vulnerable, rural blacks (and whites, too) can at the same
time be exuberant, passionate, quick-witted and as smartly
self-displaying as the well-dressed and the well-educated. She
knows, beyond that, what bounty sharecroppers must hand
over to "bossmen," and how tenant farmers struggle with
their landlords, and how subsistence farmers barely get by.
But she does not exhort. In *The Third Life of Grange Copeland,* the centuries of black life in America are virtually en-
graved on one's consciousness. Equally vivid is Grange Copeland, who is more than a representative of Georgia's black
field hands, more than someone scarred by what has been
called "the mark of oppression." In him Miss Walker has
turned dry sociological facts into a whole and alive particular
person rather than a bundle of problems and attitudes. Character portrayal is what she has accomplished, and character
portrayal is not to be confused with "motivational analysis."

Grange Copeland is a proud, sturdy black yeoman who has
the white man on his back. He picks cotton, lowers his head
when "they" appear, goes through the required postures a

segregationist society demands — the evasions, duplicities, and pretenses that degrade black men and make moral cowards out of white men. Underneath, he is strong enough to hate, and without rage a man like him might well become the ingratiating lackey he has to pretend to be. His anger is not really political or ideological. He sulks, lashes out at his wife, his young son Brownfield and her illegitimate infant. He sees too much, feels too much, dreams too much; he is like an actor who has long ago stopped trying to estimate where "he" begins and his "roles" end. He works backbreaking days in the field, comes home saddened and hungry for sleep, but tense and truculent. ("By Thursday, Grange's gloominess reached its peak and he grimaced respectfully, with veiled eyes, at the jokes told by the man who drove the truck. On Thursday nights he stalked the house from room to room and pulled himself up and swung from the rafters of the porch.") He is nearly consumed by his contempt for the white land-owners, the bossmen, but he and his wife struggle tenaciously for the little integrity and self-respect they can find. Eventually they conclude that they are losers and take to drink and promiscuity, followed by hysterical efforts at atonement on Sunday mornings. Then Grange abandons his wife, and she poisons herself and her illegitimate infant. Brownfield, the child of their hope and love, is left to wander across the land, left to learn how much a child has to pay for the hurt and pain his parents live with and convey.

I suppose it can be said that *The Third Life of Grange Copeland* is concerned with the directions a suffering people can take. His first life ends in flight, and his wandering son takes flight, too, becoming in time a ruined and thus ruinous man, bent on undermining everyone who feels worthwhile and has a sense of pride and dignity. For a while, the lives of father and son converge on the establishment run by Josie, a sensual, canny, generous, possessive madam whose café and "rooms" full of women feed off the frustrations men like Grange and Brownfield try to subdue. There are complications, accidents, sudden and surprising developments. And always there is the unpredictable and potentially violent "atmosphere" of the small Georgia towns and the dusty, rutted roads that lead from them into the countryside.

Grange's second life, in Harlem, is equally disastrous. He becomes slick, manipulative, unfeeling — the thief and confidence man our respectable world (which has its own deceptions and cruelties) is shocked to find and quick to condemn — yet not wholly unfeeling: he tries to help a white woman in distress and is rebuffed. His hatred of whites presses more relentlessly, and so he goes south, to find escape from them at any cost. Josie is waiting for him. Brownfield has married her niece, a charming girl, "above" her husband in intelligence and education and sensitivity, but step by step he goes down, systematically destroying his wife and daughters. Yet Grange finds at last — in his third life, as an exile returned home — the freedom he has asked for. The whites are everywhere still powerful, so it is not political and economic freedom he achieves. But he does take care of his son's youngest daughter after her mother is killed by her drunken husband, and, finally, he can say to his beloved granddaughter, "I know the danger of putting all the blame on somebody else for the mess you make out of your life. I fell into the trap myself. And I'm bound to believe that that's the way the white folks can corrupt you even when you done held up before. 'Cause when they got you thinking that they're to blame for *every*thing they have you thinking they's some kind of gods!"

Brownfield tries to get his daughter back, and to prevent that Grange kills him. What goes on between that daughter, that growing child, and her grandfather is told with particular grace; it is as if one were reading a long and touching poem. But Alice Walker is a fighter as well as a meditative poet and a lyrical novelist. She has taken part in the struggles her people have waged, and she knows the struggles they must yet face in this greatest of the world's democracies. She also knows that not even ample bread and wine or power and the applause of one's countrymen can give anyone the calm, the freedom that comes with a mind's acceptance of its own worth. Toward the end of his third life, Grange Copeland can at last stop being hard on himself and look with kindness upon himself — and one wonders whether any achievement can be more revolutionary.

New Yorker, 1971

PART TWO
Children and Youth

The essays to follow give an indication, I believe, of the scope of the work I first did in the South — starting, really, in the late 1950's, when I lived in Mississippi and had occasion to observe some of the tension and near-tragedy that fell upon Little Rock. Before the first volume of *Children of Crisis* appeared, I had written over a dozen articles (among them the article for Margaret Long mentioned in the introduction to this book) about the black and white children I worked with in New Orleans and Atlanta and other cities, but I consider "In the South These Children Prophesy" the one that, years later, stands up best.

Clinton, Tennessee, was one of the communities I visited in the late 1950's, when I lived in Mississippi and began to be "involved" in the South's racial struggle. I came to know Margaret Anderson, a fine Tennessee schoolteacher, and to admire her enormously — and so was happy indeed to receive her book *Children of the South* in 1966, and review it for the *New Republic*. And the article on hunger also deserves a bit of explanation. I was one of six doctors who went to Mississippi in May of 1967 to look at the way that state's children live — with particular emphasis on their health and the kind of diet they enjoy, if that is the word. We later that year testified before a Senate subcommittee, and to some extent helped call the nation's attention to the existence of serious hunger and malnutrition among the South's children. The article was written by me on our return, and published by the Southern Regional Council as part of a special report called *Hungry*

Children. I have, in the book *Still Hungry in America,* gone into the subject in far greater detail, but this brief statement deserves to be included here. Again, we were all doctors — so we tried as best we could to sound cool and calm, even as we were enraged and saddened and ashamed for our country. As for the brief article, "White People Scared," I prepared it as I was writing the last section of this book — in 1971, when the Supreme Court was still (seventeen years after 1954) handing down opinions meant to implement school desegregation in states like Louisiana.

If the essay "Serpents and Doves: Nonviolent Youth in the South" now seems too hopeful or naïve (as well as rather insistent and emotional) I can only say that many of us were all those things in 1961 or 1962, as we drove through Alabama and Mississippi, and tried to change a whole way of life, and thought we were beginning to do so — and feared for our lives all the time, but tried not to think about such matters, and in fact managed for long stretches of time to succeed in forgetting about the sheriffs and the frightened people those sheriffs can always mobilize to do their dirty work. This long piece is followed by a very short one ("We Will Overcome") in which I describe what I saw as the Mississippi Summer Project was getting under way. Later in that summer of 1964 we were all less certain that we had made a significant dent on, let alone "overcome" Mississippi's social and political system; we were, in fact, beginning to have doubts about all sorts of things, even as we seemed, outwardly, so very hopeful. In the psychiatric paper called "Social Struggle and Weariness" I try to address myself to the curiosity so many of us still continue to have, into the seventies, about our youthful social activists. By no means have I come up with "answers." That is, I have few psychological generalizations about "them" — and, I hope, little moralistic rhetoric, thinly disguised as a psychological formulation of one kind or another. (See also the last article in this section, "A Fashionable Kind of Slander.") If I have written anything that is "prophetic," it is the piece "Social Struggle and Weariness" — which I began in late 1963 and finished early in 1964, when all of us, again, were so full of optimism, and at the height, it seemed, of our efforts. Yet, I was beginning to see, in the talks I had with various young men and women, not only the "weariness" I mention, but a whole range of feelings and attitudes which only later would become more explicitly stated. Words like "black power" and "separatism" and "black rage" and "community control" had their antecedents in the disappointments that gradually were becoming obvious to many southern youths in the "movement," even in the very beginning of the sixties, even early on in the life of an organization like SNCC.

By the middle and late sixties Stokely Carmichael and others were signaling a decisive break with their own past ideals and deeds; in one article included here (many others were written) I tried to come to terms with what they were saying and doing as best I could. As the reader will see, I have never quite resolved my feelings into any clear-cut, unqualified, easy-to-declare "position." I believe many of the youths I write about in these articles have all along felt the same way.

In the South
These Children Prophesy

Children in the South today carry more than their books to school. I have spent years with some of these children, trying to find out how they manage before mobs and in quiet classrooms. I have been interested in how children begin to learn about skin color, and what lessons they grasp in this regard at the different ages of childhood. I have wanted to know what a child psychiatrist can learn about the feelings, the fears and hopes of youth in the actual situations of desegregation.

I have heard and seen some surprises. Crowds gathered daily for an entire year around two elementary schools in New Orleans. In one of them three Negro girls learned to read and write in an empty building, more abandoned than desegregated. During that first year federal marshals escorted them to school. Their parents were threatened by phone and mail. On the street the girls were cursed, and in their homes they heard worried discussions about jobs and violence. The next year, like drops in a transfusion, a few white children returned and the boycott of the school was broken. By spring there were eighteen white and five Negro children in the

school, and the three Negro girls finished the second grade in
an obscurity which felt strange after their international notoriety of the previous year. "I don't get any more letters from
people, and my picture doesn't show in the paper anymore,"
one lamented.

The lone Negro girl in the other school, Ruby Bridges, had
always had several white children with her, sometimes as few
as seven, but in the second year more than a hundred. One of
the first children to return, a girl of six with blond curls, approached Ruby, and, loyal to her mother's words, she told
Ruby that she was not supposed to play with her. A few minutes later their teacher watched them busily jumping rope
together.

The white children and their families received the attention of enraged and disorderly mobs. They suffered threats,
damage to their homes, isolation and the condemnation of
their governor and state legislature. Ruby's father, who won
the Purple Heart in Korea, lost his job, and his parents, living
in a small Mississippi town, feared lynching. Yet all the while
these children, both Negro and white, lived, played, and
learned.

Unlike many children who need psychiatric help for a variety of difficulties, these young boys and girls show little evidence of illness. They have few temper tantrums or troubles
in learning. They usually eat and sleep well. During the worst
heckling of the crowds which surrounded the schools and intimidated many of their classmates, they had the quiet support of the school routine and they were closer than ever before to their parents.

Of course, no child can ignore the cries of persistently
mean people or continual tension at home or school. However, so long as their parents and teachers survive these trials,
the children will usually be no less sturdy. The threats and
abuse become part of the many problems which would nor-

mally confront them as they develop emotionally. When they
are six, children's concern about right and wrong or the reasons for punishment is real. They wonder how things happen,
are curious about God, how He affects them, and about what
is His good and the devil's bad.

Ruby, for instance, was irritated anyway with her four
younger brothers and sisters and frightened by her normal
urge to remove them and alone possess her parents. Now she
would feel contrite as she walked through the shabby press of
accusing adults. "Am I bad?" she asked her mother often.
"Does God want to punish me and nobody else? Will I be the
only one in the family?" Several anxieties are joined in a few
brief words. She takes the world around her and uses it to
express conflict in herself, worried not only about her singu-
lar school experience but by how real her fantasies can become. Will she be the only one in the family to endure this
stress, but, also, will she be left alone in the family, without
her brothers and sisters? If so, will she be punished, perhaps at
the hands of these strangers as well as by her parents? In her
thoughts the crowd could represent a set of reproving parents
or the myriad voices of her unfolding conscience instead of a
group of obviously disturbed people.

Her mother reassured her, taking her to school, telling her
daily of her family's support. She never denied Ruby's observations that "They don't like me" but told her that her family, all of them, loved her. Most important, her mother and
father are strong and affectionate people, and it is this intimacy between basically sound parents and children which
disperses the natural fears in the young. Under such family
protection hard words and scowls are ineffective.

I soon realized how little difference skin color makes in the
way most children play and study with one another, how ironically well these battered schools held together on the inside

while storms swirled without. A white mother said, "I never worried once my children actually were in school. They had a fine time together, and developed a real school spirit. The teachers were as nervous as we were, but soon the children sang songs like 'Frantz School Will Survive,' and the police guarding them joined in too. They were like a small family, and Ruby was a hero for the children. They really enjoyed the attention and excitement. Several times I was ready to take them out; the strain was just unbearable. You'd never know what those people would do next . . . practically none of them had any children at the school. Most of the mothers around here were more scared than bothered about Ruby. But the kids, they never seemed afraid, and they wouldn't let us get too afraid either."

It is clear that the prejudices of parents do not weigh heavily on the young child's life in school. Even the strongest admonitions will often fail to dampen the natural inclination to see the other child as a playmate rather than as a racial antagonist. In a sense, the segregationists are right when they inveigh against children's "mixing" in the schools. They do romp flagrantly together. It is not that they are unaware of race, as is sometimes asserted. Children notice skin colors, and at five a child can talk in many ways about racial identity, depending on what his parents have urged.

It is astonishing how many attitudes are fixed in the first few years. I have seen Negro children draw pictures expressing their sense of rejection, of their shame and worthlessness, and their wish to rid themselves of these problems by having white skin. White children often locate their Negro classmates in separate inches of the drawing paper, sometimes encircling them with heavy black lines. Yet, even after we learn that innocence is no longer the issue, children can be seen contradicting the very fears they sketch out in their drawings. Living in an immediate world where what matters most to them is freedom of motion and the satisfactions of the moment, they end up singing and playing together with ease.

Determined parents, afraid themselves, can either transmit this fear to their sons and daughters or by example show them how to conquer it. As with animals or heights, children can become scared of dark skin or be taught to avoid it. A boy of four can associate brown skin with dirt, with what is bad or harmful. A young girl can associate black skin with the strange and forbidden. White skin can mean a powerful enemy to a Negro child or an elusive cleanliness granted only to others. Many white Southerners have customs and attitudes toward the Negro which have developed from childhood and hardened in later life. In order for these to affect their young children, they must be pushed hard on them. The passion of a phobia, the fire of real fear must be transmitted daily in their encounters with their children. I doubt whether any region can claim a monopoly of the zealously hateful, and so the children survive, despite the voluble crowds or the quieter displeasure of the more moderate. There is no emotional incompatibility that I have seen between these young Southerners and federal laws on desegregation.

When children get older they flex thoughts and opinions as well as their newly awakened bodies. Regardless of race, in every high school there are lithe, confident athletes, awkward young ladies embarrassed by the changes within themselves, shy, tentative boys, and deliciously untouched girls. In such circumstances it is not hard to imagine what could have happened when nine Negro adolescents walked into Atlanta high schools. What did happen depended to a large extent upon who the particular boy or girl was and how the student responded to the stresses of close scrutiny, or subtle or even open resentment. Equally significant determinants were the individual school, its teachers and its traditions; each school partakes of the character of its own neighborhood. Another variable is the common problems of children who are growing older. The young child draws primary strength for survival from his family. The older child begins to leave his family and grapple awkwardly with private thoughts and emotions. When a child is twelve, ideas, many of them acquired long ago, assume new strength; children start expressing in words the attitudes formerly submerged in play. As the importance of action and of immediate rewards wanes, the children begin to look around themselves and question who they are or what they will become in the future. In these older children, racial attitudes and adjustments posed by desegregation merge with the other struggles of their development.

When the Atlanta school board decided to take only a scattering of Negro children for the initial attempt at desegregation, it had to choose among many aspirants. Despite interviews and a host of psychological tests, it would be difficult for any group of educators or psychiatrists to predict the progress of many of these children. The outcome for one of the nine selected demonstrates this uncertainty. She attended the school considered most favorable for entry of Negroes; it was located in a rather elegant section and had a record of high scholastic achievement. She came from a middle-class family and was an intelligent and attractive girl. Her teachers were kindly, and of the three Negroes enrolled, she was probably their favorite. Her classmates accepted her with a nervous but friendly notice. Her first grades in November 1961 were the highest of those of all the nine Negro children in the four desegregated schools — two As and three Bs, achieved in the toughest school program. Shortly thereafter she requested transfer back to her old high school, claiming emotional exhaustion and an inability to continue under what she felt to be trying conditions.

Her collapse created a stir in Atlanta. For some it confirmed the belief that Negroes are basically inferior and cannot last in white schools. Others were saddened and put the blame upon token desegregation, which isolates a handful of Negro children in a large white throng. The governor of Georgia expressed his sorrow for the child and pictured her an unfortunate victim of the NAACP.

I had been talking with her every week as part of my study and had noticed signs of anxiety and moodiness. She was studying hard, sleeping very little. Her way of reacting to tension and possible disapproval was to work prodigiously and organize her living and thinking in great tightness and detail. She would dress neatly, smile appropriately, answer questions precisely. Being in a new and somewhat artificial situation, she and her two Negro friends were in many ways on a stage. Even with a friendly audience, this can be difficult. This girl took her role very seriously and could not turn a part of her energy to other concerns which might have made her less worried. She had never seen a psychiatrist before, and she certainly was not a disturbed or withdrawn child. But under this crisis a brittle personal and family history, hitherto balanced by a resourceful mind, became more oppressive in her daily life.

Others, perhaps less talented or gifted, often succeed because they are more flexible. You can see these children gird themselves, each in his own manner. One girl laughs away her anger. Another expresses her annoyance in sarcasm and her unfulfilled hopes in a kind of wistful, sad humor. A boy afflicted with severe headaches talks about dreams of revenge and victory. Lassitude hides tension, and fierce bursts of activity cover lurking despair. However, stubborn determination, bolstered by pride, is there too; these children are praised as well as scorned. One of them reminded me that "White folks don't realize that we're always being insulted and treated badly. . . . This is a chance to do something even though you may get the same treatment as you get downtown in a store or in the park. . . . I'd rather go through it now, because I know it's got some meaning to it. . . . I'm doing something about it by going through it this time."

Their neighbors may approve and their parents take pride in them, but the adults are also afraid, and their fear is communicated particularly to the younger children. For a month before the desegregation of the Atlanta schools, these nine families were subjected to incredible threats and abuse. In several homes even the parents, knowing full well the penalties and fearing job loss, opposed the children's wish to attend the white schools. Though these midnight callers, spewing desperate warnings, are only a small number, for the Negro families those few are a thousand, and the memory of accumulated suffering prevents calm detachment.

I have spoken with white children who were glad to have Negroes with them in class and with others made uncomfortable by them. All these children are trying to juggle ancient traditions and new realities. Some are more artful than others, but not one is unaffected by this dramatic change in a way of living. A white girl recorded the following experiences on tape: "We were as nervous as they were at first. It's strange, and you feel funny for a while. The rooms were dead silent at first. . . . I got to know them because we were together in most classes. . . . He's a fine boy, and it's the first time I've ever known a Negro the way you know a white person, his personality, or him as a real individual. . . . I never could tell the difference between how Negroes look, but now I think maybe I can. . . . Something happens in the way you think after you get to know people. . . . I was never really a segregationist. I mean, I was never an integrationist, either. My parents are in favor of obeying the law. And you've got to change in this world. . . . I could really feel for those two, sitting alone at lunch, and everyone afraid to talk with them. A few were nasty to them, but most of us needed time to get used to it — I mean, them. And we did, so it's all more natural now."

This girl has captured the quiet sympathy which many white students felt during those first stiff weeks. Sympathy means knowing what another suffers, and for many white children of this age it can be very painful to see another student ostracized. In a curious mixture of prejudicial ideas and kindness one boy said to me with great emphasis, "I didn't want them to come here. I didn't want them, the way I feel when I give my name or say I'm from Georgia. It's the way I've grown up to feel. But when they came I felt sorry for them. . . . I've gone through things like that, feeling that no one cares or will speak to me."

Few children are so instantly aware of their feelings. In Atlanta one Negro girl, having endured a year of loneliness and occasional insult, graduated with high honors but considerable relief. Toward the end of the year she gloomily said, "I can count on the fingers of one hand the friendly words said to me all year." But her words were premature. As her last day of school ended, fifteen white students approached her for the first time, asking her permission to write in her yearbook:

"Please forgive me for not being friendlier this year. I am truly sorry for my silence, but I'm sure you can understand why."

Another said, "I have enjoyed knowing you this year. I guess you know why I haven't become better acquainted with you, but I personally think I've missed a great opportunity."

A girl who once had glared at her wrote, "We have all had our problems in this year of great change, but I have come to respect you very much."

The Negro girl had sensed many unrevealed friends, often

catching a hasty furtive smile when a corridor was suitably empty, but she had never expected so direct a confrontation.

Another breed is the children who are committed, fervid segregationists. They deserve careful scrutiny, because they show us how fear can mark the white child as well as the Negro. These children can be differentiated from other white children by their stormy concern and involvement with the Negro. Several such children persuaded me of the strength of their emotions during our meetings:

"They're dragging us all down," a husky, handsome boy of considerable academic ability told me. "I'm against them because they're not like us, and they don't belong here. They're like animals. They're dirty, all of them. . . . It serves her right, what happened today in class was just a little of what she deserves. We never asked her to come here. Why don't they stay with their own? She gives me the creeps, the way she sits there and smiles. I watch her, though, and I'll bet she's really uncomfortable. . . . Gives you something to do all day, keep your eye on the nigger. . . . I almost touched one the other day on the bus, reminded me of school again. I try to keep away from them. . . . It's not only the way they look, it's just the way they are, they're not civilized."

Recurrent themes appear. These white children are afraid of contamination, of savagery, of seduction, or annihilation by these dark, promiscuous carriers of disease. Talking of these threats with a strange urgency, they reveal that when a Negro is hurt they get angrier, become more excited and critical, and shout louder and longer. Also, more and more excuses for the episode must be found. One boy described the suffering of a Negro girl with evident approval, but added, "I wish she'd leave and go back to Africa or someplace." I felt that his wish, always expressed at moments like this, meant that he was unconsciously touched by her plight and anxious to allow her some escape. Only with a show of denunciation and dismissal could he express his contradictory feelings of concern and guilt.

The teachers have shared this period of adjustment. One described the opening days as follows: "We were as nervous as the children. It was as new to us as to them, and it took getting used to, despite our preparations." When together in groups they talk about how they can ease tension with a phrase here or a question there; how their own behavior will be imitated by those children more surprised than alarmed by integration. While many of the teachers hold private opinions against integration, most are more concerned with their work and eager to keep its professional integrity. This delicate balance between firmly held prejudices and their respect for their jobs may collapse, but I think so far they have acquitted themselves impressively. Most of the Negro children have relied heavily upon the teachers in moments of panic, and these same teachers have helped white children express their natural friendliness. Errors can be found, room for improvement located, but I feel the predominant judgment of Negro and white children would be highly favorable to their southern schoolteachers.

Teachers anywhere are willing to listen to what children think of them but unwilling to allow children to determine their professional behavior. In Atlanta most teachers wisely resist letting decisions be made by plebiscite. They sense the uncertainty about desegregation among the children, and, aware that you cannot order children to love one another, they simply try to help them cooperate as a group of students. Whether or not the students get along depends to a certain extent on their teacher's attitude. Once the momentum is established, the friendliness will persist without the teacher's continuing initiative. In such cases Negro children have attended games or dances without the specific approval of nervous school officials, but had a fairly relaxed time because of the friendliness generated by certain teachers' efforts.

The first two years of desegregation in cities of the Deep South can hardly be easy for all. But young people in the South are growing up in a world which differs sharply from that of their parents. The distances between people and countries are shrinking; television brings swift news of Africa or Asia into almost every American home; and men are beginning to reach out for other planets even as they worry about the extinction of the human race. These events are very much part of the daily life of the child. Even the youngest schoolchild studies maps and draws spaceships. Parents may offer large doses of prejudice to their children, but children spot the contradictions in their parents' thinking. Particularly as they grow up, they question and doubt, showing stubborn, even fierce independence as they strive to find themselves as individuals. They may come back to some of what they have disowned, but surely what the parent believes can never fully circumscribe what the child will do.

Despite the troubles in these desegregated schools, hopeful signs persist. After a year or two of classroom contact with a Negro boy or girl, a white child will say, "I feel differently toward them, I just do. It's hard to explain, but you just get to know them." It is harder for some than for others, but there are chain reactions in which friends influence friends where no adult could succeed. Two white students stated repeatedly that their opinions changed because of the influence of some of their friends rather than the Negro children. Such distinctions are important to the young.

Also important is a slow but significant increase in the number of those sensitive to the problems of others. Small changes in attitude over a period of months point out the difference between opinions reflecting social customs and hate rising from deep fears. We can clinically separate the fretful from the violent; the single-minded preoccupations of the violent contrast with the shifting annoyances of most people.

Brought together by history in a new light of equality, each of these Negro and white children must abandon old suspicions. The white children admit surprise as they describe an intelligent answer from a Negro in a class. A child who maintained his father's militant segregationist opinions undermined them by his own observation, from a disapproving distance, of the real ability and poise of a Negro girl. The inaccuracy of many racial myths requires that they endure only with the conspiracy of the entire society. Though we cannot legislate affections or forbid hatreds, people can come to see the real world and be encouraged to give up the most blinding kinds of distortions. Often it is not just ignorance which corrupts basic reason, but the weight of social maneuver.

In many cases the white child has been reared and loved by a black maid. As he grows up he does not learn to hate her, but she remains part of his childhood, kept there because he is told that, unlike him, she is a child — full grown, often lovable and helpful, but always a child. However, today the white child finds that the black child of his own age is not necessarily dumb, silly or backward, but is another schoolmate. Many white children see more than they may presently dare to say. They hear good replies in class, and they see good marks on homework or tests. Seeing Negro children dressed like themselves, reading the same books, using similar vocabularies, they find it harder and harder to believe that their fellow students are paid conspiratorial agents or some such nonsense.

Negro children have their own share of unhappy and sometimes untruthful notions to correct. Long years of subjuga-

tion cannot be readily blotted out by newly gained rights.
The heritage of dispersed ancestors, held in bondage, lives on
in suspicion or a hesitant aloofness which masks much more
powerful hate. Many Negroes have learned only too well the
white man's sermon that they are worthless, suitable only for
menial tasks. Others can only loathe a world which so scorns
them. Whether they distrust themselves or others — or, more
likely, both — these Negro children must learn to accept
kindness from those who offer daily proof that old sins are not
always carried on. Two weeks before the end of the school
year a Negro boy said to me, "I've found that I'm not so self-
conscious anymore. I didn't trust them at first, even when
they smiled or talked with me. I thought they were just being
smart, or maybe fooling with one another at my expense. I decided to let them make the first move. But some of them are
real nice. I guess I know that now. I remember when I first
decided to walk over to a table on my own and sit with them.
I knew the kids were friendly, but it's hard to gauge how
friendly. It was probably easier for them after I did, just like
it was for me. We really got to know one another, just like
you do outside of class."

In the South today children are receiving more and more of
this informal and ungraded education. Ruby's mother in
New Orleans told me how great the contrast is between the
way she gets along with other mothers at school functions and
her daughter gets along with their children in school. Parents
in Atlanta sometimes sit back and reflect on how well things
are going and how surprising it is to them when their children bring home not only their studies but stories of a whole
new world of human contact. In a sense, we are seeing the
slow attrition of colonialism within our own country. Out of
the tragic accidents and sins of our history there developed a
nation apart of proscribed people, who could pass on to their

children little but the hardest of work and cheapest of pleasure. Their dreams of freedom are now becoming alive and real for their children.

A walk along the streets of northern cities and even a cursory look at northern schools inform us that the boundaries of segregation are not regional. Even though the South should not be defended for its habits and, worse, its laws, pride and smugness are not very attractive either, particularly when in some of our northern slums live Negroes as lost and deprived of opportunity as those in the South. Negro children of the northern slums often receive much less attention than the children I have mentioned here.

These children living in the South today, black and white alike, tell a psychiatrist much about young people under stress. But they show all of us that children can survive and flourish in spite of our many mistakes. Racial hatred may be the livelihood of some politicians, one of the few possessions of the poor and disinherited, the salve of the insecure or the indulgence of the rich, but it is not part of the baggage of human inheritance. Southern children are being liberated in order to live a fuller life than ever before.

Atlantic, 1963

Southern Children

The time is now, this year, last week, September 12, 1966. The place is Grenada, not the Caribbean island Columbus discovered and Cole Porter put to song, but an American town in one of the fifty American states, Mississippi. The audience is a large one, a worldwide one, reached by newspapers, radio and television. What they are told is both horrible and curiously familiar, while the play's scenario is all too lifelike: a mob of white citizens armed with ax handles, pipes and chains surround two newly integrated schools and attack the Negro children who want to attend them. A twelve-year-old boy is described running a gauntlet of cursing men and women, his face cut and bleeding, his clothes torn from his body. Another child is thrown to the ground and brutally beaten. A policeman watches the violence and makes no attempt to help the boy. Newsmen and photographers are set upon by men who are reported doing "all the beating," though "many women were present, cursing and yelling." It is a long-standing tradition, gallant men going off to war, while their lady-folk urge them on with fervent prayer.

Rarely in any nation's history have schoolchildren been asked to initiate social and political change with street mobs

and violence the likely reward. Yet, since 1954 that is what
this country has felt able to require of a few Negro children;
nor have we apparently considered the noisy spectacle of their
experience particularly inappropriate for the eyes and ears of
white children. Now, twelve years later, it is a fact of American politics that another generation of children will have to
continue the leadership this generation furnished in Little
Rock, in New Orleans — and among many other cities and
towns, in Clinton, Tennessee, where Margaret Anderson has
lived and taught school for many years.

Clinton is a mill town of about five thousand in the TVA
territory of east Tennessee. It is seven miles from the Norris
Dam and seven miles from the atomic research center of Oak
Ridge. Although in the South it is not possible to get any
closer to federal power than that, the town's school board
started fighting school desegregation in 1950; and the Supreme Court's 1954 decision caused no interruption in the
effort. In 1956 the federal courts finally put an end to the
litigation and ordered Clinton High School to admit Negro
students. It should be noted for the record that until then any
Negro youth who wanted a high school education had to
travel twenty-five miles away to a Negro high school in Knoxville — and pay for some of the travel, too. (When I started
studying the psychological effects of bussing upon Negro children in Boston one mother had this to say to me: "Suddenly
they're all worried about our children being hurt because of
the ride to school. They carried us halfway across the state of
Georgia when I was a girl just to keep us far away from the
whites and no one said a word; but I guess today people *care*,
bless them.")

In August of 1956 Clinton also started to care, and for a few
days it seemed to do so successfully. White schoolchildren accepted Negro children they had anyway known for years. One

Negro girl was even made a class officer, and a boy spoke of his desire to play basketball without arousing the slightest stir. As C. Vann Woodward has pointed out, the fixed habit or custom of segregation came well after the Civil War, and has its own shaky, tortuous history. While racism is a firm part of the South's past, so is a thwarted but real populism; and so is the obviously close if caste-ridden association between black and white that contrasts with what holds in northern cities.

Just as Clinton's better traditions and influences appeared able to spare the town racial-unrest, the itinerant segregationist John Kasper — do you even remember the name? — arrived and started doing his rather effective work. He had become something of an expert in exciting the South's dormant fears until finally they found expression in panicky street demonstrations. He had his connections. From all over the South its white-skinned defenders assembled in the town a nondescript, pitiable, desperate army of sufferers in search of an enemy, any enemy to blame for the unquestionable injustice they saw about and every day themselves experienced. In a matter of days, roaming bands of fanatics consolidated themselves — and eventually the town's onlookers — into mobs; Clinton's six policemen were overwhelmed; twelve Negro children whose presence in the high school set the whole affair in motion were soon facing the insults and dangers that other Negro children would face the following years. It took time, precious time, for a timid governor to act. The townspeople themselves — while pleading for state intervention — had to protect themselves against a degree of mob rule that eventually endangered the lives of newsmen and commanded national publicity. Tanks and armored cars entered Clinton. It was a sordid story and utterly unnecessary. A vacillating, uncertain climate of opinion stretching from Washington to Nashville and points south made victims not only of Clinton's Negroes but — as Mrs. Anderson emphasizes — the majority of the town's white people.

An armed peace was obtained, but once the Klan and others like them are ever allowed a bit of freedom and power they withdraw reluctantly. In the fall of 1958 the high school was completely destroyed by dynamite. A new and better school was built; but the goodwill that had been thoroughly smashed in 1956 was less easily replaced.

Through it all, the threats and terror, Clinton's high school somehow kept in session, and a handful of Negro children kept coming back for more, by the day and the year, until they graduated and thus set the stage for others to do likewise. Teaching them and their white classmates, helping them go on to college — and as this book proves, always watching them — was Margaret Anderson, who now has taken on the difficult task of sorting out her past experiences and fashioning from them whatever "advice" a shrewd mind and large heart (both of which have gone through a kind of hell) can offer.

The book *Children of the South* may be approached in several ways. It is the testimony of an unusually sensitive and courageous teacher, another southern lady in a long tradition that has produced diaries, short stories, poems, novels and perhaps the most vigorous kind of social concern the region has been able to take. Segregationist talk about the "sanctity" of white womanhood has come in large measure from nervous, worried men; and they are men rather familiar to many southern women, who have all along sensed that the Negro's confinement is to some extent theirs, too. For decades both Negroes and women were voteless; they both were kept from juries and denied education. (In parts of the South today women are as systematically excluded from juries as Negroes — and there is right now an appeal in the federal courts de-

manding the admission of both of them on Alabama juries.)
It is thus no accident that Mrs. Anderson ends her book by
quoting Lillian Smith. The two of them are both emotional
and moral in a proud, unjaded, old-fashioned way; they are
also passionate and — because there is so much cause for fear
— almost fiercely unafraid.

The lessons of Mrs. Anderson's own life come across in her
style — unashamedly personal, almost confessional. She saw
Negro children fighting hard for the good education that was
finally permitted them. She saw white children torn with resentment, guilt and forbidden kindness. She saw silent, fearful people — Negro parents, white townsfolk, her own colleagues. She did more than teach. She went to the homes of
the Negro children, and learned of the hard luck they left for
whatever good fortune might be in a first-rate school (with a
sprinkling of some second-rate, bad-mannered white children
in it). She kept the children's behavior in sight. She followed
their educational and emotional troubles. She helped them
with their college applications. (There are devastating comments on the snobbish, "aristocratic" private southern colleges that never had to comply with a Supreme Court law,
and never *did* comply with the law of any conscience they
may have had — only with what Mrs. Anderson calls the law
of "the almighty dollar.") Finally, she sat down to describe
what she experienced — year by year, child by child.

There is another way of looking at this book: it reveals an
earnest observer in an unavoidable dilemma; and to her
credit there is no effort to conceal it, or avoid coming to terms
with it by resorting to one or another ideological posture.
Again and again Mrs. Anderson found the Negro children
poorly prepared for her classes and in need of substantial support to sustain their morale and their will to learn. Their
sights are set low, their expectations are modest, their "background" not up to those of white children. They had a hard

time of it, even with the kindest and most hardworking of teachers. Yet, she remarks that "every day we are finding in these children talents and abilities neither we nor they dreamed were there. Sometimes I am absolutely amazed when I think what I have seen in Negro students the last year in high school that I could not see when they entered." She goes on to call them wryly "latent talents." (The quotation marks are hers; she is much too sensible a woman and a writer to use the jargon of educational psychology.)

How is she or anyone else going to reconcile the stresses faced by these children, the poor preparation they carry with them, the hesitant and sometimes seriously flawed performance they make, with the surprising survival — and eventual success — so many of them have also managed? Even to discuss the problem arouses the polemicists, for whom these children are but pawns in a larger game. As a result we find ordinary boys and girls not only turned into heroes, but denied the right to have erred or failed in any way. We also find from another direction a curious insistence that their every false step, their every mishap be proclaimed as if anyone who fails to do so is "sentimental" at best, or in danger of losing his credentials as one of the Negro's sympathizers. There comes a time when uncritical applause joins company with compulsive pity to reveal themselves as the gratuitous if concealed insults they both are.

In point of fact we will have to live with the ambiguity Mrs. Anderson unflinchingly documents. Negro children of the South against great odds have had a rough and dismal time in white schools, yet often enough made good, to everyone's surprise including their own. Moreover, the white South has fought to keep those children out of its schools, yet produced teachers like Mrs. Anderson — I can vouch for the fact that she is not alone — and a good number of children

who have been kind and decent rather than nasty and hurtful. It may be easier to forget all that and go whatever single-
minded way one wishes, but at least the facts as seen for years
by a teacher have been put on record.

New Republic, 1966

Children in Mississippi

We are physicians who have had a continuing interest in the medical problems of rural American children in the South and in Appalachia. One of us works every day in Mississippi with impoverished children.[1] One of us has worked throughout the South with both Negro and white children, and specifically spent two years observing migrant and sharecropper children, and treating them as a physician associated with a mobile public health clinic.[2] Two of us have recently been doing a medical study in Appalachia.[3] One of us — a pediatrician — has observed southern children at close hand,[4] and another of us — also a pediatrician — spent several weeks last summer in Lowndes County, Alabama, living in a Negro community and observing its pediatric problems.[5] And, one of us practices medicine in North Carolina and is

[1] Cyril Walwyn, M.D., in Yazoo City, Mississippi.

[2] Robert Coles, M.D. (see "Lives of Migrant Farmers," *American Journal of Psychiatry*, September 1965).

[3] Robert Coles, M.D., and Joseph Brenner, M.D. (see "Report on Appalachia," presented at Annual Meeting of American Ortho-psychiatric Association, April 1967, Washington, D.C.).

[4] Milton J. E. Senn in field trips to the South.

[5] See the paper, "Report on Medical Conditions in Lowndes County, Alabama," by Alan Mermann, M.D.

the chairman of the executive committee of the Southern Regional Council.[6]

In addition, four of us recently made a team-study of conditions in rural Mississippi, concentrating on the health of the children there. What we saw there we have seen in other areas of the South and in Appalachia, too. The issue at hand is the medical (and social and psychological) fate of those literally penniless rural families who are often enough removed from any of the services that even the poor in America can usually take for granted: that is, these families are denied medical care, adequate sanitation, welfare or relief payments of any kind, unemployment compensation, protection of the minimum wage law, coverage under Social Security, and even recourse to the various food programs administered by the federal and local governments. In sum, by the many thousands, they live outside of every legal, medical and social advance our nation has made in this century.

We are here primarily concerned with children — though obviously it is parents who have to teach children what the world has in store for them. Before reporting our recent observations in Mississippi, we want to emphasize the barest needs of infants and children, if they are to survive and grow. Even before birth or at the moment of birth a child may be decisively and permanently hurt by the poor health of the mother, or the absence of good medical and surgical care. Again and again children are born injured, deformed or retarded because their mothers could not obtain the doctor, the hospital care, they needed.

From birth on, children need food, and food that has vitamins and minerals and an adequate balance of protein, carbohydrates and fats. They also need from time to time a variety

6 Raymond Wheeler, M.D., in Charlotte, North Carolina.

of medical services — vaccines, drugs, diagnostic evaluation, corrective surgery. While all these facts are (or should be) obvious, we have to state them once again — because in various counties of Mississippi we saw families who could not take food for granted, let alone any medical care. We shall now briefly describe what such a state of affairs does to children.

In Delta counties (such as Humphreys and Leflore) recently visited by us and elsewhere in the state (such as Clarke, Wayne, Neshoba, and Greene counties, also visited by us) we saw children whose nutritional and medical condition we can only describe as shocking — even to a group of physicians whose work involves daily confrontation with disease and suffering. In child after child we saw: evidence of vitamin and mineral deficiencies; serious, untreated skin infections and ulcerations; eye and ear diseases; also unattended bone diseases secondary to poor food intake; the prevalence of bacterial and parasitic disease, as well as severe anemia, with resulting loss of energy and ability to live a normally active life; diseases of the heart and the lungs — requiring surgery — which have gone undiagnosed and untreated; epileptic and other neurological disorders; severe kidney ailments, that in other children would warrant immediate hospitalization; and finally, in boys and girls in every county we visited, obvious evidence of severe malnutrition, with injury to the body's tissues — its muscles, bones and skin, as well as an associated psychological state of fatigue, listlessness and exhaustion.

We saw children afflicted with chronic diarrhea, chronic sores, chronic leg and arm (untreated) injuries and deformities. We saw homes without running water, without electricity, without screens, in which children drink contaminated water and live with germ-bearing mosquitoes and flies everywhere around. We saw homes with children who are lucky to eat one meal a day — and that one inadequate so far as vitamins, minerals or protein is concerned. We saw children who don't get to drink milk, don't get to eat fruit, green vegetables or meat. They live on starches — grits, bread, flavored water. Their parents may be declared ineligible for commodities, ineligible for the food stamp program, even though they have literally nothing. We saw children fed communally — that is, by neighbors who give scraps of food to children whose own parents have nothing to give them. Not only are these children receiving no food from the government, they are also getting no medical attention whatsoever. They are out of sight and ignored. They are living under such primitive conditions that we found it hard to believe we were examining American children of the twentieth century.

In sum, we saw children who are hungry and who are sick — children for whom hunger is a daily fact of life, and sickness, in many forms, an inevitability. We do not want to quibble over words, but "malnutrition" is not quite what we found; the boys and girls we saw were hungry — weak, in pain, sick; their lives are being shortened; they are, in fact, visibly and predictably losing their health, their energy, their spirits. They are suffering from hunger and disease and directly or indirectly they are dying from them — which is exactly what "starvation" means.

We have the following specific medical observations to report. They were made — be it remembered — on children who are not in hospitals and not declared "sick" by any doctor. They are, in fact, children who are getting *absolutely no medical care*. In almost every child we saw in the above six counties during our visits in the May 27-30 period, we observed one or another parasitic disease: trichinosis; enterobiasis; ascariasis; and hookworm disease. Most children we saw had some kind of skin disease: dryness and shrinkage of skin due to malnutrition; ulcerations; severe sores; rashes; boils, abscesses and furuncles; impetigo; rat-bites. Almost every child we saw was in a state of negative nitrogen balance; that is, a marked inadequacy of diet has led the body to consume its own protein tissue. What we saw clinically — the result of this condition of chronic hunger and malnutrition — was as follows: wasting of muscles; enlarged hearts; edematous legs and in some cases the presence of abdominal edema (so-called "swollen" or "bloated" belly); spontaneous bleeding of the mouth or nose or evidence of internal hemorrhage; osteoporosis — a weakening of the bone structure — and, as a consequence, fractures unrelated to injury or accident; fatigue, exhaustion and weakness.

These children would need blood transfusions before any corrective surgery could be done — and we found in child after child the need for surgery: hernias; poorly healed fractures; rheumatic and congenital heart disease with attendant murmurs, difficult breathing, and chest pain; evidence of gastrointestinal bleeding, or partial obstruction; severe, suppurating, ear infections; congenital or developmental eye diseases in bad need of correction.

The teeth of practically every child we saw were in awful repair — eaten up by cavities and poorly developed. Their gums showed how severely anemic these children are; and the gums were also infected and foul-smelling.

Many of these children were suffering from degenerative joint diseases. Injuries had not been treated when they occurred. Bleeding had occurred, with infections. Now, at seven or eight, their knee joints or elbow joints might show the "range of action" that one finds in a man of seventy, suffering from crippling arthritis.

In child after child we tested for peripheral neuritis — and found it, secondary to untreated injuries, infections and food deficiencies. These children could not feel normally — feel pressure or heat or cold or applied pain the way the normal person does. What they did feel is the sensory pain that goes with disease: pricking, burning, flashes of sharp pain, or "a deep pain," as one child put it.

The children were plagued with colds and fevers — in a Mississippi late May — and with sore throats. They had enlarged glands throughout the body, secondary to the *several* infections they *chronically* suffer. Some of them revealed jaundice in their eyes, showing that liver damage was likely, or hemolysis secondary to bacterial invasion.

What particularly saddened and appalled us were the developmental anomalies and diseases that we know once were easily correctable, but now are hopelessly consolidated: bones, eyes, vital organs that should long ago have been evaluated and treated are now beyond medical assistance, if it were available. In some cases we saw children clearly stunted, smaller than their age would indicate, and drowsy or irritable.

In sum, children living under unsanitary conditions, without proper food, and with a limited intake of improper food, without access to doctors or dentists, under crowded conditions, in flimsy shacks, pay the price in a plethora of symptoms, diseases, aches and pains. No wonder that in Mississippi (whose Negroes comprise 42 percent of the state's population) the infant mortality rate among Negroes is over twice that of whites; and while the white infant mortality rate is dropping, the rate for Negroes is rising.

What are we to say? The communities we saw desperately need more and better food, and a beginning of medical care. (The communities we saw are of course not the only ones in the South where these recommendations would be applicable. Indeed, a first recommendation would be for a survey of the South to determine all places where children suffer these intolerable conditions.) Right now the government pours millions into a welfare program, a food program and a public

health service *that are not reaching these people.* We met
families who have no money coming in. The father is declared "able-bodied" and so they are ineligible for welfare.
The family does not have the money necessary to buy food
stamps; they certainly have no money for doctors or hospitals
— and they are not offered any care by the county or the
state. Welfare and food programs (including the commodity
food program) are in the hands of people who use them selec-
tively, politically, and with obvious racial considerations in
mind. What is a human need, a human right, becomes a favor
or a refusal, and if the person is "lucky," that is, given some
commodities and a welfare check, her children still don't get
the range of food they need, or the medical attention.

We therefore feel that the food stamp program should be
changed so that the rural poor can obtain food stamps free.
The food distribution activities of the states should be closely
regulated and supervised — and if necessary taken over by
the federal government or people within the particular (poor
and aggrieved) communities. The government should change
its system of welfare support, so that its funds directly reach
those who need them, without political or racial bias, and
reach them in an amount adequate to their minimum needs
for food, clothing and medical care.

Medical facilities and programs supported by the federal
government should be required to serve these people, and
emergency medical treatment provided them. The government should provide vitamin pills for such poor children, and
other drugs such as antibiotics. Local doctors can be called
upon — and paid with money provided by the government to
these families. If necessary, new medical institutions and
training centers can be created and supported. (There is now
exactly one Negro medical student in Mississippi's only medical school. Hundreds of Negro nurses are needed — and are
not being trained.) The United States Public Health Service

could place in the face of this crisis one or two doctors and nurses in each county, to work with the rural poor. Emergency dental services also are needed.

It is unbelievable to us that a nation as rich as ours, with all its technological and scientific resources, has to permit thousands and thousands of children to go hungry, go sick, and die grim and premature deaths.

Special Report, Southern Regional Council, 1967

White People Scared

The following are excerpts from a tape recording of a conversation which I had with a young black girl from New Orleans whom I have known for a decade — ever since she helped initiate school desegregation in that city:

"Ten years ago I was six. Ten years ago I had those federal marshals beside me every morning I went to school. The city of New Orleans sure had a lot of 'law and order' then; there were mobs and they didn't go away for weeks. Every day I was told I'd be killed. President Eisenhower didn't stop the mobs, and the governor of Louisiana said it was all right for white people to keep on scaring black people, and the state legislature said that the federal judge who ordered integration was a traitor.

"But people forget. I watch our southern politicians screaming about 'hypocrisy up north' and I say: yes, they're right, there's plenty of hypocrisy up north, but there sure is plenty down here. Why didn't our senators shout a long time ago that we need 'law and order' in the South? Why didn't they tell people to obey what the Supreme Court ordered and what the Congress said should be done? When I hear a senator from my Louisiana, or one from Arkansas or Mississippi

saying the whole country is ganging up on the South, I wonder to myself if they can keep a straight face when they talk
like that. Southern governors and senators have been ganging
up on black people for a long time, and no one from anywhere interfered, either.

"Sometimes a friend of mine will ask me if it was worth it,
sitting in that school building all by myself. (The whites boycotted the school for a whole year.) A lot of blacks say we
should stay away from white people altogether. They say the
whites don't want us and we shouldn't have any part of them.
But I disagree. After a while the whites came back to school,
and I've been at school with them ever since. I know some of
them and they know me. I can't say it's been a honeymoon all
these years. I can't say it's been a waste of time, either. I think
this: I'd do it again, even with all the pain, even with those
mobs and my daddy losing his job.

"I'll tell you why I think we should have black and white
together in school. I'll tell you what I say to the little black
kids I've seen — kids in Louisiana and Mississippi now starting to do what I did a long time ago. I say it's better in 1970
when I'm sixteen than it was in 1960 when I was six. It's bad,
still bad for us — all over the country, not just here in New
Orleans. But I've seen changes for the good, and I believe
we've got to keep on demanding we be treated like American
citizens should be treated.

"The white people are scared. If you're black you know
how scared the white man can get. He's afraid of his own
shadow. But I've seen white people lose their fear. Every time
I get real discouraged I remember how upset the white kids
were when they came back to school and had to be in class
with me. They'd glance over at me, and when I looked back
at them they lowered their heads. They were ashamed of
themselves. Now that I'm finishing high school I've learned to
talk a lot with white kids, and they've talked with us black

kids. If you don't know other people, and just know your own kind of people, you're never going to lose your fear.

"I don't see how people can give up so easily just because they don't get their own way immediately. I learned when I was little that you have to work and work before you begin to get what you're after. I guess some people aren't used to the kind of long fight my people have had."

New York Times, 1970

Serpents and Doves: Nonviolent Youth in the South

There are in America today young men and women, black and white, who are going to jail for the freedom of their fellow men. They are doing radical things in novel and challenging ways; and they are doing them in every man's sight, in restaurants, in stores, in movie houses, in bus terminals, and in the obscure rural offices of voting registrars. In fact, wherever they are and wherever they go, they test and defy. Here, certainly for the first time in my life, I have seen American students behave toward their society with the "ideological" concern said to possess young people in Europe or Asia. But they do not march with banners nor man barricades. They do not scream at other countries and their visiting leaders. They throw no bombs. They are concerned with their own country, and they want to become her true citizens. They very definitely want to change social and political customs, but they want to change them peacefully and in their time. They are not lost or confused; they know exactly what they want, and they are ready to give their lives for their goals. I went to study them and I came to respect them; and so I will tell their story so as to let them come to word, and through them, their tasks and their fate.

But how about the others, the men of business and the ordinary citizens of all ages and classes who come up against these students? These people have grown up with certain deeply felt assumptions about ways of getting along with one another. This happens when you grow up anywhere — you learn who you are, and who you are not. You learn who is nice and who is bad. You learn who has rights and who doesn't seem to have any. Until recently, if you were born in the South and you were white, you learned that the colored man could not go certain places, could not have certain jobs, could not expect certain rights. You learned that he took care of you, did a lot of hard and difficult things for you. You were told about his bondage, and soon learned about the Civil War. Associated in your mind with the Negro were the hard times of the South after that war, the pride and power of the North, and your unending conviction, based on the laws of human nature, that there was hypocrisy under all those words from up there.

These traditions and sentiments are not tidily bound in a cellophane bag. They are carried around by all those human beings in Greensboro, North Carolina, Atlanta, Georgia, and every other town in the South. If you look at those towns in 1962, you will see television sets and airfields. Living in these towns are young people who expect someone of their generation to land on the moon. Perhaps they think of themselves as Southerners; but they also see themselves as living on a patch of a planet which is orbited, radioactive and supersonically traveled. We all know how their parents struggled over the question of how or whether America should get involved in the problems of distant continents. Somehow we did become involved; somehow the distance between the continents has been abolished. Now we worry about countries who want to bury us and continents where new countries are rising from the ashes of old empires. We worry, and we gird ourselves for a long haul of trouble. We pull ourselves together, and parts of us get closer together. Factories move from one region to another, taking people with them, drawing people to them. Farms are left. Cities grow. People leave places where they can't work or feel hunted and go to other places where they still have their troubles but where these seem less overwhelming. Feelings about dark people persist, but must now be put on complicated scales and weighed with other feelings about work and country. Feelings about white people persist, but the white world is changing and so is the dark, and new feelings arise and demand expression. The towns and cities hold all that, grapple with paradox and contradiction and new ideas and new events; they will live or die on whether they settle in themselves how they get along with themselves.

A southern journalist emphasizes, with a newsman's special pleasure in irony, that the four young Negroes who first dared, in 1960, to ask for dimestore coffee in Greensboro, North Carolina, were prompted, even pushed, by whites impatient with the pace of the Negro's walk to full citizenship and pressing for changes. Apocryphal or not, there is truth in the story. The truth is that students are attacking conventions by picketing and by boycotts; they are going on freedom rides and risking arrest for their sit-ins. The additional truth is that when they lean hard, the walls, more often than not, crumble. It takes a certain kind of society for this to happen. In some countries the walls would not crumble. The protests would be crushed, turned into revolutionary plots. In our own country such protests have been made many times in the past with little success. There were sit-ins decades ago, which are remembered now because the present ones work. Because they work, they say something about the country and about the South. Social changes occur when a ripe moment is plucked by shrewd and hungry men. This ripe moment in the South today captures the world's interest. One of the great issues in this century is whether the different races of the world will be able to get along in some new mutual respect. The alternative is grim, but may help make it possible. The world watches a great protagonist try to make its ideals real. The South is the troubled stage, and much depends upon the resolution of the drama.

There are many actors. Some of them are storekeepers, some are governors, some are policemen. But it is students who seem to initiate much of the action and cause many of the changes; and we are here to try to look at these lean and crafty youths. We might ask ourselves about their aims and their tasks, their ages and origins, their manner of living and the ways they respond to some of the troubles thrown their way.

What they want is called "desegregation," or "integration." Some call it "mixing." Under the names are wishes and fears. The students wish that the Negro people in the South could have an easier, kinder life. They would like a Negro to feel free to vote. They would like him to hold a job which bears some connection with his interests or abilities. The time has come, they assert, when a Negro can eat in those restaurants and sit in those movies. Parks are for people, and Negroes want to feel like people. No other group of Americans has been shunted aside so long, kept in such degradation, exploited so unremittingly. The students say all these words, and that all bad things must come to an end, and that the glorious moment has come. They seem to have the idea that a secret voice has been heard and read by them. This secret voice tells them that their country can no longer endure with the old segregated ways. It goes on to suggest that the past years have shown a slow yielding of the law and a gradual improvement in the separate but equal position of the Negro. Then it bellows into their ears and scrawls on their student notebooks the advice that to freedom there are many roads. Their road is that of the direct and nonviolent protest. They are young, and they feel directly as the young do; they direct their attention to some very specific customs, and they say to one another that these exist in the middle of the twentieth century only by their own sufferance. They sense that the South as well as their country is in a bind. Both would like to be rid of this shameful relic from other years. Both feel guilty, but both are afraid, and don't quite know how. They also sense that they have not been terrorized alone; that with them have been white people in every city and state of the South, people afraid to say what they feel and for this reason not free.

Their aim is not to conspire or to destroy their country. They want what others in the country have, what others have often taken for granted. They want what their country says it is all about. They want to feel they are more a part of their country. Then, as they let their minds wander into the future, they hope for more trust and friendliness between the white and dark people of this country. They carefully distinguish between desegregation and integration. They know that you cannot legislate affection. But they suggest that if many of their exiles end, hands of acceptance may begin to reach. One of their buttons shows a white hand and a black hand clasped. I suppose that this is their wish.

What they do to get what they want is to protest. They do not carry weapons. They do not hit or hurt people, at least physically. They will not fight with sticks or stones or hands or feet. They wear suits, and they shave. They are determined to appear as presentable young Americans. Before they pro-

test they study and think about the way in which they will
protest, and they practice this too. This is the way of nonviolence. The way of nonviolence is self-explanatory. But like
many simple matters, it has complicated results, for the students and for the world they protest against.

It is complicated for them because they must control carefully some very strong feelings. It is in the nature of protest to
be unhappy over something and to be willing to assert that
unhappiness. Mild unhappiness may be endured and not protested. Overwhelming unhappiness and indignity may also be
endured and not protested, when protest is impossible because it will be crushed forthrightly. Such was the case in past
years, though protests there were, and crushed they were.
Now it is different. It is fairly clear that protest is possible,
and changes inevitable. But the emotions which have been
felt in the past, risen out of humiliation and injury, do not
disappear. They urge protest, but they are not quiet emotions. They are emotions of anger and frustration and fear.
Worse, they are those of shame and self-doubt. It is hard to
deal with these emotions when people shout at you and attack
you. When people remind you of all the lacerations and insults, it is hard to keep your cheek turned. You need the help
of others, the help of rehearsals, and the help of some of the
books which you left to make these protests. This idea has its
roots in Christ's teachings. When they had very little else, Negroes were given the Christian religion. Insofar as the student
has a tradition, insofar as his race has been allowed to develop
one, it contains large amounts of this view. It is a tradition of
bearing pain without protest. Then there is Gandhi, who
studied Christ, and loved Tolstoy, and wanted freedom for his
people, and didn't want to use violence to get it, and knew
how to make it very embarrassing for those who wouldn't give
it, and who got it.

Perhaps we should turn briefly to those protested against.

Perhaps they will help us see how the students manage the balance between getting angry and controlling their anger. It is just as complicated for the white people. Most people are hurt when others are hurt. Most people are moved by what they see and hear. If the Negro is off yonder in some shabby slum, he can be forgotten, as he is very often in the North. If he is off yonder in some field by day and then in some shack by night, he can be forgotten, as he was in the South. Some very kindly and decent people in the South, for whom he has worked and labored, have never heard him complain, and have grown up with their special ways of talking with him and caring for him. It has not all been hate. But it is a kind of love, a kind of relationship, which is no longer wanted. Nor will the hate and insults be allowed anymore. This has to be told to many people. It is important to remember that many people simply do not know of the Negro's dissatisfaction. If they did, they would not repeat so often that the Negro would be happy were it not for sinister outside forces. These are the uninformed. There are also those who really are informed and have ached for years with the injustice which they see and feel. Such white Southerners, and they are legion, have known that when others suffer, they suffer, and that the lessons their children learn are the lessons of hate and confusion, the lesson that Christian messages do not apply to large groups of human beings, not really. All of these people will be forcefully confronted. So will many frightened Negro people, unable, unwilling, afraid to do as their brothers do.

Those who keep these protests happening are of many ages and cities and families. They are mostly black men, but there are many black women, and many white men and white women. Some are from poor families, some from those in better circumstances. The son of a distinguished Negro college president works beside a very poor and orphaned boy from a rural town. There are many kinds of demonstration, and they may draw upon different participants. Some are spontaneous and astonishingly successful. In Asheville, North Carolina, some boys and girls who were going to junior high school and high school decided one day to use the library, and to try to get sodas from several stores. That was enough; and the fact that it was enough surprised the Negro community perhaps more than the white. Some demonstrations are spontaneous, but need much more planned and persistent action at later times for success. In Nashville many months were required. In Atlanta picketing of stores was followed by a boycott and long negotiation. More recently in Atlanta the movie houses were cautiously desegregated under an arrangement between the students and the owners, with the mayor acting as a friendly helper. But there are other demonstrations which are attempted in those desperate areas of last defiance, requiring careful action by experienced people. To dare to work in a small Mississippi town with Negro families, encouraging them to want to vote, tutoring them in their letters, helping them in the incredible intricacies of laws designed chiefly to discriminate against them, requires more than a college week-end of time and experience. Others leave school and devote months, years, to full-time training and action. Most protests have their origin in the local town, the local Negro college, or one nearby. The freedom rides were an obvious exception. These rides were a thrust into the heart of segregation, the bus terminals in Alabama and Mississippi. They were followed by some removal of separate rest-room signs. What they illustrated is the anxiety and concern which this country has for the welfare of these students. A policeman told one of them, "Even ten years ago you'd have been dead, all of you. Can't do that now." Though they are not sure, the students are sure enough to feel able to go ahead.

Those who go ahead seem to elude classification by class or geography or even age. College students predominate; but there have been younger boys and girls, and young married couples with children by their sides, and older people. In south Georgia or in Alabama or Mississippi or Louisiana any protest is made against heavy odds. In some towns in these states the mere act of protest is almost incredible. It is in these areas that violence is almost certain. It is here that terror stalks and danger is reliable. Police dogs are threatened in one state, and a man running for governor says that his body in front of the buildings will prevent execution of a federal law on school desegregation. He is elected. In another state students are arrested on charges of "criminal anarchy" for organizing sit-ins for coffee or encouraging campaigns to register voters. High bail is set, and some stay in prison and solitary confinement for months. In another state students escort some Negroes to register to vote. Crowds heckle and attack, arrests are made, students are kicked and hurt. But something prevents their murder, their lynching as in olden days. No one can say that such restraint in those towns is not some kind of communication from an outside world no longer so far away, so indifferent. The students leave jail, go back to their work.

Those students who leave school for some months and venture into these troublesome sections, live different lives once there. If you know the cramped, desolate, dreary quality to the Negro sections of southern towns, if you've heard the spirituals and seen the funerals, diagnosed the tuberculosis and vitamin deficiencies, smelled the cheap, bad booze which blots out poverty, persecution, the whim of the alien white lords, then you will know how some of these students live. They will often come to one of these towns and live there for months, getting to know people and finding out the usual problems of these people and suggesting new and direct responses to these problems, like a boycott, or a school where people can be helped in reading and interpreting constitutional law so that they may try to register to vote. It is not simply the hardness of the whites, many of whom are very poor and very much struggling themselves, very soft and tender people, friendly and generous with the little they have, whose voices are honey and whose eyes are sly with earthly, human affairs and constricted with money troubles and job troubles and bitter old times which are getting better, and whose ancient consolation following ancient frustration was a lowly, yelping, always handy nigger. It is the apathy of the Negroes which is more difficult to look at and most painful of all. It is their inertia and resignation which are so formidable. Death of spirit or soul, by murder, by suicide, by illness and exploitation, is worse than live, howling, frightened enemies.

Some students stay in one town for months and help local leaders plan action. Others move about from town to town, state to state, talking with young Negro students or helping them form a plan. White students will go with them, or will go to white campuses, where they will contact those who are quietly, and in ways different from those in Negro colleges, working for changes. These students are often called "field secretaries." This means that they travel in the field of southern cities and try to change that field by participating in actions which directly disregard its rules and boundaries. They receive enough money to travel and eat and sleep. When they come into a town they will look at the restaurants and the drugstore fountains. They will find out who votes, and where. They will watch parks and stand near libraries, and note who works at what job in those places where people work. Then they will get a room in some YMCA or bunk in some home or college dormitory, and start "making the rounds," hearing the many conflicting views of people, and recording and annotating them in their more than secretarial minds. After this, decisions must be made about what to do, in what order, and with whom.

When they decide, they decide their own fate, establish their own fears and hopes. Heavy odds they will be arrested and go to jail. Strong chance they will be kicked, punched, spat upon. Foul language is routine. Serious injury is possible. Most of these students have been in jail many times and in many states. Many are juggling several trial dates and bailed-free periods. They will go to court and be sentenced and appeal and, if there is money, go free and continue their activities, then interrupt them to go on trial in another state. Since most of what they do is illegal, and since they keep on in spite of this, they accumulate long prison records. Their fate is notorious. They are noticed by the press and television and radio. Their names may be given, their pictures taken. Leading newspapers and magazines will describe their behavior and, of course, its implications. This is important, because it is such news — and widely spread consideration of such news — which causes people to pay attention and become ashamed and indignant. All this is pressure on segregation, which, like many habits, works best unnoticed. When the students are noticed, they have scored a victory.

There are victories in the outside world and victories inside the mind and spirit of a person. Fears and hopes contend in us. Consider them both in some of these young people. They spend their time asking for things which they have been told they may not have. This is unpleasant enough. For asking, moreover, they are called criminals, and arrested, arraigned, imprisoned. This is unpleasant enough. As they prepare to ask, and while they ask, moreover, they risk injury and sustain insult. This is unpleasant enough. But when all is done, they must realize that what they have done is a very small beginning, and that can be very discouraging. And so there must be hope, and the mind must find ways to persist and continue when hope is sparse. It is in the nature of man for this to happen, and it does happen with these students. But not without some shifting and settling of emotions.

Abandoned are familiar routines and the comfort of daily rituals which are certain and predictable. Their clothes may be scattered over several states. There is no one bed and there may be many toothbrushes. These are students who have been brought up in homes where the discipline and routines of study are learned. In our civilization we cherish possessions and order. We learn in those early years which bed is our bed and which glass is our glass. We learn what time school opens and when it closes and how many hours we go. We learn numbers for our houses and numbers for our ages and numbers for our grades in school. We learn our private names and learn to put our writing on our books. We learn the order of classroom seating plans and graduation walking plans. We get scored in tests and ranked in classes, and we have certain pages to read for certain examinations. We all laugh when we go into the army and receive a long number beside our name; but the uneasy laugh is all too close to the long, familiar truth of our lives. When students leave college to risk punishment, leave a dormitory and classroom and library to face uncertain and changing quarters and work, they must make this possible for themselves. They are leaving what they have been brought up to value. They are leaving school, and the logical steps which they have been told to take as they become older; or they are staying in school but flirting with departure by their private, spare-time actions. They are no longer listening to their parents, or, if their parents agree with what they do, they still have the memory of the older words of their parents, words suggesting study, success, accumulation of knowledge, books, ideas, degrees. Obviously, what each student does is balance in his own mind what he wants and what he wants to do. We may be interested in how these people think and what they feel. Each of them is unique, and personal reasons mesh with public activity with different results of happiness, nervousness, fearfulness. If we are going to know how the students get along with themselves or how they get along with others, we must talk with individual students over a long enough time to get some ideas and feelings about them. All the field secretaries live almost vagabond lives, but each field secretary comes to this life with his own resources and handicaps, and for his own reasons. We can watch people live and see them act, and record that. Then we can talk with them and listen to them and hear their words and emotions, and record that, too.

Here is some information about an American man of twenty who left college in his sophomore year to engage in some of these protesting actions. Let him be called John.

He was born in a small farming town of southern Virginia in the summer of 1942, shortly after we went to war. His father was away fighting in Europe during his first three years. This was the first time his father had ever left his home. His mother worked in the home of a white lawyer, taking care of three children. John was left to his maternal grandmother. He recalls her as his childhood mother, and talks about her even now with much feeling. He remembers his father's return, and the feeling of awkwardness and strangeness. A younger brother was soon to come. His father had trouble finding a job, and seemed irritable and punishing to the boy. He remembers being beaten with a strap, and running away. He remembers being punished when about five for trying to go to a circus, trying to escape his parents and enter and go on the merry-go-round. His grandmother must have told him many times about the difference between white and colored children, but he recalls that he "really learned it" when he tried to sit beside a white lady one day on a bus.

I used to straggle after my grandmother anyway, and I must have done it on the bus. She kept on pushing to the rear, and it didn't seem to have any seats. I just sat down in the front. The woman pushed me and told me to get away and go to the back. I can remember how I felt then. I can still feel that feeling, like the world collapsing and not being liked. I felt I was bad and different, and I can still see that bus and that woman's look. Then, I was lectured by my grandmother, and her words drove everything I'd heard home for good. But my father was not happy with that, and he gave me the worst beating of my life when I got home. I can recall that too; I'll never forget him . . . telling me to keep my place. . . . My grandmother cried and so did my mother.

He tells about his schoolwork. He was a good student, and the teachers told him that he should stay in school. Most of his friends left school when about twelve or thirteen, going to the fields. His mother would tell him about big and mysterious lawbooks in her home-by-day. She would come home in the evening and tell the family about all the events in "the boss house." He recalls his fantasies about this, and the pleasure which those stories brought to the poor home. His father had by now a job in a new factory which came south after the war. The boy went to high school, and this was quite a distinction; in the entire family, spread over the nearby towns, he was the first. At fourteen he fell in love with a girl a year older, who admired him "for my brains and promise." He wanted to leave school and marry her and get a job and she wanted him to stay at studying. They fought; he stayed; she left. He graduated and was awarded a scholarship to a Negro college far enough away to be his break with home. He left, a family hero, and with great promise. "I remember," he tells in his deep and strong voice:

I can *still* remember reading about a sit-in which fellows from college were staging when I came there . . . I can *still* remember the Little Rock trouble. I used to have dreams about that. We'd sit and watch that on that television set, and we'd get angry, and my grandmother would say that those kids shouldn't try to go to that school, and my mother wouldn't say anything, and my father would curse those whites and say we should stay away from *all* of them . . . they can't be trusted, they're no good. And my mother would tell me, sometimes in a corridor away

from Dad, that that wasn't so, and then I'd hear about the lawyer and
his family . . . Mother told me one day that the lawyer's oldest son told
her that he was convinced that the South was changing, and that he
didn't mind going to school with Negroes . . . Mother told me that he
used the word "Negro" . . . she can just tell who thinks what about us
in that house . . . like when they stop talking about something when
she comes into the room. You can tell . . . I'd go to bed and dream that
I was one of those nine kids in Central High, and that Faubus came
over to the school and I killed him with a machine gun . . . or I
dreamed one day that I was ambushed by the police in Little Rock and
they wounded me and I was killing them, and then the army came and
they stopped, and one of them told me that the only reason that I lived
was because I was white. Niggers die! I can still picture that one.

In his freshman year at college he did well. The school itself was in some turmoil, with various groups advocating various pursuits in civil rights action.

We studied, but what was happening in Nashville or what happened
to those kids in New Orleans was more on our minds. . . . We talked
about that like I guess you talked about your courses when you were in
college. We'd argue about whether you should stay and get through college, or go out and participate. We'd argue about whether you can serve
your race better by just getting educated and doing your work, or whether
you should get out there and fight for freedom. I always felt you could
separate the men from the boys . . . I thought that this was our big
moment in history . . . it wouldn't be worth having a profession and a
family if they're going to grow up in semi-slavery. I wanted self-respect
more than a degree. I felt the others were cowards . . . no, I don't think
that now. I realize that not everyone feels the way I do about this. A lot
of our people don't know any better. And a lot are just scared. Some of
the guys were scared of ruining what they thought was their big chance
at college and their parents' one big hope. I thought of that, but I
thought about how can you have a chance when a segregated society
treats you only a little better than an animal? . . . My father fought in
France for this country, almost got killed. Why should he be afraid to
vote? Why should he tell me that I'm not as good as some white kid,
and why should he sit and "yes" the white man all day, and then come
home and booze it up and tell us how rotten they are? Man, it's not
worth it . . . I decided that . . . and I joined up on the freedom ride

in my spring vacation. . . . Now I was really doing something, and I couldn't go back. I thought this was the best education and the best service I could perform . . . I'll go back to school in a while, maybe a few more months . . . I just want to make sure that I've really given something to this cause . . . and there are kicks, too. You meet a lot of interesting people. You get to know the reporters. You see yourself in the papers, and really feel that you're almost single-handed in breaking some of those things . . . I get worried and nervous a lot. Mostly tired though, it's tiring, traveling and talking to other students. . . . No, I've never felt depressed. I'm in pretty good shape mentally. I get headaches sometimes, bad ones. Maybe I've got migraine . . . twenty-four times in jail, more than my age!

We do not really know John after we read this. We have some idea about some of the things that have happened to him in his short and eventful life, and we have some idea about some of his feelings. A psychiatrist would talk with him a number of hours and would tell us that he is not deluded, and not distant, and can be understood when he talks. He would tell us that he is intelligent and he would find out that before this young man became involved in his present way of life he had never entered a courtroom, let alone a jailhouse. Hearing intently, he would begin to see how this young man grew up, how he got along with his mother and his father, and, of course, in this instance, his grandmother. He would consider his behavior as well as his words. He would find him to be a tall and thin man who looks a bit younger than his twenty years; who is neat and orderly in appearance and walks slowly and, at times, hesitantly; who talks easily and with warmth; who has enjoyed good health and who has never had cause to feel unhappy enough with himself to see a doctor or a minister. His interests and hobbies and attitudes might be collected, and the roots of some of these in his earlier life might be uncovered. For example:

I think when I go back to school I'll take law . . . it's the best way to fight them [segregationists] when you get older and have to settle down . . . it's the same thing, we're doing one part of the job and they're doing another . . . we need Negro lawyers in the South . . . I'm going to stay right down here.

These comments illustrate, again, the deep involvement of this man's life in his people's struggle for freedom. What is also shown is how his family life engages with the larger, racial issue. He is a strong, tough fighter, like his father, and now in a kind of war, and he wants to go to school and be a lawyer, with dignity and self-respect, like his mother's employer. His personality and his problems are not unique. They are the problems of growing up and finding himself as a man and a working man. What is unique for him in our country is that his skin has grimly attached itself to almost all these problems, to his early years as a child and his later years as an adolescent, to his dreams and actions and fears and aspirations. Trouble with his father, longing for his mother, attempts at achieving independence — all of these are touched by his light brown color. Decisions and choices have to pass the muster of race. If he becomes like his father in many respects, his father's opinions and feelings about the Negro and the white will be there to confront him, as well as how those feelings affected his childhood. And so with his mother, and with his grandmother. Like all people, he will sift and sort and take from many people, within and without the home, those many ways and traits and habits which make up the daily lives of a person. Race, religion, ancestry, affect us all. Saying that the Negro has a special problem in this regard, saying that he is pervasively affected, intensely affected, is merely describing his lot today among us. His lot, in each person, becomes the individual's private burden and challenge. It is hard to see how other burdens and challenges in the individual will escape the magnetism of this one.

But the individual life still exists in Negroes. Each one of these students took his own road, made his detour for private as well as public reasons. It *is* a detour — away from school, into jail, toward danger and possible violence. Many youths, Negro and white, in both North and South, favor what these students actively proclaim, but for reasons in *their* lives cannot or will not join them. Here we are up against history itself, and there are no easy separations or distinctions between these two groups of people, certainly no psychiatric ones. Those who protest are not psychotic, retarded, delinquent. They are all very specific in their protests. Indeed, their college teachers have told me that they wish at moments that a portion of their defiant spirit could be applied to some of the crusty and stunted areas of college and classroom tradition. As you talk with one after another and hour by hour eliminate the broad categories of the crazed, eccentric, lawless or mentally inadequate, you soon find yourself meeting yourself and your fellow human, that vast body of mankind which is alike and unalike; sometimes sad, sometimes joyful; gifted, and tiresome.

Driven by their own motives and past lives, but united by the historical moment that selects the doers and generates deeds. There is the very bright son of a Negro law professor who could not study well at college. Every college dean knows that problem, the famous father whose son for various reasons cannot assert himself academically. It was in the midst of this kind of difficulty that the students obtained this new recruit, able, forceful, very valuable. After over a year of doing things which very conservatively might be considered brave, he could return with high efficiency and performance to a less overwhelming and frightening college career. Another shy and slow-talking boy, an only child, participated in one sit-in, for which he was arrested, lost his job, and with that, the means of support for an aged and sick parent, whose death occurred shortly thereafter. In his fierce grief he cried his accumulated rage of years after his mother's last penniless minutes in the grossly overcrowded, understaffed slum of a Negro emergency ward in the city hospital, by leaving college for a time and walking the cities in silent outrage. These two are unlike in their homes and in their experiences in roughly the same two decades of living. One is bright, well spoken, rebellious, casual in attire and, among Negroes, born to a manor. The other is poor, cautious, very neat and careful of person, and a bit sad and heavy, and unable to initiate ideas or actions. But he will follow more than the instructions of others as he walks the streets.

Walking with the Negro youth are their white friends. It is well known in the North that many white students in our universities have strong sentiments on the subject of civil rights. In the South these northern students are considered no different from the many others who have hurled accusations in that direction, some unjust, some just, but rather foolishly and inappropriately self-righteous, and all from outsiders. But in the South there are white students who are deeply of the South and who can be seen beside their colored brothers. They can be heard talking about their lives and about their rather special work and special trials. A tall, blond, twenty-two-year-old native Alabaman speaks in a soft and leisurely fashion:

I never thought much about this one way or the other until I was a sophomore at college in Montgomery. I was taking a course in sociology and one of the topics was about the Negro in Alabama. I started doing some reading, and then talked with a few teachers. Many of them would tell us their private opinions about the issue, but were afraid to speak out publicly. I started getting more and more interested. At first it was just intellectual, I wanted to write a good paper and wanted to know about what I was writing about. . . . I started noticing how Negroes existed. It suddenly occurred to me that all the things I took for granted were forbidden to them. . . . Now I was a junior and a big deal on campus, and I talked with more of the professors about this. . . . They seemed scared when I said that if everyone in Alabama said what they

really felt we wouldn't have some of these things. . . . I'm not even sure
about that, but I do know what I feel, and I have to live with myself.
. . . My father once belonged to the Klan, but it had nothing to do
with Negroes. I think the whole town joined after the First World War.
He's a minister . . . has always said that this whole segregation thing is
wrong. He's glad that I'm doing what I'm doing . . . says that if he
were my age he'd be out there fighting, too. My mother worries, but she
always worries about us. . . . We've been in this state as long as anyone,
generations . . . no, it was gradual involvement. I don't remember the
exact moment when I went from studying the problem to doing something about it. . . . I've always liked action. I think that if you believe
something you can sacrifice for it . . . this is our biggest test here in the
South, and we've got to solve it ourselves by realizing that we're not free
when we can't say what we want or associate with anyone we wish. . . .
I like tennis, swimming, anything that really gives me a workout . . .
I'd like to put in another year at this, and then maybe go back to school
and study about all this, like in sociology or psychology. Figure out why
people are so strange about all this . . . let their kids be brought up by
Negroes, let them serve them and prepare their food, then blow sky-high
if one of them tries to sit near them in a Walgreen's. . . . We have our
problems as whites in the movement. I no longer stay in white hotels
. . . I decided that as long as they were segregated and I couldn't be in
a place with my own friends, I'd stay in the colored places. I go to the
colleges and talk with students. You'd be surprised at how many people
are with us, all over the South. They have to be quiet, and do things
underground-style . . . I never push them, never try to get them to do
something that will get them expelled just to prove a point. They can
talk in the cafeteria or in the dorms, and they can find out how others
feel, and they can work from within . . . very often with the help of a
lot of the faculty, who have to keep quiet about it, too. . . . That's
what bothers me more than anything else, not being free to speak out
and say what I want to. I keep telling some of the fellows I meet that
I joined this because if I can't say what I want, I'm not any more a free
person than the Negro. . . . I used to debate, was on the team . . .
used to think I'd be a politician, run for the Senate, but not much
chance of that. . . . I've changed, learned so much about what's really
going on around me. . . . They really get enraged at me when they
can't just dismiss me as a damyankee. . . . I've been arrested so many
times I've given up counting, dozens . . . everything from disorderly
behavior, violating city ordinances, unruly assembly, criminal anarchy,

the whole range. . . . The jails vary. Some of those police know the handwriting on the wall, laugh about the whole thing with us. Others are real sadists. Turn on the hot air in summer to burn you up, or let you freeze in winter, or mess your food up, and swear, can they swear! Sometimes I think I'm becoming antiwhite, I get so disgusted . . . I can understand how some of the guys just get fed to the teeth with the whole white race . . . then we settle down . . . they remember me and a lot of others and we try to forget the whole skin thing between us. I'm black, they're white, we joke about it. I do get discouraged some-times . . . but I think about what I'm doing, and it really is more significant to me than reading books . . . I can go back to that, but then I won't just feel I've been in an ivory tower all my life. This way I've done something to make this a better country . . . I'm no complete idealist . . . I know you've got to be strategic . . . but there's a time when regardless of what you say to yourself and read, it rings hollow compared with what people have to suffer in the world, and that's the time to commit yourself to action. . . . It took me a few years, but I think you need time to find out about some of these things before you can do anything about them. It took me a long time to figure out what I could do even when I wanted to do something. . . . Sometimes some of my Negro friends think I'm nuts for putting my life on the line . . . I tell them that they've been brainwashed by the segregationists into believing they're not worth the effort, and, besides, this is my fight, be-cause the white race is really doomed if we don't solve this problem.

There is little need for comment here. This boy grew up in a deeply religious home, an active, vigorous, alert youngster who runs well, plays good tennis, reaches for prizes in express-ing himself in argument in high school, dreams of political glory, does well in college, is slowly struck by certain under-privileged people, and, in his father's own tradition, stops a while in his life to apply his restless, seeking energy to their plight, which becomes his. He outdistances his father, as each generation may, and he lives with people the life of someone who gives of himself to those less fortunate. They love and, in a sense, adore him, as people do when they meet someone who extends, even if slightly, the possibilities in man.

They also love a young girl whose eyes are hazel and hair

long, brown, and flung about when she turns her head in emphasis. Also southern, she has not left college. But she works as hard there for what she believes as she studies what is taught. A willful girl, she had a less gradual introduction to the unreason of race.

There are a few Negro girls at my college, and, honestly, at first they scared me. I didn't know them, but I just wasn't accustomed to seeing Negroes in a school or college with whites. I was brought up with them all over the house, but that's where they were supposed to be. My mother was always very good to them . . . told us they were like wonderful children with grown bodies that did all kinds of work for us, but not much mind. I believed her for a long time, but I began to question everything when she didn't want me to go to the very college she'd been hoping I'd go to all my life just because they desegregated and took in a few Negroes. You'd have thought the South was collapsing to listen to her. But I went, and one of the last things she told me was to be careful about them . . . kind of like there was a pestilence that might take every white body near it. Daddy just laughed and laughed, and used to tease mother, and tell her she was just plain scared, and letting it all out on the poor nigras. I can hear him saying, "Mother, you just leave them alone, and they'll leave you alone. They've done plenty for us, and if their day is coming, it'll be good for us as well as them. Take your fears out on something else besides them. We've used them too long already for that kind of hating and beating. I'd rather kick a tree or something when I'm not feeling good. . . ." Daddy is a lawyer . . . comes from South Carolina, but has always been liberal on race . . . he told me to take anthropology in college and find out about as many people as I could, because they're all going to be heard from in my lifetime. . . . But I was scared, kind of a physical feeling that told me to stay away from them, it's hard to explain. One day one of them was brought to the table where I was eating. I had to get a strong hold on myself to stay there and to keep on eating. I couldn't help it, I just felt sick to my stomach, sick all over. I smiled and tried to be friendly, but I was in a cold sweat . . . later, in my room, I realized that I *was* sick, that it was a kind of sickness when you react that way to another person you don't even know, just because of color . . . it's more than that, though, it's the way you've grown up, and been taught. I said that night to myself that if I could throw away some other ideas I'd heard at home, I could

throw this one away too. I just *had* to . . . it was like curing myself.
. . . I forced myself at first to get nearer to them, to talk with them or sit
with them at the table. Then I found that I really liked one of them, she
and I had lots to talk about, and she was a really attractive person . . .
then, my old reactions seemed so strange and I can't understand how I
ever could have felt that way . . . of course, when I went home and told
my mother about this, she almost died. She cried and we really had a
time. She swears that she'll send my brother only to a segregated college,
but I laugh and tell her that by the time he's ready to go to college she's
going to have a tough time living up to her word. Bobby is fourteen. A
lot is going to happen in four or five years . . . Daddy just laughs and
tells me that Mother makes a lot of fuss, but is tough underneath and
she thinks she *has* to get excited about things like this. "Your mother
hasn't it in her to hurt anyone, black or white . . . she's just changing
her ideas in her own way. She has to cry them out, and repeat them a
few times so that she can say good-bye to them. That's the South, holding to its own as long as it can, because it had precious little to hold to
for a long time. . . ." That's Daddy for you . . . after a while I decided
I'd actually *do* something about all of this, and so I started speaking up
whenever the subject came up, and you'd be surprised at how many people just are waiting for others to take the lead . . . and then we formed
our campus organization and picked certain jobs to do, like education at
our own school and helping put pressure on the movie owners and restaurant people. Most of their business comes from students, so we should
have some say in how they treat people . . .

She and her friends were having much to say, and their
words were expressed in deeds, which caused changes in the
admissions policy of local movie houses and cafeterias. In her
southern state this is possible. There are others like her in the
bottom tier of states along the Gulf of Mexico who, if they are
to stay in college, must be more circumspect, and less hopeful
of immediate translation of ideals into realities. If we play
back the hours of tapes which have recorded her voice and her
words and her story, we can sense certain themes: of her
mother and her father, and how they differ and how she gets
along with them and expresses her divided loyalties in many
ways, not the least of which is her position on the racial ques-

tion; of her childhood and training and memories as they meet a world which no longer sustains their value or truth or reality; of the crisis in her life, the discord when these old traditions in her meet upon new ways in the South, in her college; of her solutions, accompanied by fear and guilt, and brought home for their resolution; and of her emergence as a grown lady. In this case there is a more decisive experience at the supper table, which engages with not too dormant personal struggles, in themselves universal for college girls. A crisis in history is a crisis for people, and human beings yearn for ways of expressing themselves. This girl found her way.

Since the way of these students involves obvious danger, those taking the way must be able to live with this danger, must be able to persist undeterred by it. Facing danger at their own behest, devoting themselves to its encounter with such fullness and passion, they offer instructive examples of how young people manage such commitments and do not falter. The obvious dangers are from crowds and from the police and from judges and jailers. But there are other problems, too. There are problems of money, needed to eat and sleep and travel; needed to get out of jail while the judgment and sentences are appealed. Bail can be set in the thousands by a local court which so desires. There are problems of the devil: of publicity, of attracting attention to their actions, so that people will be shamed, embarrassed, or forced to act out of expediency, national interest, economic or business anxieties. In a country of interests which often conflict and whose genius is their reconciliation, they too must become versed in the practical and possible. But this means practical and possible for *them,* and if they listen too closely to the wise counsel of even their most friendly elders, they might well lose one of their greatest possessions — their own, youthful, sometimes heedless and blind momentum. The problems of momentum are problems of the flesh: of how to behave before mobs, of how to behave with one another, of how to live with oneself, and keep one's morale high.

A psychiatrist interested in how people manage these tough assignments gets to know the young men and women and watches them in action. In this age of machines his impressions can be stimulated and recalled in later months by tape recordings, and he can hover over the tapes the way others may pore over books, looking for some of the thoughts and feelings which may pass him during the conversations themselves. After he has talked to enough of the students, long enough, he gets some ideas about how they manage. How they manage can be discovered without tape, but with tapes we can hear their every word; such as when they respond to questions like "How do you feel when you walk into a situation that you know in advance will lead to violence or arrest or jail?"

I don't feel, I just go ahead. . . . We sing and encourage one another. . . . We've practiced and rehearsed. It's like I suppose my dad did in France against the Nazis, you're in a kind of an army, and you've got no choice, except that you've joined on your own, not been drafted.

I close my eyes mentally. . . . Sometimes I pray just before, or I keep on saying that nothing *too* bad can happen in America. . . . We have the reporters nearby and the federal government . . . they can't do what they used to do . . . you know . . . lynchings are harder for them . . . I know some of them would like to, but they're afraid to . . . not in this world, they can't . . .

The young wife of one of the students insists:

I'm prepared to give up my life . . . I've made that decision, and it's almost as if I'm no longer in my body. The body can be sacrificed. I just look at myself and say to myself, "Man, you can lose your body, but they can't take your soul away. They can just lose theirs. And I'm going to help them. . . ."

Another college sophomore, a young girl who wants to be a teacher someday but has taken a few months' leave hesitates, then starts with:

Every time I feel afraid I just remind myself that we've got nothing to lose. I think of all the things I've had to put up with in my life. I think of all the movies I can't go to, all the restaurants I can't eat in, all those separate rest rooms and water fountains, and, I tell you, I can get so angry that they could have atom bombs on their clubs and police dogs and I'd keep on walking or sitting. We've got our rights as human beings to gain, and absolutely nothing to lose, not a thing. So, why not? Oh, I have to get myself to thinking about this sometimes, when I get nervous, or when the jail is a bad one, and you don't know what they're going to do . . . you can do that, though, get yourself primed, like a pump or something . . .

A veteran of eighteen arrests commented:

It's almost like going into an army. Well, a better example is the Crusades, where men went off for their religious convictions, almost voluntarily. . . . You not only feel what you've always felt, but you've decided to stake your life on the line for it. You'll go to jail, face the police and those screaming seggies . . . face the whole world. . . . We help one another, keep our strength up with music and we talk a lot *after* it's happened, and joke and get some laughs out of it . . . it's fun to see your picture in the papers, and read the different accounts, a lot of them get all botched up, or completely slanted, of course . . . one thing I've heard some of my friends say is that they never really believe that those crowds will hurt them . . . heckle and scream, yes, but not really hurt. I can't quite pull that off in my mind. I know that they may hurt me, but I figure we can take it, and give it back. I've taken worse all my life . . . this is the first chance I've had to *do* something while taking it that may end the whole rotten mess . . .

Clearly, their feelings and their consciences impel them. Clearly, also, in order to endure inevitable apprehensions, they must either remove themselves or temporarily blot out some real threats. Determined minds can do this. They can abstract the mind and emotions from the body, and let *it* serve duty and risk injury. They can deny danger, wipe out or minimize hazards. They can make thorny dilemmas very simple, and they can undertake such activity, such continual movement and travel, that there is little time for nervous brooding. They can encourage singing, meeting, and praying with others, gaining the well-known strength of camaraderie. They can see fear and terror in others, in the enemy, and fail to see anger and rage in them. The enemy becomes afraid, and they are unafraid. They can urge talking and sharing in words the common dread. They can gain very human pleasure from anticipated rewards of renown, attention, approval, balancing with these all the present hesitations and doubts. They can fall back on what they call "techniques," dwelling upon the details of how to behave, where to go, what to say or do, placing their feelings in an envelope of rituals and memorized, almost automatic, maneuvers. They dribble away large doubts in small annoyances. Panic can splinter into a generally fretful day. Angry jokes can be told. Books which give comfort or release or escape can be read. There is always good food, and one can sleep longer hours. A bad headache, some vague stomach pains, these can silently express unallowed anxiety. There are daydreams, fantasies, nightmares, all perhaps lowering some pressures which may build up. Fun, movies, exercise, may help; and there can be nervously short and intense romances, almost as in war, when the lovers know they may be separated, that they have only a brief time, to which they bring so many emotions besides love. Letter-writing helps. And some of these minds can not only feel frustrated and anxious and angry and fearful, but they can hate. Often, if the alternative is despair, they can hate and hate mean and hard, can give back what they've received rather than sink into it themselves.

In courts and in jails their minds have additional difficulties. They are being accused and, usually, condemned. The charges range from disturbing the peace and loitering to criminal anarchy. Those under sixteen or eighteen may be called delinquents and sent for long periods of so-called evaluation and confinement. Some courts have even referred them to mental hospitals for psychiatric observation. With such certain punishment for their efforts, they must learn how to live in cells and under charges of criminality or insanity without losing their sense of themselves and their integrity. This requires no little effort. To do this they can deny their guilt, and turn the illegal into the just. You can hear them listing with pride their arrests and jailings. You can hear them upholding their own values against those of cities and states. You can hear them calling for the support of their government and the tradition of Western democracy. They do this out of conviction and out of need. All the time they are being told by people in black robes and people in uniforms carrying guns, by newspapers and by influential citizens, that they are bad and unruly and outcasts. All the time they are being hustled and confined, after being refused and insulted. This cannot fail to affect them, cannot fail in some parts of their minds to make them feel worthless or wrong or guilty as charged. Since all of us have gone through childhood and learned about being good and being bad, and doing good and doing bad, and being praised and being criticized, memories and anxieties of the past can return under such evocative and haunting circumstances of the present. In a sense they are being sent to a room, which is now a jail, to be alone and to repent for being bad and disobedient. This is precisely what one of the students dreamed while in prison.

Living the life of the condemned asks something of you. It asks you to have control, just as nonviolent protest requires control, except that now you are not free anymore. Control of feelings and behavior is important to these students, and in order to insure its strength they often live very ascetic lives, as if the large amount of control needed must be obtained by spreading it into almost all of their activities. In some of the front lines of Mississippi, relaxation of body or mind must be guarded. Even when they are not protesting they may be under constant surveillance. They must drive cautiously and live cautiously. Even among Negroes they must keep an image of dedication, because suppressed people are suspicious and afraid. They must control the temptation to exploit their work. Once they become heroes to some of their people easy promiscuity and many comforts may be offered them. They are anxious, and part of them responds very humanly to it. One can hear them in meetings talk about this, warn themselves in advance and point out the dangers:

> If we're going to stay in the Movement, we've got to watch ourselves, we've got to control ourselves all the time. It's like a war. They call it a fight to the finish, and so will we. If we're going into Mississippi and Alabama, then we've got to have iron discipline. . . . You either put all your energy into the Movement, or you stay behind and so do something else . . . no fooling around, we can't take risks like that, we've got enough with the "segs" without setting things up for them ourselves.

At times, under extreme danger, they go into a state which they call "commandati," which means extreme alert and caution, which measures a response to all the harassments that accumulate in a struggle such as theirs. It is not that they are by nature unruly or wild. On the contrary, they tend to be rather controlled and studious people. It is that they are under attack, and they must prepare themselves and one another for such unusual strains. To hold up under these strains requires devotion, energy and ingenuity. Perhaps only the young, the still unattached and unemployed and unsettled, can take this on.

They take on cells for homes. They must hold their sanity, keep their orientation, amidst isolation and obvious humiliation. It is one thing to go to jail for a crime committed. Many who do can even shrug off the jailing as part of the game, part of the gamble. It is another thing to have a highly developed conscience, and to be moved by that conscience to certain deeds of fulfillment, and in pursuit of these, in quest of being a fuller citizen, to be insulted, fined, sent off to solitary confinement or overcrowded cells. It is another thing because these students are not hard and tough and callous, and yet they must get along where they are often treated with more contempt than hardened lawbreakers who are there for robbery, assault or drunk and disorderly behavior.

In a Louisiana prison I talked at length with a tall, thin, twenty-year-old student who had been held in solitary confinement for two months on a charge of criminal anarchy. When all the doors had been closed behind me, the first view was of a large blackboard with the prison census divided by races first, sexes second. I wondered what genes or chromosomes made for such high numbers of male Negroes and low numbers of female whites. I was there at the request of his counsel, because this young man had written letters to friends in Atlanta requesting psychiatric help saying, "I'm beginning to think I may be cracking, I'm really getting near the edge." His criminal and anarchic behavior was organizing students in a Negro college nearby, urging them to help other Negroes vote, or be served in department-store lunch counters. When he first came to the jail he was put in close quarters with recurrent criminals, the most beaten, desperate, and lowly of his people. In the medical examining room, and later after his release, he talked about it all:

> You know, I thought until then I knew how to get along in jail. I'd been in lots of jails . . . but this was almost too much. First I had to fight to keep away from those guys . . . sodomy all the time, and I think they were egged on by the guards. What a bunch of thugs. They told me that the place had been investigated twice before, so they were going to be careful, but they let me have as much as they could . . . sent heat in the cell when I was hot anyway . . . finally moved me to solitary. I thought at first that would be better, but it gets strange after a while. You fight just to keep track of time and to get *through* time. It drags, man, it drags till you think you've just about had it. You try to write, if they'll give you paper. You dream, and try to sleep. But I couldn't

sleep. No exercise, so I didn't need sleep. If only I could have slept, or dozed all day. . . . Terrible slop for food . . . I'll tell you what it does to you, it makes you wonder whether you'll ever get out, and soon you begin to lose some of your fight. They would get their trusties to come and shine their shoes in front of me. Those pitiful Negroes, on their knees shining the shoes of the guards, and then they'd ask them, "Joe, aren't you happy with things the way they are in Louisiana?" And big Joe, big, free, independent, American citizen Joe, would look up at them and say, "Yesuh, yesuh, Mr. Boss, I sure am, yesuh." Then they'd turn and make the poor guy tell that to me. . . . The worst was when they brought those kids in, those white schoolchildren, and pointed me out as a Communist. They had me on display, like a damn guinea pig . . . I was marking the days off on the wall . . . they finally gave me two books . . . Kipling's short stories and a history of China written in 1849 or so . . . yeah, pretty funny, but not then it wasn't. . . . Those pills did help, they took the nerves out of me, let me settle down . . . they told me they didn't *have* to give them to me. . . . The doctor came around and asked me why I didn't tell him about what was aching me or bothering me . . . I couldn't trust him . . . he was probably OK . . . made sure I got the pills. I'm glad they let me write to you. Writing a letter can keep you going for days . . . I don't know if I can take another spell like that. I'm not crazy, but I began to wonder how many days I had left before I started getting there. . . .

He was indeed very anxious, and more frightened than he may have known. He was afraid of assault — sexual, personal, moral, mental and spiritual. He was afraid of losing the complicated organization of mind and emotions which we spend so long building and which is not meant to be tested by hells like this. He was afraid of losing his gritty, tough, daring ways and dissolving in tears of panic and confusion, if not disorientation and delusion. When you are alone for a long time, and you know that people want to hurt you and have that ability in their absolute power, every sound, every shadow, every movement, can signal danger and death. Fortunately he was released after three months in jail. I think it was good for him to be seen by a doctor and put on tranquilizers and allowed to write. His jailers and their superiors in the nearby district attorney's office could scarcely let him effectively lose his mind. That might hurt *their* cause. Such was his protection, and such is the way men are protected from men in some places. Sometimes they spend short periods of a day or two in jail. Often they can turn these days into frolic. They are together in cells, and they sing and laugh and talk. Or, if alone, they can send messages and whistle and sing back and forth. Many flippant, arrogant, angry phrases, sarcastic phrases, words of mock irony can be heard; sometimes smouldering resentment, neatly kept, can become a white heat of rage and hatred. This can cause shame and alarm for those who are not Negro, and are torn between their sympathy and their ability, because of different experiences, to know better, feel less desperate.

It's hard for the white student in this at times. Sometimes you have to keep quiet and listen, let them get it all out of their systems every once in a while. I feel terrible . . . it's no good if we get desegregation and they're so embittered they become just like the segregationists. That's the danger, now. Look at the Black Muslims. Some of the guys I know are not Black Muslims, but they're becoming kind of African Nationalists . . . they tear down this country and say that Africa's the place for them, to live and . . . where everything is good. That's what happens when you treat people like this . . . most of them really love this country though . . . I don't know if I would . . . after a while they cool down . . . sometimes apologize to us. . . . I understand how they have to get like that sometimes . . . I don't take it personally. I think the Movement should have whites in it, even in Mississippi, where they get so enraged when they see us together . . . that's what it's all about, that we can work side by side.

They work side by side, and then a time comes when they leave, going back to college, to work, or to a graduate school. When they decide to leave, like when they decided to come, will vary from person to person, as will the length of their stay. Some have been working at the problem for years, some

for months. They all recognize that one cannot spend a lifetime at this, at least not in the capacity of a student. Perhaps
more of a problem now for them is the inevitable consequence of their various successes. Like any gathering of
human beings who are trying to do things together, they have
to come to some settlement with the nature of themselves as a
group or organization. In 1960 when four of them went into a
store in Greensboro, that was not a problem. It still isn't in
the many spontaneous instances where a group of high school
or college students simply decide to take on a specific job, like
a movie house in their town. But if a systematic assault is to
be made through direct protest, and if considerable resistance
is met, requiring planning and more time and effort than
originally estimated, there must be distribution of work and
energy and direction. Living in a highly organized society,
the students learn that it will not necessarily fall under an
attack of the moment. And so they pool efforts, and since
there are many colleges, many cities and many states, they
come together and meet and talk and argue, and try to regu-
late themselves, and they belong to different organizations
and call themselves by different names. They find, in the continuing irony of human existence, that adversity has its own
joys and success its own trials. They worry about losing their
freedom and spontaneity in a mass of constitutions and by-
laws and regulations. They worry about exhausting themselves in bureaucratic tangles, in endless appeals for money.
They fear the futile absorption in stamp machines, mimeograph machines and filing cabinets, even as they know how
much these are needed. They struggle with these new and
petty tyrannies, trying for the needed balance of personal action and staff action. This struggle may be harder, in the very
long run, than even that for the rights of the Negro. Wherever
there are men there are rivalries, envies, competing needs for
power. Wherever there are men there are also possibilities

that great and decisive things will be done and ideas conceived. They are struggling for the right to be human, to be men in the many senses of that word, and so this, too, will mark their progress; when they can wrangle with the fruits of their labor like all other free men.

Their harvest becomes a harvest for all and a source of challenge to many. Those who are interested in how people manage to change things around them will study these students. The various social scientists will consider their case. Certainly they offer interesting challenges to psychiatrists. Psychiatrists are asked today to help the courts decide, not only whether a person knows the difference between right and wrong, but also whether he is so constituted that he can adhere to this understood difference. We have urged considering motives and impulses as well as facts and strict rationality. We have urged changes in laws where we have felt them to be unfair or harsh or not in accordance with our view of the nature of the human mind and its development. We urge understanding of people, and help for people who are not well. Finally, we are asked, not only to do our healing and our research and teaching, but to advise the general public, as well as the courts, on the widest variety of subjects. We are consulted about the nature of delinquency, what it is, who the delinquents are, and what can be done. We venture more and more into prisons to work with prisoners, on the good premise that people impelled to crime have some disorder of impulse as well as a record of wrongdoing, and should be treated with more than custodial reckoning. We are asked about problems in schools and colleges, problems of learning, of behavior, of suitability for certain programs. We are consulted by many professions, to help them choose candidates for the ministry or to screen applicants for crucial places in business or the government. Presumably, then, our capacity to evaluate human beings and their behavior is considered by others and by ourselves to be of some practical as well as theoretical value. Presumably, also, our knowledge is felt to extend beyond the mental hospitals and consultation rooms and into the life of the community.

The lives of many of our communities today are endangered by troubles between groups of people. Large numbers of people gather themselves around certain names describing religions or nations or sections of nations or races, or combinations of these. They declare themselves apart by rituals or flags or color or customs or locations. In their behavior with one another these multitudes are often like individuals: they get along or they fight, they help one another or they try to control one another. It has been this way for a long time. New collections of people emerge and old ones die as new bonds and ties appear and old sources of allegiance seem less compelling. It has been and still is a part of growing up in most of the world to find out about oneself, and many of these associations — national, sectional, racial — help in this and contribute to it through traditions, customs, knowledge, security. Perhaps when people know themselves, and are not too afraid of themselves, and are relaxed and at ease, they do not have to lose themselves in overworked assertions of themselves as members of particular groups rather than as persons.

Certainly these students have shown that American youth can look around and see things that are hurtful to themselves and to others, and venture forth to change them. Certainly their work is important, and certainly it should be evaluated if we are concerned with changing life in our community. As psychiatrists we have this concern, and our society asks this concern of us. Our challenge with these students is, as always, to gather observations and descriptions; then attempt to sort them out and come to some estimate, always tentative, of what their behavior means and what it may portend. To do this may be easier than to reconcile some of our own professional problems. But, in a stimulating fashion, the behavior of these students may help clarify some of our professional problems.

Not the least of our problems is that elusive idea, "normal." We wonder what it is and how to use it; we wonder whether it exists and we are struck by the curious obsession which it inspires in many around us. Not the least of our problems is deciding what is "sick" and what is "healthy." We should use these words carefully, too. Then, we have to decide at times who can best take on a particular job or perform well in a certain situation. We thus start evaluating "creative" and "destructive" parts of the person, and find them often entangled enough to blur their separate meanings. We also have to worry about our own values, our own hopes and ideas of what is desirable for man, what helps him grow, and what is crippling and harmful.

How, then, do we comprehend these protesting students who break laws and go to jail and are sent to detention centers as delinquents or to mental hospitals for suspected insanity? How do we evaluate their departure from college, their radical departure from established customs and habits, their defiance of law and order, their public display of themselves and its resultant public uproar? How do we evaluate their desire to do things even though they know they will be insulted, attacked, injured? How do we evaluate this stubborn, sly, systematic assault upon the laws and conventions of our society by youths of both races? Casting a glance elsewhere, we can ask some other questions. How do we comprehend those students who don't participate in these demonstrations? How do we evaluate their attitudes toward themselves if they are Negro, or toward others if they are white? How do we evaluate their willingness to endure, or see endured by others, these restrictions and deprivations of person, property and dignity? How do we look at them in school, or in their obedience to laws which curb and isolate them or others? Finally, do we dare look at our society and ourselves in it with any questions? What in laws and customs will help people to be secure or to maintain health, and what is injurious? What do we mean when we use the words "well adjusted" or "poorly adjusted"? We certainly use them. Should a boy who has been arrested twenty-five times and put in jail eighteen times and charged by his society with criminal anarchy be called "well adjusted," "delinquent," "anti-social" or "creative"? Does he have a "problem with authority," and, if he does, why don't more people have it? Should we call it a problem? A problem for whom? Students like these challenge the unrestrained application of adjectives. Such nouns as "masochism" and "acting-out" are also challenged by these students. Are they "acting-out," are they masochistic, are they troublesome deviants? Or are they other words we use, like well integrated, or "mature," with "good defenses" and highly developed sublimations? Finally, what do we do about applying what we know about people — what is healthy and sickly in them — to these problems? These students are denounced and praised. Should we, can we, evaluate their actions with some sense and fairness? Or do we find such problems too prickly, too dangerous to our positions in society, too risky for involvement? Perhaps these students challenge our assumptions, our concepts, our language, our present ability to answer many problems; they make us aware of some of our limitations, despite society's importunate requests of us and some of our indiscreet replies. If so, they will have given us a measure of humility. This would be a large gift. With humility, we need not apologize for some of our present ignorance. Ignorance is a challenge, and it is a high honor to engage with it. We lose honor only when we see victory when there is still a long struggle ahead. Perhaps these students of social change and we students of human nature can meet in that struggle.

For there can be no doubt that many of their problems are also ours. Daily they show us how they must refuse the arbitrary and absurd confinements of skin color. Each of them is an individual, and they hope that someday they will be known to their fellows by themselves, by who they are and what they do. Pigment seems to them, to those who are white as well as black, a frivolous and tragic standard for human knowledge of one another, an irrelevant distinction, indeed. It is, then, the meaningless word, the hollow hurtful evocation which bothers them. With us, too, categories and labels of soothing certainty abound. We have no little ability or wish to add to these terms and to these conceptual separations of the mind within a person and of people from one another. Our peril is that, driven by the need to find out about ourselves, we may find ourselves more puzzled than ever by our own thinking and the conflicting faiths to which our thoughts adhere. We must challenge our concepts and categories just as the nonviolent youth of our South challenge those of others. If our terms fail to describe what is happening in the world of people and their lives, they must be discarded. If they are contradictory, inadequate, misleading, they must go. If they fail to account for human effort and courage and man's deeds toward a more decent world, if they fail to envision and honor the reality of the heroic in the smallest, quietest assertion of a deeply ethical youth at a southern lunch counter or in a southern jail, they must depart. If these students will help to draw us to such considerations and clarifications, their efforts will be our accidental but most fortunate and timely gain.

Youth: Change and Challenge,
Erik H. Erikson, ed., Basic Books, 1963

We Will Overcome

Oxford, Ohio

I doubt that one could willfully arrange a more motley assortment of racial, social, cultural and economic backgrounds than this college town has seen in the past several weeks. The youngsters spent days talking about themselves and their different pasts in the hope that such an effort would weld them into an instrument of education for Negro communities in Mississippi — teaching them how to register to vote, how to read and spell or improve their health.

I've seen this before in smaller doses: idealistic college youths from our harshly criticized middle class confronting tough, skilled fieldworkers, most of them Negroes reared in the predominant poverty that is their racial lot. If there had been tensions on such previous encounters, what might one reasonably expect from this unique venture, with its recruitment of hundreds of college students facing dozens of sometimes tired and even cynical "regulars"?

It worked, though. They met, kept good distance from one another, groped toward one another, argued. Then they started leaving, more intent on work than on self-

examination or analysis of motives. Their *job*, after all, was to
work with Negro families in the backward regions of a backward state. We shall see later as we follow them in the summer how their minds and spirits hold up under uncertainty,
likely threats, and continually possible violence.

As a psychiatrist, I've treated my fair share of delinquents
and of odd or variously impossible college students. In comparison, these students at Oxford seemed solid, sane and far
from fatuous. By and large they've given much thought and
more than a moment's hesitation to their project.

I came here to help "process" and "evaluate" them, vulgar
words to describe offering some medical and psychiatric assistance. Well, they certainly did manage their bruises, cuts, infections and allergies; and they were often afraid and anxious,
too. But they also developed purpose and resolve. They are
sensitive young men and women — do you remember the
time in your own life? — motivated by ideals and seized by a
moment in history which offers those ideals fulfillment. If I
had been looking for disturbed minds — I have come to know
better — I would have been disappointed.

They are nobody's cannon fodder. I have never heard more
honest talk among leaders and followers. Yes, these young
people are being "used" in a desperate effort to effect change
in Mississippi. (I suppose we all "use" one another in many
ways.) They have chosen just that fate. Most of them, as a
matter of fact, clearly possess all of this century's psychological and political sophistication which makes the best of us
aware and the worst of us cynical. What I find impressive
about them is that they are not yet jaded and paralyzed. Their
heads may face future gunshot, but at least they do not carry
their intelligence and knowledge like a millstone around
their necks.

Social Struggle and Weariness

Struggle to make our world a better one for more people demands effort and commitment, and these are sometimes repaid with exhaustion and despair. I am writing this paper to describe the onset of weariness in veteran activists of the civil rights movement in America and to indicate that there are ways to help diminish its paralyzing effect upon those who suffer from it.

Though I have never taken part in a "sit-in," or picketed, or accompanied a Negro trying to register or vote, I have watched demonstrations of all kinds all over the South for four years. I have lived with the students staging these demonstrations, followed them about, interviewed them at great length, visited them in jail and even treated some of them there, in consultation with prison doctors, for temporary episodes of anxiety, borderline psychosis and severe depression. In addition, I have attended their meetings and conducted "groups" at their request, groups where they could talk about their feelings and problems. The Student Non-Violent Coordinating Committee (SNCC) called me their "staff psychiatrist"; and the real heart of the work, besides leading many discussion groups, consisted of my prolonged interviews with — relationship with — twenty-three students, white and Negro, men and women, over a span of four years and under the various conditions mentioned above.

Young men and women in the American South have been staging nonviolent protest demonstrations against segregationist laws and customs for several years. How do they manage the various inner stresses and outer trials of their lives, engaged as they are in full-fledged social struggle? Some understanding of this question can perhaps be gained, I propose, by looking at how an increasing number of them *don't* manage; how they grow weary and lose interest in themselves and their cause.

Sit-ins are not as new as they seem to many of us. A number of them were staged spontaneously in the earlier years of this century, isolated, ineffective expressions of resentment by Negroes at their peculiarly hard lot in this country.[1] The fact that such efforts in our time have emerged as a "movement" illustrates the intersection of private struggles with the historical enablement of them. That is, events in the life of our nation have transformed random discontent into a highly complicated, organized, social and political phenomenon. This development contrasts with other kinds of social protest which have from the start been more deliberate and planned, or with those which have been taken up by groups already firmly in existence.

The demonstrations have had several purposes: To call attention to the exclusion of Negroes from hotels, restaurants, movie houses, even voting booths; to try to end this practice by entering such places in the hope of being served or accepted; to exert moral, social and economic pressure on pri-

---

[1] See, for example, E. Franklin Frazier, *The Negro in the United States,* New York, Macmillan, 1957.

vate businesses or on public institutions such as schools and libraries so that they will reconsider their policies; or to prepare the basis for litigation by testing customs clearly illegal constitutionally. The persons taking part in the demonstrations may not all have these aims precisely in mind. Many of them think of their goal in terms of abstractions like "justice," and rely much more heavily on feelings, such as their sense of being denied and scorned.

In the South this kind of social struggle has been chosen by a relative handful in the face of strong resistance, open and devious. Indeed, any discussion of nonviolent protest in that region must somehow establish the psychological quality of the southern Negro's life and, reciprocally, that of his white neighbors, grounded as they both are in history, customs and hard legal, economic and political realities. The Negro's daily life is determined by his terrible past and his present condition of relative poverty, powerlessness, restriction and isolation from his fellow countrymen. There may be no reason to repeat such obvious facts; they have been fully established by historians, political scientists, economists and sociologists. Yet, there is every reason for a psychiatrist studying the adjustment of students involved in social protest to keep constantly in mind what it means to grow up as a Negro; how it feels; how the world is seen and engaged; what is lacking for these people and what they expect, and how much of either is grounded in fantasy and how much in reality. The reality of the southern Negro's life is unrelentingly menial in its public and private relationship to the white world; to appreciate this fact fully, perhaps, one must have had some residence in the South.

No convenient generalizations quite do justice to the astonishing number of ways in which the mind can handle an unpleasant or curbed fate. The rationalizations, denials, projections and reaction-formations developed under such circumstances will easily be imagined by psychiatrists, as conscious as we are now of "ego psychology." Such information, in fact, cautions us against any supposition that *all* Negroes feel alike, respond to their situation in like fashion, or are prepared to take similar arms against their "sea of troubles."

On the contrary, we are presented with the question of who *does* join these demonstrations, or who, given what kind of personality and background, *would*.

Many reasons indeed have caused Negroes, and for that matter whites, to join the several protest movements. They may generally be stated as combinations of private experiences or emotions engaging with public events in the context of a summoning historical time. I have seen the most diverse kinds of youths join sit-ins for a wide variety of personal reasons, and participate in them in highly individual ways, briefly and fearfully, steadfastly, defiantly, quietly, exhibitionistically.

Those who contribute the largest numbers to the southern movement and are most influential in it are Negro college students or recent graduates from college. Several reasons explain this fact. This is their generation's time. Their parents could scarcely have envisaged, let alone help bring about, what has happened in race relations in the past fifteen years. This is also their *own*, their personal time, when they are grown enough to leave home and develop their own attitudes, yet, most of them, still young enough to be spared the heavy social and economic responsibilities of parenthood, while granted the flexibility and mobility of studenthood. Many are only fresh out of college and their condition has been best described by Erik H. Erikson. They are trying to figure out who they are, what they believe, how to live their lives, and with what ideals to guide them; or they are a bit older and have been storing their energies for a ripe kind of exertion of them.[2]

There are, of course, much older men and women in the Movement too, persons who have found their professions in social work, the ministry, teaching or law, but have found also that their "work" is impossible without prior dedication to the achievement of their dignity as human beings. For the most part they are the well-known leaders, particularly so in the more established Negro civil rights organizations. Yet a good deal of the most earnest social struggle, in the hardest, most unyielding counties of the "deepest" South, is today carried on by youths, and indeed is organized and directed by them. These are the ones who rode the freedom buses, and the same ones who are often called by newsmen "the shock troops" of the Movement; their work demands almost impossible sacrifices of living conditions and freedom in towns whose existence and character in this nation are perhaps unbelievable if not seen and confronted in some depth of experience.

The work of these students is not totally the action caught by cameras or reported in the news. The brunt of it is taking actual residence in towns where their goals are considered illegal at best and often seditious; considered so by local police and judges, by state police and judges, by business and political leaders. Their very presence in these towns, in fact, is regarded as a violation of law and order. Most significantly, they are feared, and resented too, by their own kind, by Negroes as well as whites. The job of organizing southern Negroes into effective groups for sustained assertion of their rights is a hard one, and one not suitably described by a rhetoric which de-

---

[2] Erikson's discussion of "moratorium," for example, in his study of Luther's life is helpful in looking at these students in the midst of a similar kind of struggle; that is, inward as well as outward, in their growing up as well as their demonstrating on streets.

nounces segregation and fails to consider what such a system does to those segregated, or, for that matter, to those born to enforce, believe in, and often profit from segregation.

Negroes in southern towns are heavily apathetic, widely illiterate, predominantly anxious and afraid of any protest in their own behalf; they are stubbornly reluctant to believe those who advocate such protests, let alone to join them. At the same time, these Negroes are largely poor, menially worked, constantly susceptible to unemployment, and subject to laws often hardly sensitive to their civil rights, though acutely sensitive to their history and their customary position in society. These are grim psychological realities for those youths who take up the struggle. They are the facts of the oppressor's disposition, of the victim's submission, of the fear they both share for different reasons. Every tape I have from every student tells these facts, and they help explain the development of some of the psychiatric symptoms this paper aims to describe.

What unites all of these students is the development in each of them of certain specific clinical symptoms. These symptoms emerge in youths of different classes and ages and with different reasons for participating in such struggles; they crop up in people whose character structures vary, whose choice of defense mechanisms encompasses the entire range of the ego's possibilities. To develop they take time and certain kinds of experiences; but given both, they occur, in my experience, almost universally. They are clinical signs of depression. They constitute "battle fatigue." They indicate exhaustion, weariness, despair, frustration and rage. They mark a crisis in the lives of those youths who experience them, and also one in the cities which may experience the results, translated into action, of such symptoms.

Because of these symptoms students may depart the Movement, go "back to the world" of schools, jobs, pursuit of career, to be replaced by younger or fresher cadres. Or they may linger on, disabled. Or they may stay on but become troublesome, bitter, and a source of worry, of unpredictable action, of potential danger to themselves and their "cause." The development of these symptoms, these depressive episodes, is a problem for civil rights organizations, and for the country too. Leaders of the civil rights organizations well know that their struggle is a long one, not to be resolved in a year or two. In a sense they are more than leaders of organizations; they are generals worried about "war-neuroses" in their front-line troops. The rest of the country is the scene of the battle, and thus has good reason for regarding closely the state of mind that develops in many of these young men and women.

Briefly the symptoms reveal fear, anxiety and anger no longer "controlled" or "managed." Depressions occur, characterized by loss of hope for victory, loss of a sense of purpose and acceptance of the power of the enemy where before such power was challenged with apparent fearlessness. The youth affected may take to heavy drinking or become silent, sulky and uncooperative. Frequently one sees real gloom, loss of appetite, withdrawal from social contacts as well as from useful daily work in the Movement. Sometimes withdrawal from the Movement becomes a precursor of the abandonment of a commitment to nonviolence, the advocacy of total, disruptive assault upon the society, or complete, hateful disengagement from it. In such cases the nonviolent movement itself may be attacked instead of the segregated society formerly felt to be the enemy. One very bright and exceptionally intuitive young man summarized his feelings very concisely:

I feel I've lost those years. They've come to nothing, really. No real change. So I feel betrayed by the Movement, and I guess it's easier to get angry at it than at the white world. I just want to *pull out* of the

white world. I mean you can't hate it the way I do and live with it. . . .
That's it, my hate for the Movement is a release or something. . . . I
can hate it and do something about it. You know, attack them or under-
mine them. But what can a Negro do to the white world without getting
destroyed eventually?

There are warning signs, and they are increasingly spotted
these days by certain leaders. But full-fledged depressions still
appear without being anticipated, and I have treated several
of them. They are difficult to treat because they seem to have
developed over a long period of time and in people resourceful at concealing them. Once they make their appearance,
they seem refractory to anything but the strongest of medical
and psychiatric measures — medication, psychotherapy, a
change of environment, even temporary hospitalization. On
the other hand, increasing sophistication has enabled certain
key "officers" to recognize the beginning of weariness, the first
stages foreshadowing collapse, with their signs of anxiety and
fretfulness and with their subtle changes in thinking and feeling.

For example, minor complaints of insomnia or headaches
may herald depression. So also may comments like, "What's
the use?" or, "Why fight them, they're too strong?" Such remarks may be quickly denied even by those making them, but
experience in the Movement has shown that it is wise not to
ignore their significance. Somatic complaints are also significant: stomach pains, or menstrual cramps newly bothersome
and disabling, or vague skin itching and nondescript and self-
ascribed "allergies." Then there are the "accidents," with
bikes, with cars; and the injuries, due to drinking, or to
"friendly" fighting, or "horsing around," or suffered in ath-
letic games. They are often the result of rising tensions de-
flected by consciences not easily prone to acknowledge their
presence, let alone their strength and pervasive influence.

The forms of despair and exhaustion are really only limited

by the ingenuity of the human mind. We have seen pregnancy serve as an "escape," not only for women who must
leave to have a baby, but for men who must leave for mar-
riage. We have seen parental disapproval of protest activity
suddenly accepted and embraced as a means of dodging one's
own depression and guilty wish to leave the struggle. We have
seen reckless, defiant behavior adopted to deal with the guilt
over the wish to leave, as if severe punishment at the hands of
the segregationists would satisfy the demands — often quite
unconscious — of the student's conscience. It is as if a voice
tells them, "For wanting to leave you must seek and get punishment, and from the very people you were up to this point
managing so well through your controlled, nonviolent behavior." Two young men showed bursts of dedication, a kind
of outlandish zeal quickly recognized for its compulsive and
strange quality by others; the denial of other feelings, of
inertia and apathy based on depression, explained their actions. And I have seen exhaustion attributed to others; or
young people become exquisitely sensitive to the weakness of
others as they struggle with their own budding feelings of de-
jection.

The very institutional development of the sit-in movement
parallels such individual psychological developments. At first
there were simply youths — vigorous, unfatigued, keen to
protest, indifferent to organizational concerns and inexperienced in just how to sustain their momentum — that is, how
to raise social, political and economic support for themselves.
But as it became clear that sit-ins were "working," more participants became available, and organizational developments
began: The students formed committees, they met, elected
leaders, opened up offices, bought equipment for them, appealed for money, became conscious of publicity. The mak-
ings of a bureaucracy were thus established, and with time
came the tensions, the rivalries, rigidities and inertia associ-

ated with such developments. One student — a political science major — put it quite bluntly:

I'm tired, but so is the whole Movement. We're busy worrying about our position or our finances, so we don't *do* anything anymore. . . . We're becoming lifeless, just like all revolutions when they lose their first momentum and become more interested in preserving what they've won than going on to new challenges. . . . Only with us we haven't won that much, and we're either holding to the little we have as an organization, or we get bitter, and want to create a new revolution. . . . You know, one like the Muslims want, which is the opposite of what we say we're for. It's as if we completely reverse ourselves because we can't get what we want.

Both bitterness and organizational preoccupations can be a refuge or outlet for anxious, depressed veterans of active protest, and often these two developments occur together. For example, a twenty-four-year-old veteran of numerous sit-ins came to see me because he knew he had been depressed for several weeks, and more recently had become aware of his reluctance to join any active demonstration. Even the "softest" demonstrations in the more northerly South bothered him. He was afraid, hence unwilling to do anything but work in the regional headquarters of the organization. The thought of going to jail, which he had once regarded as a laughing matter and almost welcomed as a means of earning pride in himself and esteem from others, terrified him now. He had trouble sleeping, and nightmares afflicted him:

I dream I'm going to be hurt, you know, kicked and manhandled by those jailers. [There had always been reason for him to fear such possibilities as probabilities; but until now he had been able to "dismiss" or make light of such "reality."] Sometimes I wake up in a cold sweat, and I remember that I've actually dreamed that the whole Movement was arrested. . . . I mean all of us were taken in custody, and then I escape and a few of us get a boat and go to Africa, or we take refuge in one of the African embassies. . . . I mean to get away from whites, all of them, that's what the dream says; the reverse of integration, you might call it.

This young man was actually quite agitated when he came to see me, and he was "furloughed" for "rest and rehabilitation." (The language of the students is commonly "war language.") He became a member of a small group I was asked to lead as a means of dealing with such "casualties."

The problem of just what *can* be done to help such students is not easily solved. Some simply leave, to go back to school or work. Others are torn idealistically between their rage at an unfair society and their fear of its punishment of their protests, their despair at their own ineffectiveness in social struggle, and their natural worry at the personal sacrifice of valuable time and energy. ("I'm giving the best years of my life; and what will I have at the end to show? . . . How will I make a living and support myself? . . . and will it all do any good, anyway?") These youths may express their ambivalence with symptoms; and, in my experience, psychiatric care, individually and in groups, has been helpful.

Yet, working with these students, I have found, is not the most conventional psychotherapeutic task. Many of them are profoundly distrustful of outsiders, even those recommended to them by their fellows; and I am white, an obstacle for many southern Negroes who need time and experience to feel even remotely comfortable with *any* white, even those standing beside them in demonstrations, let alone a watching psychiatrist.

Some of these problems of suspicion and aloofness yielded to the slow formation of relationships between many of these students and me. Such relationships took a good deal of time to develop, months becoming several years, and they took several forms: Casual "consultations in the field"; more formal prison visits to certain students in clear need of emergency sedation, tranquilization and support; participation in general discussions on policies, strategy and tactics, occasions

which made more "formal" my association with the students
and their goals; teaching certain students specifically assembled for lectures on such topics as the "psychological development of prejudice"; and, finally, repeated meetings with individual students, many self-referred ("I'm depressed," or
"My nerves are thin") and many evaluated as troubled by
others ("They say I'm jittery, but who isn't?").

In general, a variety of responses were needed to the complaints brought forth. Some students were clearly seriously
disturbed — a very few psychotic — and had to be encouraged to leave the Movement and eventually be referred to
whatever psychiatric facilities were available in their home
states. Others were comparatively less disturbed, but heavily
enough depressed to suggest both to them and me that separation was the indicated choice for them too. These were also
few in number, and all of them were to recover within several
months of a more "normal" life. The majority of students
treated individually for clinical signs of depression (thirteen
of seventeen) responded encouragingly to a relatively small
number of visits, as few as three and as many as ten.[3]

These meetings were both "supportive" and "clarifying."
By those words I mean that my intention was to talk openly
and warmly, yet firmly and realistically about what it means

[3] Of the twenty-three students I have followed intensively, eight became
depressed enough to request more "formal" interviews with me relating to
their symptoms. They would call or write me from their various "homes" or
"battle stations" over the South. I would frequently go to see them, or they
would come to see me in Atlanta or New Orleans, where most of my time
was spent. All of these eight students (six Negro and two white; two Negro
women and one white woman) responded favorably to treatment. Five additional students also responded well. But four students, all Negro and all from
very poor families with little education, if much persistence and determination, became deeply enough depressed to warrant prolonged separation from
the Movement. Two of the four were clearly in psychotic depressions. There
were many more students who needed — in some cases, urgently — and requested interviews. The limiting factor was, as might be expected, my time
and energy. I worked with larger numbers in four groups which met for vary-
ing lengths of time, six sessions in one case to fourteen in another.

to take on a resistant and powerful social system, what it means generally to groups and individually to their members. I rarely had trouble in hearing the various symptoms of depression and anxiety. Hearing them, I would relate them to their precipitating causes, the stresses of social struggle and protest, and then discuss with the individual students or groups the *ways* of handling such stresses, the limits which *all* people have, variable for different people but at some point of tension inclusive of all humanity. We would then usually relate the particular difficulty or symptom, often hidden from others, to the *real* provocations for them, and try to assess alternatives to continued suffering — withdrawal, rest or vacation, change of scene or type of job (from "field" to office), or reduction of responsibilities with some help from tranquilizers and further medical and psychiatric visits.

As I review my notes and listen to my tapes, I can now see what I must have somehow realized all along, that the chief purposes of psychiatric intervention in work like this were quick evaluation of who could stay "on the firing line" and who had to be relieved, and the provision of several kinds of support to those who could stay. Furthermore, in working with those who were to stay, the problems of guilt and the *real* nature of the external threats were the two most common challenges.

In most cases, after all, these were highly ethical and idealistic youths, perhaps prematurely so in contrast to those from certain more comfortable, white middle-class homes where aggressive feelings are more easily or variously indulged and consciences are less quickly and fearfully buttressed by social customs or laws. The "morality" of many of these students is a rather complex development. Either with the help of their parents or by themselves they have had to reject the stereotype of the lazy, indifferent, apathetic and "instinctual" — drunken, promiscuous — Negro. At the same time they have had to live under the powerful coercion of a segregationist society, and the restrictions of such a society have become part of their own consciences long before they decide to abandon them and even fight them. They must, therefore, in Erikson's terms, abandon an old identity, achieve a new one, and fight for it. They must reject an old morality, that of their own society, and fight for a new one against strong odds.

Small wonder that many of them feel anxious and guilty, then depressed. Often, they do not recognize the guilt they feel; and often, in order to function, they have had to "forget" the really tough, often unshakable, frequently treacherous and punitive social and political resistance they face. When disabled, they feel additionally guilty for *that*. What often seems to help is coming to grips with the guilt directly and relating it to some larger perspective of the relationship between personal effort and social reform. To explain this last statement, I shall draw on my work with a young man, recently graduated from college, who interrupted his law school career to join a major sit-in movement in Alabama.

Charles came to me — a twenty-three-year-old veteran of eighteen arrests for countless sit-ins — with a recent history of severe insomnia, restlessness and increasingly chronic fatigue. A friend of his, an officer in the organization, felt him to be depressed and recommended that he see me. In our first meeting Charles acknowledged "some depression" but quickly followed the admission with protestations of his own worthlessness. He had no "right" to be depressed. People had gone through "worse" and had suffered no ailments or grievances doing it. Why should he, then? Why *did* he feel so low? He was bad. He didn't want to go on, go on with our talk, or go on with his participation in sit-ins. He would either have to "stop this silliness" or quit.

In the course of eight interviews in six weeks' time it was possible for us to explore his feelings, his fears and his sense of badness and failure. Fairly directly I defined what I had come to know were his likely troubles: He felt depressed, felt bad even to know that, and was struggling hard to push his feelings aside, to mention them to nobody, including, if possible, himself. He was slowly feeling "out of touch" and "different." Others weren't so "weak," and their bravado, their light-hearted humor, proved it.

Of course their overworked jesting and often fairly hurtful games and quarrelsome scuffles showed just the opposite, how nervous and worried *they* were, too. I mentioned that, and from there we were able slowly to go into his feelings of loneliness and failure, and how he used guile and pretenses to hide such feelings from others, only to feel lonelier and guiltier. His father was a minister and disapproved of his son's "illegal" activities. One day Charles summarized the grim linkage of external and internal accusations confronting him: "I'm damned by my own parents and damned by the police, and then I feel I'm not doing the best for the movement either."

He was clearly helped by talking about such matters, and I actively defined for him his feelings as I heard them and told him how similar they were to those of other students I'd met in the Movement. Several times I told him that I thought he was unduly "rough" on himself and that he was blaming himself for crimes of fantasy rather than fact. In moments like this I would take up with him the *facts* of the struggle he was helping support. I tried to relate his aims to those of the Movement. Many of these students, and he was one of the them, come from the Negro schools and colleges of the South; and many of these institutions, state owned and supported, are hardly places likely to kindle the fire of social protest or furnish some social, political and economic context for its occurrence.

Charles had first become aware of the Movement through

watching television. He had long endured various restrictions
in his Alabama town, but now they had become harder to
bear precisely because similar segregationist confinements
seemed to be crumbling all over the South. He knew about
that, saw them collapsing before his eyes on nightly news programs. One day he boarded a bus in his hometown and tried
to sit in front. "Actually I didn't think I was going to do
that," he says, and thus qualifies the story as he tries to convey
the subtleties of human courage and fear blended into the
flash of a moment's decision. "I just started for the rear as
usual, and found I didn't get there, but had sat down in the
front." He was quickly rebuked by the bus driver and the few
white passengers, while the Negroes in the rear sat silently
looking on. He would not budge. He was arrested for "disorderly conduct." It was this deed which set his engagement
with the sit-in movement going. When he joined, he was, in
his own words,

. . . optimistic, that's what I was, plain optimistic. I thought we'd demonstrate and then they'd fold up before us. But it's been tougher than
I ever dreamed . . . you know you learn slowly how this country runs
and how it's not so easy to get what you want if you're colored. . . . I
suppose if I'd known that when I first joined I never would have done it.

The naïveté and its slow loss described by Charles defines
a very real stage in the psychological development of most of
these youths. Much of their most fearless and vigorous protest
occurs in this first period, a time of both innocence and
denial, where much isn't known and much that is slowly per-
ceived can still be blotted out or pushed aside. Soon, however,
it becomes harder and harder to do so. Victories are not permanent, and sometimes not to be had at all. In the Deep
South, Negro students find that they must make do with the
long, wearisome job of working with their own people rather
than the more dramatic and satisfying assaults upon white
storekeepers. (The silent Negroes on that bus were a portent

of what Charles was later to recognize as the most frustrating part of his work: Fighting his own race's — and his own — long-developed fears and inhibitions.)

Psychiatric intervention was most helpful in this time of transition. It seemed helpful for the students to hear their moodiness and gloom "approved" by relating them to their very real causes. It was also helpful that we talked about what could and could not be done by them, separating the possibilities of their actions from their larger hopes for our society. In this regard some very realistic balance had to be achieved between concentrating too much on socioeconomic abstractions, usually pessimistic ("What's the use?" or "You can't really change much because of the whole system," or "Very little really comes of our actions"), and overly optimistic heroism in its last nostalgically hopeful moments like the following: "If we really pulled off a mass demonstration, I mean one where a few of us might have to die, then the whole country would be so electrified that I think Mississippi would crack wide open . . . we would get federal troops in there because of the riots and deaths, and that would change the whole state."

The point to be emphasized is that there are some very real things which *can* be done, and done to great purpose and accomplishment, but that they must be chosen and approached carefully and with specific goals in mind. Or, as Charles told me after his depression had lifted: "If we're in a war, we've got to be professional about it and have our tactics and strategy and not just beat ourselves against a wall and then fold up."

He was right. He had been bloodied doing just that, physically and emotionally. Now he recognized more fully his job and its relationship to his broader wishes for his country. He had been able to talk about his guilt and fear and to realize that they are shared by others, certainly shared by his co-workers. He had been able to look at how he had come to join the Movement, how he had changed in it, and how his symptoms reflected that change but did not necessarily doom his continued if different participation. "Now," he told me in our last formal meeting, "I suppose I won't be as hopeful as I once was, but I still think I'll be able to knock down a few barriers to freedom. Even if I persuade one man to register to vote, that's worth it."

It is a delicate equilibrium these students see, and one we psychiatrists must respect if we are to work with them: Trying to keep their courage and initiative while accepting the often sour lessons that come with growing older and living through unexpected and dismaying experiences. They must keep their moral initiative, maintain their ethical resolve, yet somehow avoid succumbing either to depression as an inward expression of frustration or to disorganized rage and antisocial behavior as equivalent outward forms.

It is, of course, tempting for social scientists to simplify lives — which, after all, are often lived in considerable and continual ambiguity and even contradiction — by dividing them into "stages" or "periods." There is no denying the value of outlining predominant or preponderant trends in life. There is no doubt that our struggles — personal and social — change in content and intensity over time. Yet, I am reluctant to make easy generalizations about the personal histories of these youths in the Movement, including the development in many of them of exhaustion or "battle fatigue."

I am no statistician, no expert in culling attitudes from large groups and tallying them. But my own observations and those of many leaders in the civil rights groups lead me to say that weariness touches almost all the students who stay in the Movement for any significant period of time — that is, long enough to taste its hard, grinding daily demands which are not always relieved by spectacular successes and are often encumbered with the additional burden of hopes sparked but not realized.

It might well be asked what students are most *likely* to become incapacitated by this common weariness, and what, precisely, the various *alternatives* are for those who become involved in the Movement — to stay for short or long spells only to leave, to combine "normal life" with bouts of protest, or to stay involved "permanently."

I have seen no one kind of person that is more vulnerable to this "battle-fatigue" than another. Constant exposure to frustrating social struggle seems to be the critical element in a "syndrome" which affects those with widely different characters and ways of handling stress. I have seen youths prone to depression *before* involvement in the Movement manage perfectly well — that is, use their cynicism, their concealed anger, with detached, gloomy effectiveness — until the *reality* of the hard struggle and its very *actual* wounds of insults, threats, jailing or disappointment became felt. I have seen, on the other hand, hopeful, winningly active and energetic youths give way under the same cumulative burdens.

These youths are not mere adventurers. Their voluntary and prolonged exposure to hardship qualifies them as conscientious, steadfast people, and the story of their relationship to the civil rights movement is not yet concluded. It is true, of course, that personal struggles of growing have found expression in this social struggle. But many of these young men and women are now grown, married, with families, graduated from schools and colleges, in pursuit of specialized professional training, and are still heavily involved in this movement. Since the Movement *itself* is only a few years old, it would be indeed presumptuous of me to define too closely the complicated and — I really think — highly personal and variable course of its members' relationship to it. Some join, stay to fight hard, leave in a time whose length is defined by a desire to return to school or a job. Others stay and are still staying after participation from the very beginning of the student movement in 1960. *One* important factor in deciding whether a person stays or leaves is how he handles (and is helped to handle) this period of tired, fateful realization of the difficulties ahead as well as at hand. Working against continued involvement may be family pressures, public pressures, or private wishes — the desire to be a doctor; a fiancée who opposes this kind of life; an ailing father who needs his son at home to take up new financial responsibilities; social and economic harassment which extends to a family, to brothers and sisters, to parents.

What will be needed is further documentation on how these young men and women decide the coming questions of their relationship to this movement. The battles — even with new legislation — are still being waged. The fatigue arrives. They can muster themselves out of service — go back to home, school, *other* jobs — or they can persist.

Meanwhile, in such dilemmas certain psychiatrists, psychologists and social workers, interested in their cause and anxious to help them, may indeed be of considerable service. I suspect that we shall not soon see the end of many kinds of protests; and, hopefully, they will be useful, constructive and self-fulfilling. That is, they will spend themselves in the achievement of their purposes. The problems these students face are clearly not all psychiatric, but social, political or economic. But some of them *are* psychiatric. Many of these youths are increasingly recognizing their own need for medical and psychiatric help, and have begun seeking it out in certain cities and from certain doctors who, they feel, are likely to be attentive and sympathetic to their needs and aims.

In many ways these young civil rights workers are in a war and exposed to the stresses of warfare. And in many ways they can be helped to deal with these stresses. Such help would perhaps, by strengthening their movement, enable it to be more successful; and, as a result, freedom would be more universally enjoyed in our country. This seems to me a worthy objective for psychiatrists to pursue.

Psychiatry, 1964

A Psychiatrist
Joins "The Movement"

I first came to the Atlanta office of SNCC (Student Non-Violent Coordinating Committee, often called "Snick") in late 1961. I was studying Atlanta's first episode of school desegregation, and a sixteen-year-old Negro boy whom I knew particularly well suggested I visit "the office." The student sit-in movement at that time was in its infancy; the SNCC office had been in existence only a few months.

Right off I had doubts and suspicions. What did I, a doctor, and a psychiatrist, want there? I was told then that if I wanted to help I could work stamping envelopes or typing. If anyone wanted to talk with me, or I with anyone, that would be allowed. It seemed a good idea to me, a good way to get to know the students and learn how they spent their time and managed their tasks. Also it might help to dissolve the distrust felt toward me, an older, white, middle-class professional man, and a psychiatrist to boot.

It took months for us to relax with one another. But once that had happened, there was no question about what I should do. They decided that others could stamp envelopes. I would be their physician and psychiatrist. As such, I heard their various medical and emotional complaints, and offered what treatment I could. I did so quite informally, in many places and many ways. At times I kept fairly regular "hours," using the office to talk with the students. At other times I followed them "into the field." At the request of attorneys I visited them in jails, to appraise their survival under often unjust and wretched conditions. Finally, when the Mississippi Summer Project of 1964 to increase voter registration was being organized, I took part in its planning, and I followed through the orientation period of two weeks in Oxford, Ohio, and the operations as they unfolded in Mississippi.

Isolated forays had been made into Mississippi before. Several leaders of the 1964 project had already experienced the threats, jailings, beatings and injuries that go hand in hand with trying to work for the voting rights of Negroes in that state. The segregationists in those towns are so solidly established, and their living is so effectively removed from the will or practices of the rest of the nation, that centuries seem to separate one from the other.

Before the Summer Project began the SNCC youths traveled over the country making their plans known and discussing them with students, sympathetic educators and religious and political leaders. By the spring of 1964 recruitment on campuses was well on its way, and plans were firm for a preliminary, two-week period of orientation followed by a summer's work likely to bring hundreds of students converging on dozens of Negro communities.

Even before Oxford I had noted that the students interested in the project seemed consistently serious, dedicated and well aware of the serious implications of the kind of work they were asking to do. Every effort was made to acquaint them with the hard facts of life facing the Negro citizens of that state, and the firm conviction of its leading white citizens that no change could occur. Some students decided well before the orientation meeting that the risk to life or limb was not only real and substantial, but too much for them. Some of these students were afraid, others insufficiently concerned about civil rights. "I thought it might be an *interesting* summer," one college junior told me, "but I frankly don't care enough to risk my life."

The real time when motivations were tested and responses to fear and tension were quite apparent came at Oxford, Ohio, where for two weeks, on the lovely campus of Western College for Women, about 400 college students assembled to learn about their coming summer, and once and for all decide whether it would suit their wishes and capacities. I can only suggest the background here: the constant presence of reporters and television cameras; the anxiety in the nation and over the world; the threats spoken in Mississippi. Within a few days three members of the project disappeared in Mississippi. First their death seemed an increasing likelihood, then a certainty. Such a grim general atmosphere became for each volunteer a specific confrontation: Going to Mississippi meant the concrete, explicit risk of death.

The veterans also were under strain. Some Negro Southerners resented outsiders even as they welcomed and needed them — and particularly white and relatively privileged ones. Many were afraid, not as they had been before in their comparative isolation and powerlessness, but in the face of the new significance that had come upon their struggle, and the tensions, rivalries and fears of the increasing organizational life which accompanied it. Some felt guilty. Did they have the right to ask aid of others, knowing — as only those who have fought for civil rights in a small town in the Delta can possibly know — the fateful hazards and gambles attached to the work, the constant jeopardy of its achievement?

Within all of the students — veterans and new volunteers — lived the slowly awakening conscience of much of their country. Yet, there were really few people or groups giving them clear support. Even many morally sympathetic people felt hesitant, doubtful or fearful before their actions as they slowly took shape. Nor were these volunteers simply lonely or isolated from the approval of others. An aroused conscience does not automatically generate the will to change things. Even given the will, such events in the life of the mind as fear, inertia, the onset of rationalizations and denials — or the legitimate rise of feelings of helplessness or despair before the magnitude of a difficult ordeal — combine to stay action, to spread doubt, to start anxieties in motion that can become paralyzing worries, suspicions or tensions between people.

It was thus apparent from the very beginning that each one of this tiny handful of young people, a fraction of one percent of the college population of this country, would have to come to some conclusion — even if in his private thoughts, fantasies or dreams — about why he was taking on this kind of summer, and how he expected to manage it.

They hassled and argued with their guilt and self-doubt, the racking accusations, the continual analysis of motives which bespeak inner uncertainty coming to grips with outer uncertainty. Many of them wondered whether they were hopelessly "neurotic" or "masochistic," doing the right thing for the wrong reasons. Some could resolve such conflicts quickly; others did so only with difficulty, or only over time, or only with the help of a person or event which somehow "made it all clear."

For example, during one long, heated meeting a young Negro woman from Mississippi replied to a series of remarks which largely reflected apprehension and hesitation with the following words, spoken with a gentleness and simplicity which only added to their force:

I've been listening to you all for two hours and I suppose if I didn't
get up to speak you might be talking two days or two years from now
about whether you should go and what will happen when you do. But
I'm going to tell you something: I don't want to know why you're here.
I want to know what's taken you so long to come; and I want to be
thankful you're here.

Another issue besides those of anticipatory fear or personal
motivation was that of racial attitudes. The very problem
summoning them to Mississippi was also part of their own
problem as a group of white and Negro Americans with
widely different backgrounds and experiences. For many of
the white volunteers this was the first time they would be living on "equal" terms both physically and psychologically
with Negroes; living with them as a preparatory group in
Ohio, and then in the Negro quarters of southern towns and
villages under the strongly disapproving eye of a white society. The common nervousness of all concerned, from poor
southern Negroes to wealthy northern whites (there were
southern whites and northern Negroes there, too) was variously expressed: in sly avoidance, in forced, awkward encounters at mealtime, in humorous exchanges while watching
television, in all the ways that people find to meet and accommodate themselves to one another.

There were some medical and psychiatric problems of a
serious nature, requiring the usual clinical diagnostic work-up
and finally a decision about the person's fitness for the project. We encountered three youths near psychosis — one suspicious and withdrawn, the other two clearly near panic. It
was of interest that they were referred to by the students themselves as a bit odd or seemingly "troubled" or "distracted"
and in need of help. They were willing to leave the project,
in fact pleased to do it for medical reasons.

A more difficult few to evaluate were those with "neurotic"
personalities or "character disorders." Five students knew

they were "in trouble," realized that however well they had managed before, they were headed for serious difficulty under the stresses likely in Mississippi. Three of them sought us out fairly quickly, and were helped to leave without excessive guilt or sense of failure. Two others were spotted by their roommates or friends, and similarly helped to decide upon departure from the project. They themselves had wanted to see us, hesitating out of guilt at abandoning their summer's objectives. Three of these five had previously been in treatment for depression, anxiety or phobias. The other two were of rather rigid, brittle makeup, each of them attached to an orderly, punctual kind of living. They were bothered by the "confusion" of Oxford — that is, the lack of precise timing for meetings, the tendency for lectures and discussions not to terminate so long as there were intense preoccupations and uncertainties to be aired. Their distress showed them and us that the similar but even more marked disorder (and consequent need for flexibility) of active social struggle was not for them.

Overall, we were struck at how successfully the students kept their spirits high, their resolve undiminished. The orientation session was to instruct the students in what they would be doing, and where; to help them get to know one another, and form some cohesive bond; to prepare them for the challenge and problems ahead, by lectures, demonstrations and even films; and to filter and select out those not quite suited. The terrible news from Philadelphia, Mississippi, revealed how effectively these aims had been accomplished.

After the killings at Philadelphia, there was a noticeable increase in the consultations made. We worked almost round the clock. Minor medical complaints, bruises, cuts, aches and pains came in higher numbers — we thought because many students were doubtful of their strength of body and mind to face their own possible Philadelphias. There was an increase in those openly anxious, fearful or unable to sleep. Yet the general drift of those tense hours and days was toward a final consolidation of the entire group of several hundred youths. They assembled in song and prayer, in silent marches, in circular, hand-holding communication and recital of their determination to proceed. The emotional power and support of those songs can hardly be conveyed. One has to be there, feel the strength and reassurance of the words, the melodies, the young people united in saying and singing.

Looking back, what did I find as I worked alongside, but not quite in the midst of, these young Americans both in 1964 and in the summer of 1965?

Initially I wanted to know why civil rights workers undertook such obviously dangerous tasks. Then, I wanted to know how, in fact, they survived. They are a diverse lot, embracing a wide range of personality types and social, cultural and economic backgrounds. Traditional psychiatric classifications are not really very helpful in thinking of these youths, though Freud's psychodynamic view of the mind does give insight into the essential conflicts facing them. What united them — poor, rural Negro youth and rich, urban white ones; neat, slow-acting, earnestly thoughtful ones and untidy, dramatic, moody ones — was a common willingness to dedicate energy and, in some cases, life itself, to an ideal. Whatever first brought them there — elementary self-interest, or defiance, or wish for adventure, or rebellion — they found themselves facing the same questions and the same ordeal. I have heard again and again: "However we got into the Movement, it's the same in jail and the same with the police or the Klan." There are many ways to be defiant, adventurous or rebellious that are less idealistic and dangerous than civil rights work.

I have learned that there are definite phases in the adjustment of civil rights workers to their jobs. First, the transition from "ordinary" life: whether the volunteer comes from a wealthy home and a first-rate eastern college, or is a high school dropout reared in a sharecropper cabin, the confusions and dangers of social protest soon become forcibly clear. Jailings are always possible; harassment by local people (including law-enforcement officials) is constant. The civil rights worker lives in a climate of apprehension. The routine of school and work disappear. Periods of boredom and inactivity alternate with hectic, chaotic, exceedingly tense episodes of protest or activity. The worker must accommodate himself to this life, using whatever mental defenses can help him.

Quite common at this time are the so-called psychosomatic complaints: headaches, colds, sore muscles, back pain, stomach pains, skin disorders. In my experience their incidence can almost be graphed, reaching a fast peak in the first days and weeks of the volunteer's exposure to his new life. Even those who commit themselves to a short spell of participation may, all through it, remark upon a pain in this limb, a little disorder in that organ.

Why physical symptoms? Evidence of psychiatric pathology is noticeably absent at this time. Fear and anxiety are stubbornly denied. Any doubts about the wisdom of a particular activity or the danger involved in carrying it out must be overlooked. The novice realizes he is inexperienced and he eagerly wishes to be accepted by his newfound companions. Thus, in the two-week orientation session that preceded the Mississippi Project, another physician and I were kept busy day and night with basically healthy youths who were afraid, but also afraid to be afraid. In our society a sore back is unlikely to suggest a judgment of cowardice.

The attitude of the youth (or, indeed, the older participant) toward the "outside" world also begins to change fairly quickly after his involvement in civil rights work. Usually he is exposed to danger, or at the very least isolated from many others in our society. Particularly in the South, he is likely to find himself in a relatively small group, constantly scorned or harassed by everyone from the police to various frightened and aroused citizens. His common response is to pull himself closer to his fellow volunteers and further away from "others." I heard one civil rights worker, a thirty-two-year-old white, middle-class schoolteacher, put it this way:

> After a few days you throw out a lot of baggage, your habits and expectations, from running water and inside plumbing to brushing your teeth regularly; and you become "men against the sea" — a small group rowing against odds that are sometimes heavy. . . . You think of yourself as removed from a lot you once took for granted; when I go past a bank or a restaurant now, it's like I'm looking into another world. . . . I guess, in a nutshell, you become an outsider.

Many had never been South, had never been face-to-face with the kinds of poverty they now lived with intimately, had never had to contend with the gap in social and cultural customs between them and their Negro hosts and the equally significant gulf that separated them from the white people of the state. It may be one thing to read of poverty in the Delta; it is another matter to enter a sharecropper's cabin and live there — eat and sleep there, attempt to make conversation there. Here are the recorded words of one volunteer, summing up for many:

> It's like I never could have imagined. I read all the books, but they don't tell you what to say when you're left with a family and you're there to help them, but you find they're scared stiff of you, and pretty soon you're scared of them. . . . They treated me as if I was some strange god, and I mean a dangerous one as well as a good one. They tried to be nice, but they were so respectful; and I kept trying to be equal with them, because that's what we were there to do. . . . Well, it was awkward as hell. First I told them not to call me "Sir." Then I could see they couldn't help it . . . and I stopped trying to pretend, too. I didn't like being without running water and good toilet facilities; and I didn't like some

of their food either. It was too fried and greasy. . . . Well, we grew accustomed to one another, and then we'd slip up once in a while, let our guard down; *really* let it down, like getting annoyed, or just plain speaking the truth of how we felt. . . . And the work we did was what made a go of it for us.

That same volunteer described the other part of his difficult accommodation as follows:

You know, at first I thought, "Who cares about the whites? They're blind, and we'll just show them the light." Well, it's not that simple. You go downtown to mail a letter, or buy some razor blades, and they stare at you, and make you feel like an enemy spy. . . . It's not the way we dress. They call us beatnik if we don't wear a tie in 100-degree weather, when they don't *themselves.* Look at the way the Klansmen dress; not just "on duty" but "off duty" with sweatshirts and khakis just like ours. . . . What you slowly begin to realize is that they're not just enemies. They're *you,* in a different society; or what you're struggling with yourself. . . . So, sometimes I feel lonely for them; just to have a good talk with them. It's easier in ways than with the people I'm with. All I have to do, though, is think about what the whole system of segregation does to half of those in it, and I lose that idea pretty fast. . . .

With such isolation comes, in many instances, scorn or even hate for the world that has been left (in the case of whites) or challenged (in the case of Negroes). Detachment from the world being picketed or in various ways defied or confronted requires from many the price of strict criticism of that world. "You have to become a little bitter and sour," one summed it up.

In time several modes of "adjustment" occur, as these earnest, mostly hardworking people come to terms with the hard life they have chosen. Many of them become exhausted, victims of real "battle fatigue." They become tired and moody. They lose interest in their work, or even leave it. On the other hand, they may stay, unaware of just how weary and sulky they feel, and consequently at the mercy of their own unacknowledged despair, or rage, or sense of frustration.

Some manage to survive this syndrome of fatigue and eventually consolidate their involvement in "the Movement." They face their exhaustion and prevail over it. They take "vacations" and return strengthened. They turn to psychiatrists or psychologists, to friends, relatives, or ministers, "talking out" their experiences and in the process determining their own future. If they "go back" they usually do so "the wiser," that is less grandly hopeful and expectant, more accurately if painfully aware of how difficult social change can be — for those effecting it as well as those experiencing it. If their aims are more cautious, their capacity to endure is perhaps greater.

Many do not go back. A year or two, even a summer, is all they can take of heat and humidity, fear and brutality, doubt and ambiguity. "You sweat it out a summer," a northern college student, a Negro, told me, "and you leave wondering whether anything you did makes any difference. You can't help wondering what will happen when you're gone; whether the people will settle right back to their old ways, the whites and Negroes both."

For some the decision to leave comes from more than personal fatigue; they recognize that to remain not only time and energy must be spent. Often enough goodwill must yield to fierce determination, and the worker senses his kindly feelings giving way to an increasing cynicism. Toward the end of the Mississippi Project one college girl remarked:

If I stay here much longer, I'll become hard. That's what happens. You get so tired and angry that you become like the enemy you're fighting, and anything goes to win. You lose patience with anyone that's not right square on your side, the liberals and the moderates and "the good people" caught in the middle, and the Negroes who won't cooperate or are indifferent. They all become enemies . . . I've never realized how *soon* you can become bitter or change your mind and your perspective, if the pressure on you is great enough.

While some may flee such a threat to their own values or ideals, others stay, and the lives of such people have their own natural history. As noted, such civil rights workers become tired and depressed. A second point of separation occurs then, some leaving permanently, some leaving for a while to come back refreshed, and some never really giving up the daily struggle.

Those in this last group, in my experience, present a recognizable and characteristic clinical picture. I use the word "clinical" with some hesitation, fearful of dubbing such a word upon the actions and attitudes of brave and hard-working young men and women. Yet, I think it fair to say that there are some civil rights workers in whom long and hard exposure to the stresses of their kind of work has produced more than a temporary period of "battle fatigue." Fixed anger and suspicion plague them. They lose not only perspective and humor, but they begin to distrust the intentions and aspirations of others, so that fewer and fewer people, even among their own co-workers, can be trusted. Hate and its moral and psychological equivalents appear: scorn for newcomers in civil rights, distrust of anyone, black or white, connected ever so slightly or innocently with the "power structure."

In five years, by the way, I have heard the term "power structure" spread from a specific description (of social and political institutions) to an indiscriminate word thrown about in anger so willingly and arbitrarily as to lose all its meaning and value. If I have second thoughts about this or that idea, I am selling out to the "power structure." If I wonder and shudder at the spectacle of arrogance in myself and my fellow civil rights workers, I am heeding the rationalizations or seductions of the "power structure." If I worry about my job, my family, this comfort or that private interest, I am in danger of being "processed" by the "power structure."

Smaller and smaller are the number of those whose motives can be genuinely trusted, whose actions are above reproach. Angrier and angrier become the discussions between some of the veteran fighters and the newer recruits. It is not simply a matter of nerves shaken, tempers for a while let loose. I am describing those for whom anxiety, depression and misgivings of one sort or another have turned to chronic withdrawal, un- compromising suspiciousness and a readiness to anger, even to hate, that is destructive to every goal espoused by the Move- ment.

How many are so affected, and how seriously do they threaten the others with whom they work? It is hard to say precisely, but I would suggest that working strongly to mini- mize the influences of such people is necessary to the continu- ing success of the overall cause of civil rights, not to mention the very value of work in that cause.

It is, for example, hard to justify complete bitterness in the face of what has happened these past few years in the South. Not simply the Civil Rights Laws of 1964 and 1965, but the thrust of the poverty program have all been felt throughout the region, and not only by a few Negro middle-class citizens. I spent a portion of the summer of 1965 as a consultant to Operation Head-Start, and particularly its program in Missis- sippi. While there I met up again with many of the volunteers I had come to know the previous summer during the Missis- sippi Project. Yes, some of them were wiser, wearier, less flushed with that mixture of excitement and single-minded devotion I saw in many of them as they had prepared, in Ox- ford, Ohio, for the Mississippi Project. However clear it was to them a year later that Mississippi's segregation had not yielded to their courage, their freedom schools and voter registration drives, it was also clear to them that the state *had* changed. Its schools *were* desegregating. (In 1960 few indeed thought school desegregation would come to Mississippi by 1965.) Its major hotels and motels, restaurants and movie chains were also open to all.

I remember the Freedom Riders setting off in 1961; I have their tape-recorded descriptions of Jackson's police in 1961. Jackson's police in 1965 were reported by some to be brutal; yet all agreed their behavior *was* different, decidedly so. Social changes such as Mississippi has seen in the past five years cannot escape the notice of civil rights workers no matter how tired and overworked and frustrated they are. "Just when I get really fed up, I see enough real hope, real change to keep me going," I heard from a young Ivy Leaguer, a resident of the Delta for over a year.

The psychological adjustment of volunteers who return to school is by no means an easy one. Consider the differences between school life on American campuses and life as some college students have known it recently in the deep South. From safe classrooms and comfortable dormitories they have gone to rural cabins, many of them as primitive as there are in America, and done so to face constant danger.

I have seen quiet, even timid young men become vigorous teachers, shrewd organizers and adaptive fighters in what often has been, in many senses, a real war — between sheriffs and the police on the one hand and students on the other, between angry white mobs and determined Negro and white demonstrators.

The list of accomplishments wrought by these young workers is more than impressive, or even stirring. Confronted with what many of them have shown they can do, what they *will* do, the puzzled psychiatrist begins to wonder about the human mind: What accounts for such resourcefulness and ethical development? I cannot frankly say that I ever would have been able to predict the courage and ability I have seen these youths demonstrate. Is it not time for us in medicine and psychiatry to acknowledge more than the vague "influence" of "environmental factors" upon man's health and state of mind?

As a doctor privileged as much by accident as reasons within his own life to see the actions of many of these people, as well as get to know them as individuals, I am thankful that my clinical impressions are what they are. I would frankly worry hard were there not a puzzling diversity to these youths, and to their manner of behavior and survival. Either I would be doing them an injustice, not seeing the many truths of their many lives in the interests of my own tidy, categorical inclinations; or they themselves would be indeed united and similar — in ideology, in behavior, in professed aims.

We have seen such uniform, mass youth movements in our time; I find it significant and a cause for gratitude that for five years — while their ambitions had deepened and broadened — the overwhelming majority of these civil rights workers have refused to march to any such cadence.

Transaction, 1966

Two Minds about Carmichael

In a recent issue of *New South,* a quarterly published by
the Southern Regional Council, space was given to a "dia-
logue" between Stokely Carmichael of the Student Non-
Violent Coordinating Committee and Randolph Blackwell of
Dr. Martin Luther King's Southern Christian Leadership
Conference. The contrast between the words of the two
speakers, both Negro, was striking — enough so to prove once
again that membership in the civil rights "movement," like
skin color itself, tells only so much about a person. Throughout, Mr. Blackwell was on guard for the irrational, sensitive
to the ironies and almost boring repetitions that history forces
upon mankind, unwilling to deny the value of a broad number of interpretations for any issue; in sum, thoughtful.

For example, when the subject of "black power" came up,
as it did immediately, Mr. Blackwell was able to summon
a retrospective view: Frederick Douglass and certainly Dr.
W. E. B. Du Bois long ago were talking about black power, or
something very much like it. We have to be specific. We have
to "clear the air precisely as to what we are saying." He then
goes on to do so, in the most enlightened and reasonable way,
by putting not only the issue of "black power" but the entire

civil rights struggle in the following perspective: "Twentieth-century civilization is infinitely more complicated than just the race problem and because of that we have to be concerned with advancing technology . . . with expanding population . . . with a number of social forces that we feel are . . . compelling decisions that cannot be answered surely by viewing our concern as just one of the position of the Negro people."

A little further on Mr. Blackwell again demonstrates how reluctant he is to dwell on race alone, or to place the struggle that he himself is fighting in any but the very broadest of contexts. The populism of the last century will be revived, he hopes. The populists of 1890 transcended race, he asserts; they saw the needs of all people — for land, for work, for decent wages. So did the labor movement in the thirties, when it insisted upon "the fact that poor people, regardless of race or color, have basically the same needs and motivations." For Mr. Blackwell, it was the Second World War that stopped everything, or at least stopped the development of a genuine populist movement that would change the life of the poor for the better. Although he did not spell it out in this particular instance, he presumably intended to say that in spite of the enormous increase in our national wealth and in the size of the American middle class since 1941, millions have stood by with little to show for themselves but the increases in the size of their welfare checks. Such people — farm workers, the people of Appalachia, the urban poor — have no organized means of redressing their grievances. The labor movement is largely part of the middle class, and the distinct minority of poor people in this country has no significant political power of its own. For Dr. King, and his aide Mr. Blackwell, and presumably for the other leaders of established civil rights organizations that is the problem, and increasingly it is the one big problem they face not only as Negroes, but as members of a relatively stable if inequitable society. The vote and access to restaurants does little for most Negroes, and not only SNCC but all civil rights organizations realize that. Proposals for huge federal programs (up to $100 billion) are made repeatedly by men who have easy access to the White House. If Mr. Carmichael only insisted that his people get much more money (and the power that goes with that money) it is hard to see how he would differ from Mr. Blackwell, Roy Wilkins and Whitney Young.

Stokely Carmichael's responses to Mr. Blackwell show that what separates him from them and their respective supporters is a matter of substance as well as emphasis or mood. In one sentence he demolishes any conceivable coalition in present-day American politics: "I've worked on the assumption that this country from top to bottom, from right to left, is racist," and has been from the start. Populism was doomed because black men had no one and nothing reliable of their own to fall back upon. Populism tended to "absorb" the Negro, as indeed do its contemporary successors; but they never can manage to do the job because racism is everywhere, in everyone's mind, a psychological inheritance that curses this nation as a result of the slavery it codified into law and justified through an astonishing and instructive variety of religious and intellectual rationalizations.

It is an interesting pair of horses that Mr. Carmichael rides. Like other Negro leaders he wants an end to the hungry bellies and idle hours that plague his people, and like them he emphasizes the economic struggle that still faces the Negro, in contrast, say, to a legal and social struggle for minimal citizenship. Yet, he is no economic determinist, despite what many observers (and more enemies) of SNCC say. With all the names SNCC has been called these days it is interesting to note what much of the public refuses to grasp about Stokely Carmichael's message and state of mind, for the two are quite inseparable. In a curious way he is far less a hard-line "materialist" than his critics, the "moderates." If I read Stokely Carmichael correctly — at least in this exchange with Mr. Blackwell — he believes the Negro is up against a wall that dollars will not bring down. Yes, the Negro needs money and power, but this country will not give him much of either — no matter how hard he tries to get them — because he is Negro. What the Negro needs to do, then, is withdraw, pull himself together independently, and after that is done exert his new presence as the new form of power it will in fact turn out to be.

The more he talks about white people, the civil rights movement and the Negro's position in American society, the more Stokely Carmichael emerges as a would-be leader of an immigrant group that is, finally, here — even if its more recent point of departure is our own (plantation) soil. His premises, his assumptions about the nature of the Negro's position in American society differ markedly from those of his liberal critics of whatever color. He insists that a new ball game is at least starting for the Negro, while their reply is that the same old game is going on — only it is in the last and hardest inning. For SNCC (as it is now constituted) all its own work of the past years was not really in vain; it was simply and literally a means of deliverance, of bringing hitherto exiled Negroes into the initial confrontation with American society. The rest of this nation's minorities had this confrontation, I suppose, at places like Ellis Island — where, it has to be admitted, they received right off guarantees the Negro always lacked and has only recently been able to claim with some assurance of success. Two years ago I heard it put this way by a Negro man who had voted for the first time in his life: "I feel like I just came here from across the ocean, and today is my second day in America, because yesterday was the first, when I walked in there and voted. So now maybe that we can vote, we'll get somewhere, like everybody else has."

Today we forget the past (or even present) clannishness of this country's various "nationalities." They came scattered and forlorn, foreigners from different nations, cities, towns or villages, united only by the misery they wanted to escape and the promise our shores offered. They settled near but not among those already here. They drew together, crowded into sections, neighborhoods, whatever; and they lived in fear, suspicion and defensive withdrawal. Eventually they no longer felt it necessary to turn all the hurt and scorn they experienced upon themselves. Meek, self-effacing, obliging people fought the shame they had grown to believe their due, and shocked the sensibilities of the "older" groups (particularly, I would imagine, the more sensitive and kindly members of those groups) by appearing newly assertive and demanding — utterly ungrateful for small favors. Instead of feeling hopelessly marked by their origins, they proclaimed them in pride and defiance — and used them with a vengeance in politics.

If that is all very familiar when we talk about the past, it still seems hard for us to have any perspective on what in the present may be quite similar: the migration of Negroes from national exile (including its more patronized and subsidized forms) to a condition of aroused, insistent *presence*. Here is what the grandmother of a child I know in Boston has to say about the change she has both seen and experienced in her sixty years: "If you want to know the difference, I'll tell you how it is. Before, we were in the closet, and under the rug, and you know the white people in this country, they have big homes, so they have a lot of closets to hide us, and rugs all over the place. (I know, because I've worked in about two dozen of those homes myself, if I recall right.) Then just a few years back we started getting out of the closet, because we pushed hard, and besides, the white men, they're fighting between themselves, and so they had to let go of their greedy grip on us. So out we've been coming, and the more we see the more we know we've been robbed all our lives, and before that. So we say, look, white man: you have to give us our share, or if you don't we're going to make you tear your hair and bite your nails, and you'll turn whiter than you are — so pale you'll faint — because we want our own legs to stand on, and not your canes, and your crutches, and your leftover shoes, and your pieces of gum and maybe a corner in your attic, and an invitation to come have a Coke every election day, so you can all feel so good about yourselves.

"The way I see it, they can try shoving us back in the closet, but let them go ahead and see what that'll cost them. Or they can keep telling us we're their equal, and be satisfied with equality, and eat it three times a day, and use it to keep the rats around here from biting our kids and if it gets cold and the landlord says no, there's no heat for you, then go down on our knees and thank the white man for telling us how equal we are, and for saying we can pull the voting machines just like him, and get the same crooks he does to boss over him.

"If they're smart, they'll leave us be, out of the closet like everyone else, and they'll give us what's our right, after all they got from us since the country was started. They say we're lazy, but we've been working on their land and taking care of their dirty dishes and cleaning as long as they've been here. They grabbed us and put us to work, and they pushed the Indians all over the place, and shot them up, one tribe after the other, and now they call us lazy and the Indians lazy, and they call us bad and wild because we're stuffed in corners of the closet, and we can barely breathe, and we're trying to force the door open, and want to get out — not to go live with them whites, but to live, period."

My job is to observe, to hear and record her voice and see how her granddaughter manages the "strain" of riding twenty minutes from her "neighborhood" school to one across town

— where white children eye her with mixed interest, kindness and fear. The grandmother and I have talked about that, too: "I tell her it's OK to go to school with whites, but don't get the idea *they're* the reason she's going. It's that they have the better schools, and we want them, the same as they. If black and white can like each other, that's one thing, but we shouldn't go begging them to like us, so they can smile back and pat us on the head, and want to hold hands with us and say how we're all brothers. I tell my grandchildren the only way you get real respect in this country is by demanding it, and when you get it, keep it as *yours,* because otherwise all you're doing is helping the white man keep his own respect, by showing off how nice he is to you, and how many pennies he'll give you every now and then. That's the truth; we have to make sure it's our freedom we're after, and not the white man's, or else we'll be like a hobby of his — to come take a look at us and see how we play jazz and eat the fried chicken and all that."

She is no advocate of "black power," no member of a civil rights organization. She is an aging, tired woman, whose hands show how very intimately she has known the homes of white people. As I read Stokely Carmichael's remarks I thought of her. She and Mr. Carmichael and many other Negroes feel cornered. The country basks in wealth, even amid an exhausting war fought halfway around the earth; black people live on, by the millions "permanently poor." There is talk about this or that kind of coalition to change things, to secure a little something for powerless, voiceless black people, but instead the pressures of bulging Negro ghettoes upon hard-pressed and fearful white neighborhoods produce a wave of panic, and a quick congressional response that enfeebles the few existing laws and kills the chance of any new ones — even pitifully modest ones — being enacted. A Negro youth in the South once put it this way to me: "The white man gets dust in his eye, and everyone rushes to take notice; the Negro screams because he's dying, and they don't even hear, or they come to finish the job, or if they say they're friends, they stoop down to put a washcloth on his head, when he needs blood."

Cornered people become excited and find trouble maintaining a "long view" of history. Their language I have found to be strikingly aphoristic, right to the point and without the circumlocutions the rest of us learn in order to keep within the bounds of "reality" whatever stirrings of conscience we have. The words lance my middle-class mind — and in response I try to sort out the terrible, unsettling mixture of truth, anger and despair they mean to convey. I want to say no to Mr. Carmichael; it is unfair to go away, to be apart from the "mainstream," to shout so loud and mercilessly when in fact things are getting better than anyone dared dream even a few years ago. I think of all the books, all the graphs and charts that would prove conclusively — to anyone, I am certain — how much is being done, how far a reasonable and basically decent society can go to right its wrongs. Instead, from what I judge to be an increasing number of Negroes, I hear bitter or sad or indifferent refusals. "What is there to say? There's only our feelings we have, and the white man, he's letting us know his limit. He's back-lashing us, and we're feeling it, baby. The skin is raw from all the other times, so we're feeling it good, because you can be sure the skin is raw." I didn't hear that at a meeting or rally of any kind. A white teacher showed me a short composition written by a youth whose "adjustment" I've been following. No doubt about it: He's doing it — making his adjustment.

One afternoon as I was leaving his home I heard on his sister's radio a song of Irving Berlin's from *Mr. President,* "Empty Pockets Filled with Love." Driving away, my car radio picked up the song as it came to an end. I pictured the boy I had just seen a few years from now, older, his skin still raw. If he then were to join a riot — and who knows how long this country will live in nervous fear of them — someone like me might try to tell him to "cool it," tell him how much the liberal people of this country like him and want to do for him. For all I know, in some part of his mind at that moment the memory of a song might yet persist — "Empty Pockets Filled with Love." All the pieties in the world would not then placate him, because it is work and money that his family needs now and will continue to need.

New Republic, 1966

The Words and Music
of Social Change

Oxford, Ohio, is a town of about 10,000 located about forty miles north of Cincinnati. Gentle hills are nearby, and farms and roads go a long way before meeting other ones. The people in rural Ohio are white, conservative and generally prosperous. They vote Republican. They want their children to get educated, though not "too educated," by which they mean a lot of philosophy and poetry and leftist political science or sociology. True to its name, Oxford claims Miami University and Western College for Women, both of which were founded well back in the nineteenth century, and both of which (so I heard from a doctor in the town) occasionally stimulate the "wrong ideas" in students. "They read everything these days," I can remember him saying. A second later he pointedly added something else: "and they're not fussy about who they let use their buildings."

Yes, indeed, in June of 1964 Western College for Women had offered its entire campus to the Student Non-Violent Coordinating Committee and CORE and God knows who else — for God knows what purpose. The year 1964 right now seems like much more than five years in the past, perhaps five times five years. Yet for all the changes since then the historical significance of the Mississippi Summer Project of 1964 cannot be questioned: A decade of sporadic, lonely, and occasionally fierce social struggle — most of it connected with southern racial problems that arose as a result of the Supreme Court's decision of 1954 — had finally become a political crisis of national significance. Black youths who for years had been hunted down by the police and called "delinquent" or "psychopathic" by judges (and sent away for psychiatric observation as well as imprisonment) were now leaders and heroes to hundreds of middle-class white college students — and those students took their ideals seriously. They came to Oxford, Ohio, because of those ideals, and after two weeks of orientation they would go to Mississippi because of those ideals.

Within a few days, however, three young men, who had left Oxford well before the rest of us, were found missing and immediately presumed dead. "They're dead, they're absolutely dead," I was told by Stokely Carmichael, with whom I shared the responsibility for a seminar rather wryly and with mock pretense called "methods and techniques of nonviolence." In those days Stokely Carmichael believed in nonviolent protest — and believed that yet another demonstration, yet another summer's blood, would bring "freedom, oh delicious freedom, freedom at last," as one song put it. Then, even the death of three comrades was somehow a beginning and not an end, a measure of success rather than a failure. Then I could hear this, record this — on a tape which now can only be considered a document of sorts from another era:

They killed them, but they can't kill the summer, and what we're going to do this summer. They can't kill our spirit, only our bodies. They'll find out what they did when they murdered our people, our brothers. They'll find that they made us stronger, that we'll beat them sooner, be-

cause of what they've done. The whole nation will rally round — but
even more important, *we'll* rally round.

Well, how did they "rally round"? Did they — the leaders
of the project — ask me to talk with people, analyze their obviously increased sense of fear and gloom? Did they suggest a
"group" or two, perhaps a bit of "sensitivity training," as it is
put by all those "group leaders"? Did they call in advisers —
political scientists and social scientists and doctors and lawyers — so that those several hundred young men and women
would feel better advised, better protected? Did they rush to
Washington, to the newspapers and magazines, to the television cameras?

In fact, they did worry about the collective mood of their
new recruits, many of whom had never been south — and
now had to face the distinct possibility that a first trip might
be a last one. They also wondered about morale, about everyone's morale, about the ways people affect one another when
they feel sad and anxious and in a way suspended — not at
home, not in Mississippi, "just waiting," which were the
words one heard again and again from youths terribly hurt
by the sudden loss of three good friends, under conditions that
the mind could only imagine, and know to have been as awful
as any fantasy could possibly be. And finally, the young civil
rights workers knew how self-conscious things would have to
be: The press didn't have to be sought out, nor the cameras;
the entire county had become involved in that project. Again,
in Stokely Carmichael's words: *"We'll have to show them,
show them we're not afraid, we won't pull back, we'll go
there, and stay there and outlast them; show them they can't
scare us."*

As we now know, they were not scared. At least private
fears never became a public display of terror, or turned into
something like T. S. Eliot's "compromise, complacency and
confusion." How did they manage? How did they dare, con-

tinue to dare? Again, in Eliot's word, how could they "presume" — presume to go on, to believe there was any justifiable "going on" in the face of such brute force, such longstanding power, now instantly and arbitrarily summoned? Choices there were: to reconsider, to retreat, to "regroup," to wait and only later go south — and, above all, to consult with advisers, all sorts of knowledgeable and experienced and welltrained people, who I can remember appeared as if out of nowhere, whether or not asked, to have their say, to express fear or worry or, occasionally, a bit of hope.

Suddenly, though, in a couple of days, something quite surprising and wonderful and (I can only use the word) awesome happened. Suddenly hundreds of young Americans became charged with new energy and determination. Suddenly I saw fear turn into toughness, vacillation into quiet conviction. Suddenly waves of emotion swept over that landlocked town of Oxford. Even the doctor I mentioned at the start of this essay became shaken, touched, affected, and, in the end, very much moved. What, how, why — those are the words invoked by observers like me, however "involved" or "participant" or whatever we are. For a while I wanted to banish all the questions, all the analytic propositions and scientific explorations that my nicely trained mind could not help raising with itself. Yet eventually I realized how needlessly protective I was — of students, black and white, whose words and deeds and purposes could quite definitely tolerate any scrutiny I felt driven to make.

"How did we do it?" I had asked a black youth from Mississippi how he and others had converted a grim piece of news into an unforgettable occasion, an almost spectacular kind of moral and philosophical experience for an entire midwestern town, and he replied right off by asking himself my question. In a way, the earnest way he did so should have been my clue, but as it turned out I didn't need one, because he was pre-

pared to go on: *"We never thought we had anything to 'do.'*
We had to get going, and we decided the best way to get going
was to get going."

I knew there was more to say, because I had been with him
and others at Oxford all along. I had in fact seen and heard a
powerful and lovely and stirring spectacle (that is the word)
take place over a span of two days. Still, he was right; it had
developed, grown, almost bloomed, and if guile had helped
things along, the unself-conscious, direct, spontaneous character of the activities and meetings — which in fact were *rites*
— cannot be denied. So, I asked him simply to tell me what
had occurred. I knew and he knew that I knew the facts. I had
been part of the scene. But I felt his account would tell me
something else — not facts, not data, not even clues to overall
"attitudes" or emotional states. I suppose I believed that the
effort of narrative can be revelatory (not revealing), and
even redemptive (not therapeutic). I suppose I believed that
in talking, in telling, we could not so much clarify as be properly amazed and surprised and, yes, even stunned. In this
century, among the West's intelligentsia, the look backward
has become such a sober and serious matter. We are puzzled
or troubled. We try to find the first causes of our bewilderment, our present pain. But perhaps old sorrows can indeed
make themselves felt later — but in new assertions of pride
and wonder and hope, as I discovered in Oxford, Ohio, when
I saw tired, hurt victims of the civil rights movement:

> If things had fallen apart there'd have been no Summer Project, no
> Selma, nothing. They'd have known they could scare us, make us back
> down. There'd have been no civil rights laws — on voting and all the
> rest. I know you can't two years later say that, say it was one point in
> time that was so important; but I can say no *other* moment was more
> important, that I know.
>
> We thought about what to do, and then we fell to arguing a lot.
> Finally we decided we should become religious, real religious. We de-
> cided we should go to church — and until then we didn't even know

where the chapel was on that campus. We decided we had to get together, *really* get together. We decided we all had to stop and think, that's what, that's what we kept saying, stop and think and figure out the meaning of things. It was as if we wanted everyone to become philosophical — and face it, real head-on: to risk their lives or not to risk their lives; to fight or surrender; to know what's important, really important, and stand up for it, or run home and say later, later — because it's too dangerous now.

That's the kind of thing we wanted them to think about, the kind we thought about, the few of us sitting up through the night wondering what to do. And we started asking each other what to say, what to do, what to read in the church, what to sing. We wanted each volunteer to stop and think — but feel close to the next person, who would be doing the same thing. We wanted to have silence, so people could ask themselves things, and we wanted a lot of talking, too — a lot of music and arms locked together, all that, you know — so that people wouldn't be scared, at least not too scared.

Well, I knew the rest. I took part in the rest. I heard the folk songs. I heard the poems, the selections from John Donne and Shakespeare and Dostoevsky and Thoreau and Tolstoy and W. H. Auden. I heard the phonographs play Beethoven and Brahms and Berlioz. I saw several hundred young men and women — black and white, rich and poor, northern and southern — form themselves into a huge circle, hands held together or arms locked into one another. I saw that circle close in on itself and then expand. I saw it break up into smaller circles: to dance and embrace and shout words of sadness and determination and anger and outrage and pity and vengeance and most of all soreness, in all the senses of that old and powerful word.

In between the public moments, the times when we were all together, all listening or singing or praying or reciting, we went off in two's and four's and six's to wonder and be afraid and straighten up suddenly and say yes, not no. Then, too, the writers and artists and composers appeared, as if out of nowhere. I was astonished at the sight of those books — among people told to come with very little, to travel light, to bring only essentials. Essentials they brought: *The Plague, Crime and Punishment, Light in August, The Mind of the South, All the King's Men,* the poems of Wallace Stevens or W. C. Williams or W. H. Auden. In a moment of fear, of decision, of social struggle, I saw books, inert books (and symphonies and postcards from this or that museum) become — well, if it has to be said that way, "relevant" and "useful." In those desperate moments, when actually more than the outcome of a Summer Project hung in balance, what can loosely be called the "humanities" had an emphatic and remarkable effect on a large group of bewildered, mourning, hesitant activists — who then wanted and needed wisdom, not knowledge, a sense of moral purpose rather than "goals" or "programs" or "data" or "interpretations."

In a way, as an observer and a friend, I found myself taken aback. The Bible and the Classics figured prominently in my life. My parents — correctly I believe — had little faith that some combination of technological ingenuity, socialist politics and psychoanalytic discovery would put us all within sight of the New Jerusalem. By the same token, they urged upon me an ethical code grounded in the past, the distant past. I came to college familiar with Jeremiah and Isaiah; with Matthew, Mark and Luke; indeed with St. John's apocalyptic Revelations; and I came there grounded in years and years of Latin and Greek. In contrast, most — though not all — of the white college students in that Mississippi Summer Project had spent a good deal of time weighing the "meaning," the "message," the "value" of books I simply (and all too naïvely) considered novels, or poems, or "contemporary literature," pure if not so simple.

So, as I look back and think about it all, I have to conclude that for a long time I felt closer to the black youths from the rural South than many of the northern students. For example, I favored the Supreme Court's 1954 decision (striking down the legal fiction called "separate-but-equal" schools) because what was right — ethically, philosophically, religiously, *humanly* — had to prevail. It seemed almost (and literally) blasphemous that the Court had to bulwark its decision with all sorts of psychological and sociological testimony. Many times during our night-long talks and arguments I heard the Supreme Court's wisdom upheld as modern, as sophisticated; as tied to discoveries made here or there, and written up in this or that book — only to hear in reply (from a young black "fieldworker," a civil rights activist) an outburst that came across almost like a gospel song. Here is one cry, recorded in Hattiesburg:

> You all have your books, and you tell me I've got to read *The Plague* (is it?) and something else, the one with the long title about "'praising men," and the poems you have. But to me it's in plain sight what has to be done and I don't need anyone telling me from a book. My book, it's the Bible. When I was a little kid, my mother would tell us we should listen to what the Book says, and someday, if we're lucky, we'd get a chance to *do* something, and then the Bible would tell us how to behave and do it right. Maybe — I admit it — maybe you need a lot more than the Bible today; but as I hear some of you talk — well, I say to myself, they've got their bibles and I've got mine, and when you come right down to it, there might not be too much difference. The guy who wrote *The Plague,* he must have been sweating about some of these things; like Matthew and Mark did, they surely did. And maybe the one thing the summer has taught me is: with different people, you get different saints that they listen to. In fact, I don't believe there's a man alive who doesn't have at least one saint he listens to, even if we'd call him a devil, not a saint. I'll bet over in the Klan meeting, over there across town, they're quoting somebody, yes sir.

His closing verb had summarized a lot of that summer. We had all been quoting people left and right, day and night. Lines or whole stanzas from Auden or Spender had been underlined, or paragraphs from Agee and Camus bracketed. Songs were sung not only for "release" or to achieve solidarity, but to say something, to declare, to affirm and sing out.

Still, in the face of that experience, and others like it, if less dramatic, I hear the humanities questioned. Are they of any value, of any possible interest to today's students? Yes, it is nice to read a novel sometimes, and listen to a symphony; but the world is full of immediate problems and enormous challenges, all of which requires from young people an almost single-minded sense of competence and purpose. And, of course, some who claim to speak for literature and art can be impossible: deliberately arrogant, aloof, condescending, priggish, stuffy and all the rest. Writers and artists sweat and suffer and finally manage a lucid moment here and there — only to be worked over by cold and mannered pedants and declared their property. No wonder many people, even among the well-to-do, are put off or walk away in disgust and anger. Yet in spite of everything — the fake and self-appointed connoisseurs, the smug literary coteries and the petty, artistic salons, the schools that thrive on jealousy and exclusiveness and hauteur and vengeance — the world's Melvilles and Faulkners, its Balzacs and Tolstoys and Picassos continue to confront us with everything, with pain and suffering and tenderness and love, with moral choices and ethical conflicts and most of all with an effort toward coherence, toward a vision that inspires, that summons, that makes us, at least from time to time, a little more than we usually are, than we possibly can be for very long. Perhaps what I am trying to say can be best said by someone else. Here is what one leader of the Mississippi Summer Project said to me in Greenville, right near the great mythic river, in late July of 1964:

Well, we did it, I don't know how, but we did. We all were scared. Who wouldn't be after what they did in Neshoba County, so fast — like a challenge to us. You ask where it came from, the guts it took to stay in Oxford, and then drive down here. I don't know. You find it, you find it in people — and I guess you call it guts or courage or things like that. You're scared, but you've asked yourselves some questions and find the answers. You know, it's like living in a novel or a play, this whole summer is. Everything is bigger, bigger than usual — the way writers picture things they write.

Yet, four years ago in Mississippi during one of those interminable "soul sessions" uncannily and unself-consciously used by civil rights workers to weaken fear and trembling, I heard another message, this time an outcry:

> Whatever we do, it'll be the white man who will benefit the most. We'll ask for school desegregation and they'll get better schools. We'll say that we get no medical care at all, and they'll get health insurance and more medical schools. We'll criticize the values of this society, and they'll start asking themselves what they really believe in. The Negro may come out of all this with the vote, but it'll be white people again who really win. They'll have better schools and better doctors and better everything because we helped wake them up. Our pain made them look at themselves, and then they said, "Here, boy, here's a Band-Aid" — while they went rushing off to the hospital to try and get their *own* sickness cured.

Of course I knew he was "upset" then — because a freedom house had been dynamited the night before. I also knew how *complicated* things are. I could allow him his stark, polemic rhetoric — and go on to remind myself how much he had omitted from his "analysis." Yet I could not forget the important point he was making. America's present-day political and racial unrest has strengthened the hand of all sorts of social and educational critics. We in the upper-middle-class academic and professional world have indeed been asked to look both inward and outward — asked once again to look at what we are doing and for whom. Our assumptions and values have indeed been questioned. Our purposes have been attacked. We have been called narrow-minded, parochial, self-centered.

We are not "involved"; our interests and work are not "relevant." We are race-bound, class-bound. We are crusty and snobbish. We are dying.

All those charges have to be answered. Here I can only list some ideas and feelings I have acquired during ten years of what I suppose could be called "fieldwork" — done by a child psychiatrist in the South and the North, among Appalachian families, migrant farm families and ghetto families.

I have learned to question a number of medical and psychiatric tenets I had never before doubted. I have learned to give "ordinary" people more credit for courage, guile, discretion and, yes, those "higher things" like sensibility, restraint, tact, generosity. I have learned to draw upon a book like Ellison's *Invisible Man* instead of a book called *The Mark of Oppression,* which offers "in depth" — of course! — psychiatric case studies of the Negro. I have learned that one does not have to be a political or social or philosophical "romantic" to comprehend and appreciate the kind of truth that binds a Faulkner to a Tolstoy, an Agee to a Bernanos, a Simon Weil to an Orwell.

I think that more than anything else I have learned to *know* what social scientists know, but *see* what a Eudora Welty, a Flannery O'Connor, a Richard Wright, a Robert Penn Warren, a Walker Percy demand and suggest and hint and urge one like me to see. What a far from tragic poet has called "the things of this world" defies all categories, man-made and inborn.

Above all, in Roxbury's ghetto, and among people grimly and all too easily and condescendingly dismissed as the "backlash" I continue to see evidence of both hope and failure. I hear strong language that is unharnessed. I see visions, valuable and imaginative visions, that are on the point of being crushed or abandoned. I see children paint poetry and put to word the landscapes of their minds. I watch them come home from school — tired and bored and ready in a back alley to reclaim their humanity, their right to test themselves and learn about one another.

And on the other side of town, "across town" as the children put it, I hear college students and college teachers speak and think in language that on good days can perhaps cause a resigned smile. Ghetto children need and crave coherence, a sense of what the world is truly about. But students and graduate students and professors can stand a few lessons too. Clear, direct and strong language is no luxury. Our words reveal our thoughts. Cloudy minds and murky disciplines need more than a few hundred editorial assistants to "clean things up."

We the enlightened cram our children with facts and figures. We ask our teachers to be sensitive, to understand psychology, child development, the nature of prejudice, the facts of "group experience." We offer "the new math," and we crowd our classrooms with teaching machines to make French easier and (I suppose, soon) Chinese possible. But I talk with and teach college students who do not know how to struggle for a straight thought and put such a victory down on paper. They may know that they can't "write," but they do not know that they have been denied what they must (and can) have, a mind that works — lives and breathes rather than digests facts, theories, and "data."

I hear from some that Henry James or T. S. Eliot is reactionary; or Carson McCullers merely odd in a clever and powerful way. If you would know America, take courses in "race relations" and political theory. Know the social system, the power structure, the latent this and the unconscious that. And know the facts, man, the facts — who owns what and who is bigger than whom. Yet I believe I find the whole world in the letters of van Gogh, not to mention his paintings; in a story by Flannery O'Connor; in one of Eliot's quartets; in a "decadent" novel by that great, curious, stubborn, long-winded, ambitious, shrewd observer and artist Henry James. I believe that ghetto children and suburban children can learn the most important "facts" that can possibly be learned from Rembrandt's "Life of Christ," from his canvases and from the Scripture that he brings alive: how long man has suffered and how much man can do to redeem himself, to win a little ground from life's built-in ironies, ambiguities and terrors — enemies far more dangerous than particular men or even social systems.

Finally, I believe that we can actively struggle with the world, but also sit back and wonder at things, understand them and be amused or scornful at how "it all" works out, comes to pass, whatever. And I believe that from "culturally deprived" and "culturally disadvantaged" ghetto children we in medicine and law and business and education, we right in the middle of the universities, might learn much more than we dare realize.

Whatever troubles "us," the well-off and supposedly well-educated, we still have all of "them" to trouble us. They just don't learn how to read very well. They seem to have their own music, which we find and treasure — out of our sophisticated interest in everything, everywhere, however "primitive" or "parochial." Yes, in the Delta, in Appalachia, out west on reservations, they have their jazz and their folk songs, their crafts and ballads and myths and rites — but how, exactly how, are they going to become more literate, more industrious, more like us: able to read and understand Max Weber's *The Protestant Ethic and the Spirit of Capitalism,* but, most of all, *feel* the book's truth — that is, remember it as an experience out of one's life?

At this point, with such questions in mind, I have to get very specific and, God forbid, talk about "educational materi-

als" that I have seen, heard sung, watched being used — both
down in Mississippi, and also up north in the ghetto of a large
city. In 1965 I saw a Head Start program get under way, but a
most unusual one: Hundreds of small children from sharecropper cabins all over Mississippi's Delta were suddenly confronted with schools that meant business, schools that were
not meant to be a mere formality, a half-gesture of "separate-
but-equal" education, but schools that had behind them —
oh, I suppose it could be called a "philosophy," though I
would like to call it a burning sense of conviction. Here is
how one of the teachers described the effort she and others
were making:

> We believe we can reach these little kids, and be reached by them. We
> believe that they can learn — learn a million things — if we keep believ-
> ing that they can learn. The trouble is that for too long their teachers
> have been convinced that they're hopeless. (A lot of them never even go
> to school more than a day or two a week, and they drop out when
> they're about ten). And the trouble is that a lot of the teachers, the
> more sophisticated ones — the outsiders who come here — keep on
> dwelling on how *bad* things are in the state, and how peculiar and
> different these kids are. You know: they have a special culture, and
> they don't trust you, or understand you, and all the rest. Well, they *do*
> have a special culture. It's different, the way they live. That's for sure.
> But they are children, and they can learn, and they can desire to learn.
> You have to forget yourself, and stop trying to impose on them all
> you've gone through, all the rote memory you had to accept, all the
> business of speaking clearly and learning the alphabet and reading the
> books your parents read — the Dick and Jane books that are handed
> down from one generation to the other. You have to get around *words*.
> Remember, black people were slaves — still are, in many respects. They
> were told to keep quiet, to mind their every step, to obey, obey, obey.
> They were denied the right to have a family, to vote — to build up a
> social and political tradition. They were kept from books and magazines
> and newspapers. Their children were kept ignorant and poor. They were
> called "uppity" if they spoke out, even spoke at all. No wonder they
> learned to be quiet, to fear words and distrust talk. No wonder they
> don't have books — most of them are lucky to eat half-well. But they are

men and women, and they see the world and respond to it — and from that comes a whole culture. I mean "culture" in the sense of style of looking at the world, in the sense of a particular form and structure to one's vision, one's feelings about things.

You — you people talk about "cultures" and "subcultures" as if men are only what they do and think: They live here and pray there and have this custom or that one. But the poorest sharecroppers developed secret, clever things: musical rhythms, sayings, songs. You can call it folk music and of course jazz; but the point is to recognize that it isn't just you, the outsiders, who "appreciate" such things, who see the beauty and subtlety in them. Poor, illiterate blacks sung and spoke their way to — to jazz, to the blues, to a rich tradition that we love to enjoy on our long-playing records. And to make a long story short: We believe that these children can learn, can learn like thousands and thousands of blacks have learned, learned every day — even though they'd be found on the bottom of every IQ test in America. We believe they see and hear and listen and feel things going on inside them and look outside themselves and take stock of the world and figure out how they have to act and what they have to say and how the world is run and who runs it — all of which is learning, I'll tell you, sad learning. So, we go ahead and do things, with all that in mind, I guess.

I spent a summer (1965) watching what she and others like her and hundreds of Mississippi's black children (ages three to six) all did, together. I have to admit it, I was surprised — as were others like me, who came from all over the country to observe, inspect, study, whatever, and left, invariably, scratching their puzzled heads. Children from rural cabins were learning all sorts of things: first how to own and wear clothes; then, how to eat food and enjoy it and come to believe that there will be yet another meal, yes sir and for real; and finally, how to do things and make things and look at things (and at one another) and, in sum, breathe life into the body's senses and the mind's already developing sensibilities. Paints, crayons, dances, movies, walks, exercises — all of that and more enabled children to become alert and delightfully self-conscious. But one child told me something I hope I never forget, particularly when I congratulate myself and others on a Head Start Project well done, or any other achievement: *You go to the Head Start place and they want you to see everything and tell it to the teacher — just like my little sister does when she comes shouting at me and pulling on me, to tell me that she saw a bird up there, and did I see it."* Her sister was then two years old, not quite eligible for Head Start. Does anyone really believe that "preliterate" and "illiterate" people don't learn, learn, learn — from the beginning of life on?

The schools I visited in Mississippi had at last caught up with the possibilities that exist in all children, even the children of sharecroppers. In Boston's ghetto, in Appalachia, in migrant labor camps, I have seen young, idealistic (sober, not starry-eyed) youths do similar things: such as give cameras to "culturally deprived" children, who then take pictures and movies — that we all might not have expected, might not have looked for or dreamed possible, from "them," from "poor them." I know that many photographers or movie directors would be fascinated by what such boys and girls have done, though I am not so sure about any number of thoroughly accredited and certified teachers.

Can there really be any doubt that the "humanities" mean everything to children — whose eyes and ears are still alive, have yet to be killed. Elizabeth Bowen knew that "death of the heart" is, to use the expression, a "cross-cultural phenomenon," as anyone knows who lives near rich and well-educated parents, whose children have learned how to glut themselves with facts and utterly dread a mere suggestion, an unanswerable question, a little bit of mystery. By the same token, poor and illiterate children die every moment — in the end spiritually, if not earlier because of hunger, malnutrition, and untreated diseases of all sorts. Yet how many people are really hopeless, really damned outright and forever? In 1965 I watched young black children from Holmes County, Mississippi, sit around a teacher and listen to her as she read some of William Faulkner's pastoral writing. Yes, a lot went unnoticed; indeed, a lot was bothersome or thoroughly unclear. But every once in a while — and, I noticed, with increasing frequency as the minutes followed one another — a word or a phrase or an observation struck the right chord: in a child here, another one over there, and from time to time in all of us. And last year, I heard students at Harvard — who already love records like "The Original Sonny Boy Williamson" or "The Blues of Alabama" or "The Sound of the Delta" — marvel at some photographs taken by a group of children from Boston's ghetto. They're amazing, we all thought. They remind one of postwar Italian movies — you know, *Open City* and *Bicycle Thief* — where violence is everywhere; yet the lives portrayed were meant to show that beauty lives on — in people crushed by wars, revolution and a history of virtual slavery and poverty. It took an artist like DeSica to pull all that together, the sadness and misery with the stubborn, lovely pride and the hope that never quite disappears.

For generations writers and artists and musicians — the men and women who *make* the humanities — have done that, have tried to give life and coherence to our ambiguous, ironic fate on this earth. For generations to come it will be the same: People will live, and some of them will write about it all, sing about it, draw and paint it, capture it on film. Certainly those who use their senses and then their minds to record and comment on life, in all its variety and complexity, have no quarrel with one another, are not "alienated" from one another, do not naturally feel "irrelevant" to one another. But in between them stand us — the mediators, the scholars and educators and teachers and just plain citizens — with our own ideas about what is possible, appropriate, suitable, "right" or "wrong" for children, and of course for writers and artists, too. I fear the rub is there, where the writer, say, in all his clever and calculated and summoning childishness is kept away from his audience, the child and the child in us, by censors of all sorts, who often enough are murderers, pure and simple. In the words of that Head Start teacher I quoted: *"Some teachers, some people, they don't really like writers and artists, so they turn them into dust, and make the kids try to eat the dust, and if the kids start vomiting — well, it just goes to show you that the writers are no good, or not suitable for such kids, or don't speak their language, the right language. Can you beat that for dishonesty?"* I fear the answer is no.

Yet, teachers can be different. They can in fact learn with their students, offer them fire, spirit and force; offer them ideas and doubts and questions; offer them a willingness to experiment, admit error, take risks and chances. Writers, artists, composers — all of them mean to teach, to enliven; even as the rest of us, young and old, crave the breath of life that their stories, pictures and songs all offer. If Tolstoy or Faulkner or Mozart or Big Joe Williams, the bluesman from Mississippi's Delta, cannot bring professors and students, older people and youths together, make them one and all readers and listeners, human beings who share and respond to something that transcends time and space, then who and what possibly can?

This question of Theodore Roethke's was rhetorical:

> *Stupor of knowledge lacking inwardness —*
> *What book, O learned man, will set me right?*

He knew that no book can provide the Word, that any book, however lovely and even exalted, can be inadequate to life's awful moments. But as a poet he persisted; he wrote his words, "words for the wind," and he hoped they would inform, excite, alarm, deliver courage and something one can only call a moment of quietness, a truce for a brief spell in the wars we all know. I believe that the winds he enriched naturally seek us out in classrooms as well as in a field, a hill, a place lonely and apart. Do we hear — we together, we in those classrooms? We can hear. *Do* we, though? Or does the life of a man like Roethke, his vitality, become his lyrics, scare us to — oh, in fact, scare us to death?

Daedalus, 1969

A Fashionable
Kind of Slander

It may seem strange now, six or eight years later, but in respected and moderate circles of the South, and the rest of the nation, the southern Freedom Riders and the Mississippi Project volunteers of 1964 were thought to be (were declared) wild, impetuous, thoughtless, self-destructive and masochistic; and the plan to challenge the state of Mississippi was considered a crazy and romantic scheme, doomed from the start and potentially dangerous, or even ruinous, because of the response that powerful men like James Eastland and John Stennis and their allies would no doubt make.

I would like to single out three of the expressions I just used: *masochistic, crazy* and *self-destructive*. For years in the South I heard those words directed at civil rights workers, and when I went to Appalachia to work with the Appalachian Volunteers, a similar group of dedicated, youthful political activists, I again heard the same thing. The line goes as follows: What's the matter with them? What kind of people do things like that? Why do they do such things? Do they really think anything will come of antics like theirs, rash and impul-

sive assaults? They are mistaken if they believe a small minority like them can prevail against the powers-that-be. Maybe
they *want* to lose, though. Maybe they are stubbornly, un-
compromisingly bent on the kind of confrontation that can
lead only to violence, disorder — and a kind of retaliation
that will not only put an end to their protest but set things
even further back, create an even worse climate of fear and
repression. In short, maybe those youths are irrational, deluded by a host of absurd and dangerous fantasies, violence-
prone and in some serious way, antisocial.

In 1963 I heard a decidedly sensitive and well-educated
southern judge send a youthful black civil rights worker to a
state hospital, where he was to be "observed," where his
"mental status" was to be evaluated, where possible "delinquent" and "sociopathic" trends would be ascertained and
studied — and where, perhaps, the young man would begin
to get some "treatment." Though he received no treatment
the youth did have a chance to think, and what I heard from
him was for me a professional confrontation of sorts, something I have never been able to forget, especially because I
had worked with delinquent youth in the course of my training in child psychiatry: "It's quite a setup they've got. We
protest our inability to vote, to go into a movie or restaurant
everyone else uses, and they call us crazy, and send us away to
be looked over by psychiatrists and psychologists and social
workers and all the rest of them. The questions I've had put
to me since I've been here! Were you a *loner* when you were a
boy? Did people consider you *rebellious?* Were you *popular*
or *unpopular* as a child? When you were younger did you
have trouble *taking orders* from your parents or your
teachers? Did your mother *discipline* you firmly, or did she
more or less let you do as you please? And on and on they go,
one question after another, and none of them very subtle.

"The guy doing the questioning told me he is a doctor, a

psychiatrist, and I asked him why he wasn't interested in *what* I've done, and the *objective reasons* I've acted as I have. But he said he knew 'all that.' He told me his job is to examine my mind and find out what my 'motivations' are. He kept on asking me whether I feel angry at this person and that one, and if I have a temper, and how do I 'handle tension,' and he wanted to know whether people in 'authority' make me anxious, and whether I have trouble in 'controlling' myself, and whether I 'rush out and act' when I come upon an unpleasant situation, or instead do I stop and think and try to figure out the best possible 'attitude' to have. I wrote them down, as many of his words and questions as I could, because the way he put those questions was to me more abusive than anything I've ever heard from the poor, ignorant red-necks. At least they have the decency to insult you right to your face; so you know exactly where they stand and no one's fooling anyone, least of all himself. That doctor (I can tell from talking with him over a week) considers himself way above the red-neck; in his mind he is a careful, thoughtful, temperate man. He used that word 'temperate' two or three times with me. He kept on contrasting 'temperate behavior' with 'impulsive behavior,' and after we got talking more casually he told me that some people have a 'need' — that's right, a *need* — to disrupt the lives of others, and hurt them, and get hurt themselves. Did I think I was that kind of person?

"Soon you just slip into the whole scene. I mean, you stop noticing all the assumptions a guy like that constantly makes, and you simply try to answer him as best you can. And anyway, if you protest and tell him off, tell him what you think is implicit in his questions and his whole way of thinking, he's not going to take your argument seriously; he's going to go after *you* — and call you 'hostile' and 'defensive' and full of 'problems' and all the rest. He as much as told me so, that doctor did. He said a lot was going on inside my mind, and until I found out what 'really' was prompting some of my 'behavior,' I'd probably continue what I've been doing. He told me he was going to recommend to the court that I not be sent to jail. He said I needed treatment — but he was worried that I would be 'resistant' to it, and that would be 'too bad' for me, and later I would be sorry."

The youth then pointed out to me what I hope is obvious: the smug, self-righteous arrogance, the pejorative use of psychiatric terminology, the limitless display of self-satisfaction and condescension, the essentially illogical and totalitarian nature of a mode of thought that claims to have the authority to decide who has a right even to discuss certain matters, and who (whatever he *thinks* he is saying or doing or trying to say or trying to do) is *really* "sick" or "resistant" or seriously in need of "help," and therefore thoroughly, hopelessly suspect. I was prepared to accept much of that from him — I had heard patients endlessly labeled in ways that robbed them of their dignity, and I had seen in myself as a psychiatric resident the awful tendency to dismiss a patient's disagreement or criticism as evidence of just about anything but his or her good judgment. But I was not so prepared to see how convenient it could be for that judge, and many like him, to have people around who would summon all the authority of medicine and science to the task of defending the status quo — which meant putting firmly in their place (a hospital or a clinic) those who choose to wage a struggle against that status quo.

Only over time did I begin to realize, often because I was brought up short by some very bright and clearheaded youths, that all sorts of phrases and concepts bandied about rather freely by me and my kind reveal as much about us as about those we describe. What indeed is "mental health"? Who indeed is "normal"? Were slaveholders "normal"? Did Nat Turner have a "problem with authority"? If a man tells

me he is going to kill himself, I call him "suicidal" and want
to hospitalize him. If a man in Vietnam runs into a burst of
machine-gun fire, urging his comrades to do likewise, I call
him a hero. If a man wants to kill someone, he is homicidal
and needs confinement. If a man drops a bomb on people he
doesn't even see or know, he is doing his duty. And if a man is
afraid he might want to kill someone, he, of course, needs
help or guidance or treatment to prevent a fear from becoming a deed; whereas if a pilot should become horrified at the
thought of what *he* might do, the bombs he might cause to
fall on fellow human beings, he would need that same "treatment" — presumably so that he will get over his hesitations
and "do his duty." Certainly if he starts making a lot of noise
about his fears and his misgivings he will be sent for "evaluation." And, of course, if the pilot never once has such hesitations and qualms, he is "normal" or "patriotic" or a "good
soldier" or whatever.

Such ironies and vexing discrepancies ought to make us all
at the very least aware that psychiatric judgments about what
is or is not "appropriate" are not rendered in some scientific
vacuum, but are made at a particular moment of history and
in a given society by men who are distinctly part of that society — namely, its upper middle class.

The southern youth who was just quoted knew in his bones
what it takes some of us longer to realize, if indeed we ever
do, no matter how thoroughly we analyze ourselves — that
the assumptions we make about a person's social and political
behavior have to do with the kinds of lives we ourselves live,
and that the doctor in that mental hospital was nothing less
than a willing and indeed eager representative of a particular
kind of entrenched power, which wanted those protesting its
authority discredited and knocked out of commission, one way
or another. In the distant past, but also in recent times, dis-
senters have been banished to prison or sent to their death (or

sent to America!) for their noisy, unorthodox, unsettling and provocative words and acts. Many of us no doubt find such out-and-out repression distasteful, but we are not beyond our own ability to call a person we oppose only thinly disguised names, to insult him and at the same time ignore the thrust of his declared purposes, his stated intentions, his deeds — which surely ought to be open for discussion on their own merits, rather than the merits of one or another person's psychiatric status. We dismiss, belittle, and run down those we disagree with *substantively* by doing them in *personally.*

For example, in response to a questionnaire put out by a magazine, a substantial number of American psychiatrists were willing just a few years ago to signify that yes, Barry Goldwater is not "psychologically fit" to be President of the United States. Later, we heard that George Wallace might also be "neurotic" and "unstable." I would prefer to have as my friend Barry Goldwater to Lyndon Johnson. Mr. Goldwater is more open as a person, less self-centered, and less given to pettiness or meanness — but I voted for Mr. Johnson because in 1964 his position on all sorts of issues seemed far wiser to me than Mr. Goldwater's. In 1964, to a supporter of Lyndon Johnson, his moodiness, his arrogance, his secretiveness seemed the foibles of a great, warmhearted humanitarian, just as to Richard Nixon's supporters today, his aloofness, his outbursts of anger when things have not gone as he likes are the way he chooses to deal with a difficult job, or the way he responds to outrageous provocations. Put differently, psychological evaluations inevitably are influenced by our disposition to like or dislike a person or his views; and that holds for psychiatrists, too — who can misuse their own professional language and applaud or condemn deeds or individuals with words like "egosyntonic" (which means "good") and "pre-oedipal" (which means "bad").

Then there are today's students and demonstrators. What

we don't hear about them! They are "products of permissive child-rearing practices." They are sons of self-made men who abhor the materialism of their fathers, and more than that, are struggling with some version of an "oedipal conflict." They are "immature." They have "poor ego controls." They are not in touch with "reality." They are "passive-aggressive." They are "exhibitionistic" or plagued by "omnipotent fantasies." They are "acting out" one or another "problem." Their words and thoughts and actions show them "paranoid," even in some cases "psychotic." Nor are those whose serious and carefully thought out ideas happen to capture the interest of the young immune from that kind of comment. The distinguished British psychoanalyst R. D. Laing, whose many books and papers require patient study, whose ideas are bold and challenging and singularly free of the banal and the pompous, is called a host of psychiatric names and ignored in all too many centers of psychiatric and psychoanalytic training. The well-known American psychiatrist Thomas Szasz, whose books constantly demand from his colleagues a willingness to look at the way unconventional people are commonly enough labeled "mentally ill" and locked up permanently, is himself called "paranoid" or possessed of a "one-track mind" or an "obsession" — as if men like Pasteur or Freud were not grandly preoccupied and maybe even "obsessed."

Needless to say, there are no limits to the abuses that can be perpetrated in the name of any ideological system. In the Soviet Union social critics and writers and scientists are regularly carted off to psychiatric hospitals, where they are called various high-sounding names and kept locked up. Here things are by no means as blatant and absurd, but with shrill rhetoric becoming almost our daily fare, it is hard to imagine any line of argument as off-limits today. And if young people or political activists are to be condemned for their "personality problems" rather than listened to (and thoroughly ap-

plauded or severely criticized) for the substance of what they
propose or advocate, then surely we ought to turn the tables
and ask some questions about other people — in order to end
once and for all a silly and insulting way of dealing with
issues.

What are we to say, for instance, about the "early childhood" or "mental state" of political leaders or business
leaders or labor leaders who lie or cheat or order thousands to
go off to fight and kill? What kind of "psychological conflict"
enables a man to be an agent of the Central Intelligence
Agency, or a pilot who drops napalm bombs, or a congressman who wants to use atomic and hydrogen bombs so that a
nation will be "turned into a parking lot"? What kind of
"oedipal conflict" enables so many people to demonstrate
their obvious lack of real concern for millions of poor Americans — out of work, ailing, hungry? Do we inquire about the
psychological "factors" that enable a man to be hard-driving,
competitive, on the rise, always on the rise, often over the
backs of everyone else around? Do we question the "unconscious reasons" so many of us "adjust" to the injustice around
us, become indifferent, become caught up in what is called a
"rat race" or a "grind" even by those utterly uninterested in
social change or protest? Moreover, if students are out to kill
their "parent surrogates," what indeed about our desire as
grown-ups to squelch the young, subtly and not so subtly degrade them, be rid of them — because they inspire envy in us;
because they confront us with all the chances we forsook, all
the opportunities we have lost, all the tricks and evasions and
compromises and duplicities we have long since *rationalized*
or *repressed* or *projected?*

So it goes, and so do we all suffer, I believe. Step by step we
become the victims of various kinds of slander and invective,
some obvious, some indirect and clothed in pietistic, sancti-
monious language or in the jargon of the social sciences or

psychiatry. Words like "fascist" and "elitist" are hurled indiscriminately and viciously at anyone and everyone, and of
course "Communists" crop up everywhere in the minds of
some. And if those more political modes of assault don't work,
the rest of us, more "moderate" and maybe just as desperate
and confused, can always dispense with a bothersome individual or political question by raising our eyebrows and calling
into question a person's "psychodynamics" or damning an entire group with some psychological or sociological generaliza-
tion. Why bother, after all, to remind ourselves that every
single human being has "problems," struggles with love and
hate and envy and fear and all the rest? Why bother to ask
whose "law" and *whose* "order" are being assaulted, and for
what *purpose?* Why bother asking ourselves what *in fact* so
many youths, from so many different backgrounds and regions, are actually saying and asking of us? And finally, why
trouble ourselves by asking how it has come about that we
have lost faith in our ethical convictions, and so have to attack
or defend people and entire political movements by resorting
to words and concepts originally meant only to help doctors
clarify for themselves the sorrow and pain felt by particular
patients?

Atlantic, 1970

PART THREE

Changes

I wrote most of this section in 1971. Much of "A Black Civil Rights Worker" was first published in *Harvard Today* (1971), and was originally delivered, in slightly different form (on December 16, 1970), as the William James Lecture on Religious Experience at the Harvard Divinity School. The title of the lecture was "Psychological Sanctity and Social Protest." "The Weather of the Years" was previously published in *Daedalus;* the American Academy of Arts and Sciences sponsored a series of discussions on adolescence, with an emphasis on *early* adolescence — that is, ages twelve to sixteen — and eventually a special issue of the Academy's journal was given over to the papers those discussions prompted. All the rest of "Changes" was written in middle 1971 especially for the present book. As the reader will see, I try to describe what has happened to some of the black and white children and youth I once described in various articles, some of which are reprinted here in Part Two, and also described at greater length in the first volume of *Children of Crisis,* which was written in 1965 and 1966. And finally, one of the young blacks I write about in "The Weather of the Years" has repeatedly asked me whether I have kept track of the changes in *me.* I try to do so here, even as I say good-bye, in a way, to a whole range of the South's black and white youths and men and women I have known for a good long time.

The Weather of the Years

Late November in New Orleans the rain comes down hard. With it a chill can challenge the city's sense of itself as deeply southern and a gateway to Latin America. For the poor those damp, cold days are particularly difficult; they have to be fought off, and to do so requires money that is scarce indeed. So, children go to school shivering or even wet, because they haven't good sweaters, and often enough lack a raincoat; and families hover around old and dangerous gas burners, the only source of heat for many who live in the port city's black slums.

In the autumn of 1960, when four black children, each of them six years old, prepared themselves for the ordeal of initiating school desegregation in New Orleans, the weather (of all things) was very much on their minds — just as the weather was on their minds ten autumns later in 1970. Here is what one little girl said to me in November of 1960: "It's bad. It's real bad — the weather. I'm afraid that when I get to the school those white kids will have sweaters and they'll have raincoats and they'll have umbrellas — and I'll be wet through and through. My daddy said I should pray for rain, the more the better, because then people won't leave their homes to cause trouble for us outside the school, but I told him that I'd rather have the people shouting at me with the sun out and no clouds than no one around except the rain. When you go inside the building, you close the door on the bad people and all their words. But if you're soaking wet and your bones are shaking from the cold, you might as well not go to school, because all day you're trying to warm up and dry out, and the teacher won't look on you as very nice."

For a while the girl had no worries, at least none supplied by "those white kids." The school she attended was almost totally boycotted, and every day her main problem was to get by mobs — angry, noisy, threatening mobs. With the help of federal marshals the mobs did not achieve their often stated purpose: "to keep that little nigger girl out of our schools." The girl appeared every morning; men and women were waiting to shout obscenities every morning; the girl emerged every afternoon and left for home — and they were back, shouting and screaming. In the words of one of the federal marshals: "It's a regular game we have here between the little child and these so-called grown-ups. They just have to see her and swear their hearts out at her. And I tell you, I don't believe she lets them bother her much. She worries about her teacher and how sad the other teachers must be, because the white kids aren't coming to school. But when it's raining and there's no one there to heckle her and taunt her and scream at her, she looks as if she almost misses them. I guess you get used to almost anything, isn't that right?"

The little girl did indeed get used to anything. She got used to rudeness and meanness and loneliness. She got used to uncertainty and a kind of lingering sadness she could sometimes shake off — only to find it return unexpectedly. And yes, she got used to being inward. Under constant stress, she stood fast and went to school and learned and moved along from grade to grade, but all along she wondered about things to herself, asked herself questions, became her own rather severe task-master. I have already described how she (and others like her) managed the immediate months of school desegregation in the South — at a time when the region was jittery and sullen and all too openly violent.[1] Now I would like to describe how those same young children have grown up, have lived through the 1960's; and in doing so become sixteen and seventeen, become what one young lady I have known these last ten years calls "worldly."

Here she is at age fourteen using that word, and contrasting herself "no longer a child" and herself years before, when she and her struggle prompted from a federal marshal the remarks I have just quoted: "I'm coming to be a grown woman, I guess. It's hard to know when you're all grown and when you've still got some growing to do. My grandmother tells me there's no one alive who doesn't have growing to do. She says I've been wise for a long time — because of what I went through. She says I should go on up to Washington, D.C., and talk to those people who run our government. But I don't know what I'd say. I don't feel any wiser than anyone else. I feel I know a lot about white people that some of my friends don't know; but I'm a girl of fourteen, and we're all just beginning to find out about the world, that's what I think — so I'm as worldly as the others, but no more. Every once in a while one of them will be just like my grandmother; she'll tell me I know everything, because I had my picture on television and in the newspaper and I got all those letters and I've been with the whites for so long, and she'll keep on talking — until I tell her to stop, please, and let me speak. Then I remind her that I was a little girl like her, and there was just so much I could learn. In the last few years, I'd say since I was ten or eleven, I've been learning things I never knew before.

---

[1] In *Children of Crisis I: A Study of Courage and Fear*, Atlantic–Little, Brown, 1967.

I'm no longer a child now. I know what's going on in the world, and sometimes I think this to myself: If I ever knew what I know now about people back when I was a little girl and going past those mobs outside the school — well, I would have told those people a few things, yes, I would have given them something to go home and think about, just like they gave me a lot to get upset about."

What has she been learning these recent years? How is one to describe the particular way she has slowly been growing up, and at the same time indicate the things she shares with others in New Orleans, in Louisiana, in the South and in the United States? And is there any point in getting schematic about her life? Is there something all that different about the character of her mind now, in 1971, when she is going on seventeen, something that contrasts with her manner of thinking five years ago or ten years ago? I again turn to her. I turn to her at fifteen, in late 1969: "In some ways I don't feel much different now than I did when you first started visiting us. I'm the same me is what I'm trying to say. Of course, I'm older. I'd be a fool if I didn't say that! But I'll get to talking with my grandmother, and we both agree that if you stop and look around, you will see that a lot of time the world doesn't change as much as you think. Because you've added ten years on to your life and you've seen a lot happen doesn't mean you've come into a different world. I will say this, though: I'm always wondering what will happen next. I mean, I'm not bored. Well, I'm not *often* bored. Sometimes I just sit and listen to my records and they don't do anything to me, they don't register. That's when I know I'm bored. Another time is when I watch the news on TV, or look at a newspaper. It looks to me as if there are good things happening in the world — but the bad side is always waiting, ready to get even and set us back. We've lost Dr. King and we've lost Robert Kennedy. My grandmother keeps on saying they were so

young, and it was terrible — but the minister told us Jesus
Christ was even younger when they killed Him, so I guess you
have to expect the worst all the time, even when it does look
good, the world you're a part of.

"I'm sure I'd be thinking a lot different now if I wasn't
living in the city here, but was over in Mississippi, living with
my cousins. As bad as it is for us, it's worse for them. I don't
think they minded when they were smaller, but they're getting big, growing up, like I am — and they tell me there's
nothing for them to do, there's nothing ahead of them. I'll ask
them why they don't pack up and come on down to New Orleans. They'll glare and glare — as if to tell me they know I'm
trying to be smart, but instead I'm just fresh and sassy. Then
I'll know I've said the wrong thing. Then I'll know I haven't
stopped and thought about *them*. My grandmother says a person can't just up and leave, not unless she wants to or she has
to. My cousins want to and they have to, but even so they're
scared and they think it's bad all over, so they stay put. They
tell me I'm headed for trouble, they're sure of it, because I
have 'big notions,' that's what they say. I tell them that all I
want is to finish high school and meet a man who is good and
God-fearing, and then marry him and have a girl and a boy —
no more than those two children. I tell them I'd like to live
free — yes, that's how I say it. And I don't have to explain
myself; a black woman who talks about 'living free' has only
one subject on her mind: the white people. You can't grow
up and be black and not have the whites on your mind. I
know I'm special. I know I've been with them all these years
— and you know my friends tell me I've been whitewashed.
But I do believe, I honestly do, that those friends of mine are
more under the spell of them, under a white spell, than I am.
I'll tell you why. I've learned all about the white people. I've
seen them. I've heard them. I've talked with them. I've listened to them talking about me. By now I've become tired of

them — tired of thinking about them and tired of talking about them. All I want is to be myself and think of my own life. Do you know, the black person has a hard time growing up and finding herself, because she can't shake them off — all those white girls and those white boys, and all the grown-up whites who won't stop running everyone's life, even if she's a black girl like me.

"I'm no girl anymore. I have to say that. To a white man, we're all girls. I have two white friends, white girls, who have admitted to me it's true: we're *never* looked on as grown-ups by a lot of white people, and not only those who live in the South, I'm sure of that. Some kids can be sure they're grown up; I'm speaking of white kids. If you're black and live in the state of Louisiana you can't be sure everyone is going to look upon you as grown if you're seventy, never mind seventeen or fifteen. Sure, the country is changing. Even Louisiana is changing. I've been with whites in every grade. They don't shout at me anymore. They don't boycott me. They leave me alone. I think they're glad to leave me alone. I heard one say the other day (she was walking ahead of me and she didn't see me behind her) that we never grow up, not really, because we don't have the intelligence to grow up. I almost ran up to her. I almost made some trouble. But I have enough intelligence to know there's no point in trying to talk with a little child like that in the corridor of a high school. She's worrying about us; she thinks we'll never be men and women. Maybe we won't. Maybe you're not really a man or a woman until you can look at yourself in the mirror and feel there's no one owning your life. But I believe a white girl who can't do any better than call black people *children* is a baby herself. She's not a child, mind you. She's not up to my little sister in intelligence. She's a baby; she's one or two, and she gets nervous when she sees a new face.

"Once my grandmother saw my sister start crying; she was

about a year old, I believe, maybe less, and a stranger came and tried to be nice to her. Well, she got scared. She cried. She stared for a second, and tried to smile, but she couldn't, so she burst out into a long, long cry for herself. I tried to do everything to stop her. I talked to her and I sang to her; but all she wanted was to go away. She didn't want to see any strange faces in front of her. She wanted to be with us, and with no one else. She was a baby, that's what. My grandmother came over and told me that; she said a baby is afraid of everyone except the few people she knows, so the only thing you can do is indulge her, that's right. 'Someday she'll grow up,' that's what I can remember my grandmother saying. And you know, for a second in school I wanted to go up to that white girl, that white child, that white baby she is, and tell her that I'm praying for her, yes I am; I'm praying that she won't forever be a little baby — all dressed up as a big girl, a woman I guess we're becoming these days, but still a baby in her head.

"Don't ask me what it takes to become all grown up. I'm halfway there; that's what my grandmother says, and I think she's right. I asked her when she got all the way there — and she said no one ever does. I guess I didn't follow her, because my face looked puzzled, and she said I shouldn't be a child, and I asked her what I was thinking that was wrong, and she said that a child is someone who thinks she's going to stop being a child one of these days. I scratched my head and said I couldn't see what that meant. My grandmother didn't explain herself. She just told me I was twelve, going on thirteen, and when I was seventy I'd be six going on seven and twelve going on thirteen and twenty going on twenty-one, because she's found out it happens that way in life.

"I'm old enough now to understand more and more of the advice I heard when I was small from my grandmother. I think you're no longer a child when you catch yourself thinking back. I used to think I'd be all grown up when I'd have a million things to anticipate as around the corner. I used to think the day would come when I couldn't hardly keep up with all the plans I'd be making. But now I'll catch myself wondering how I ever got by those people in front of the school, and I'll pinch myself and say I never *did* get by them, it was only a dream. But it wasn't a dream, I know. If you were to ask me whether I'd go through the same thing over again, now that I've had almost ten years to think about it, I'd say yes; I'd say I can't imagine what I'd be like if I hadn't gone past that crowd (that mob, the marshals always called them) every day. And I can't imagine who I'd be if I hadn't stayed and stayed and stayed, until I saw one white girl and then another one come back to school, and after a while even sit near me in the classroom. 'Don't try to think of some other life you might have had'; that was my daddy's advice before he died. My grandmother told me she'd whispered that in his ears when he was a little boy, and he was always asking her why he couldn't be rich and white and up in some city like Chicago. I learned what the white people are like when I was six years old, so I never wanted to be white. I wouldn't mind being rich, but I'd never want to go to Chicago. I'm from the South, and I hope to stay right here all my life. Now that I'm in high school I've been doing some thinking about where I'd like to live. I've thought of other cities, like in Florida or up in Atlanta. But I think I'll stay here. It depends on the man I meet and marry, of course. But maybe he'll listen to me as much as I listen to him. Like my grandmother says, women aren't the niggers they used to be!

"I'd like to be able to understand the world like my grandmother does — that's my chief ambition. Then I could talk to my children and my grandchildren the way she does. I used to think that when I got to high school I'd be like my grandmother — I'd be smart and I'd know what to think and what to say, no matter how tough the trouble I was in. But you can't race ahead of yourself. You can only keep up with yourself, if you keep at it. And it's hard, not falling behind. If you don't watch out you're losing ground in your schoolwork and you're slow about what to wear and what to say and what records to buy and what to watch on television. There was a time when I'd only look forward to lunch or supper after I had breakfast; now I'm worrying about what I'll wear when I graduate from high school, and that's two or three years from now. And by then they may have new styles, so there's no percentage in figuring out what you'll be wearing that far ahead.

"My boyfriend says I should be wise about all that — the newest clothes, the best food to eat if you don't want to get fat. He thinks the white folks know everything, and they taught what they know to me. I tell him he's a child. Fred, I say, when you were five or six you probably thought your own parents knew everything; now you think it's the white man who is so clever. You're twice wrong, I tell him. He should grow up and know there's more to this world than anyone can figure out, no matter how old he is, or how white. But I do believe you learn new things each and every year, and that's what growing up is all about."

As I go over all I have heard her say and try to summarize something called her "psychological development" I keep on wondering whether the rather unusual experiences she went through as a young child may have caused her to be especially thoughtful and almost uncannily ironic and detached. All the insults and near-disasters, all the fear and doubt she knew, all the special attention she received from her own community, may have fostered in her mind a kind of precocious resignation such as philosophers struggle to obtain and demonstrate to others — or so I sometimes think. Yet she has never let me get away with that line of reasoning. She sees herself as a rather "ordinary teen-ager." She sees herself as thirteen or fourteen or fifteen. She sees herself as black, as a resident of New Orleans, as a Southerner who lives in Louisiana. She reminds herself from time to time that she is more and more a woman, and is becoming a woman at a moment in history when women all over the United States are breaking down barriers, even as she began doing likewise in late 1960. And there is more: She calls herself "fortunate," and at other times, "lucky"; and she has in mind a whole range of circumstances when she uses those words. She does not go hungry. She is going to graduate from high school. She has some attractive clothes. She owns a record machine and some good music to play when the mood suits her. She has (and has had) the attention of boys she likes.

Not that the young lady comes from a well-to-do family. Be cause she was a pioneer, neighbors and friends have saluted her over the years — and perhaps more than made up for the suffering a bewildered little girl went through day after day for two years, really; by which time a degree of "quiet" (as the girl once put it) if not full-fledged normalcy had settled upon her daily school life. So, no doubt about it, she has been given much, singled out again and again — by grateful neighbors who know well how white men and women singled out the first black children to enter the South's white schools. On the other hand she reminds me again and again that her grandmother has lived a long and hard life, has known extreme poverty and trembled in her own time before whites, perhaps not assembled in front of a school building, but no less desperate and vindictive. And in the face of that life the old lady has more than survived; she has sustained her children and her grandchildren: "She has taught us how to grow up."

By no means does the grandmother constantly figure in her granddaughter's conversation; nor is the young lady I am writing about constantly talking self-consciously about "growing up." We who think and write about "adolescence" can turn the youths we presumably hope to understand into cannon fodder for the theoretical wars we so often wage. And for me it is especially dangerous to quote from a girl at such-and-such an age, then from the same person later — now become a "youth" or a "young lady," as her grandmother refers to her. By selecting this or that remark I make a case of sorts — and run the risk of failing somehow to indicate the breadth and depth of a particular life. Perhaps others should be allowed to speak about the black woman I have been seeing all these years, even as she should be given a chance to reply in kind. For example, a white girl who returned eventually (in 1961) to the boycotted school once had this to say about her black classmate: "I've been at school with her for most of the year now. She's nervous, I believe. She doesn't look at me unless she can't help it. She's not nearly as dirty as my mother told me they are. She's just another girl, only she's colored — and they're different. I don't mind her. There isn't anything we can do: They're here because the federal government in Washington, D.C., has forced them on us. But I play with her sometimes; I do. It's only for a few minutes, and she's all right. She smiles a lot."

Later, years later, the same "girl," now fourteen and in high school, looks both back and ahead: "I remember all that trouble every once in a while; there will be something in the news about Negroes and I listen and think of all we lived through. Then I'll see her in the corridor, and we'll say hello. I don't harbor any bad feelings against her. She's a nice person — quiet and neat. She has good manners. If only all the colored people had the poise she has. I think they mature faster than we do. I read someplace that they do. That's why they're good athletes, and the girls look so grown up. They have a rhythm to them; it's hard to describe — and I don't only mean that they're musical. They seem to move along faster than us down the corridor, and they laugh more easily — some of them. Of course it's like with us, you find all kinds, provided you get to meet enough people. Maybe the day will come, like our minister says, when we all trust one another in this country. But like I've said before, it's only natural that the races stay apart from each other in a lot of ways. I still believe that."

She believes many things. She is also growing up, parting company with her childhood, feeling herself more aware of a future, less tied to the immediate, concrete present of the school and the neighborhood. As a result, she makes comments and observations about an increasing number of people and customs and events, not because she is becoming a social analyst of sorts, but because she too is getting some distance on herself and her life, and yes, on life in general, on time's flow as each of us comes to know it. At nine and ten she would make particular remarks about one or another black child she sat near in class or watched playing in the schoolyard. At thirteen and fourteen she would talk more generally, more philosophically, it can be said, more conceptually — though I hesitate to describe what comes across as natural and unselfconscious with words that straitjacket a rather subtle development, much of it not a matter of phrases used or ideas mobilized, but rather "thoughts that get really felt." I use that last expression because I once heard the white girl just mentioned speak so, and I can't at all improve on her way of putting what she has been going through these recent years: "When you start going to high school you realize that you're really on the way — yes sir. I never thought much about life until now. I never asked myself any important questions. I guess I never really looked around and stopped and considered what was ahead of me. But now I catch myself hearing a song or listening to what a man says on a television program —

and all of a sudden it's *me* who's there, and I have a picture of myself getting married, or I recall something I did five years ago, maybe, and I wonder if my own child will go through the same experience I had.

"With the colored kids I know, I'll bet their children won't look upon us whites with the same amount of fear. For us white people it will be different, too: when we're parents, we won't talk about the colored the same way our parents did, so naturally our children will grow up with different ideas on the subject of race. Who you are depends on where you grow up as much as what your parents believe, don't you think? Our minister said that, and I couldn't help turning his words over and over again in my mind. There are some thoughts that get really felt — you just can't put them out of your head. That's why I think I'll always be a Southerner, even if I meet someone who comes from another part of the country, and he takes me away to live there and not here."

Yes, there is nothing all that surprising or original in her remarks. Like many millions of young adolescents she daydreams about her future and becomes moody, introspective, sentimental, hesitant, then thoroughly sure of herself. Most of all, though, she feels herself emerging from the day-to-day life of childhood; and as she does so she summons her mind to the task of finding for herself a certain coherence. As I have gone back South to talk with her I have watched that coherence develop, heard it revealed now in an aside, now in a full-fledged declaration. That is to say, I have heard her take note of the music she likes, the politics she finds appealing, the reading she does, the hopes she nourishes, the fears she sometimes can't quite (but mostly does manage to) put aside, the hobbies and "interests" she pursues, the food she is "partial to," the clothes she has or wants to have, the television programs she won't under any circumstances miss, the sermon she has heard in church and not by any means forgotten the next day, the nation she is proud to call her own, the region she loves, the state she refers to as "our Louisiana," the city she wishes never to leave, the streets she walks down, the buildings she passes every day, the stores she goes to, the house that is unmistakably hers (however much it strikes an observer as like all the others nearby), the bus she boards, the soldiers she sees walking, the policeman she sees driving by, the firemen who stand outside and smile at her and talk to her — because her uncle is one of them, but also because she is "getting pretty," they tell her, "looking real nice," they declare, "becoming quite a young lady," they comment, "growing up real fast," they observe, "turning into a real, lovely woman," they remind both me and themselves.

What those men take note of does not escape the young lady. She recognizes her growing attractiveness. She dresses in such a way, walks and sits in such a way, touches her hair and moves her bracelet in such a way as to make clear her developing sense of herself as a woman, "a real lovely woman" whom men stare at and no doubt think about in their thoughts and daydreams (their "fantasies" some call them) just as she can "catch sight of" a young man and find herself much later on wondering whether he looks like the man she one day will marry, and, again, quite possibly move with to another city or state. In her few but important words: "A woman takes a man's name and becomes fulfilled by making a home and family for him, wherever the place may be." Nor can the pieties she learns from her parents and at school or at church be dismissed as mere chatter. All sorts of high-sounding notions (her "femininity," her "unconscious attitudes," her "sexual identification," her "role" as a woman) can in a flash come across as not necessarily a great confusing mystery to her — but rather as something settled and lived with, or, as we psychiatrists say, "resolved."

Meanwhile there are her boyfriends, and she is careful to

watch them, even as she is anxious to have them keep an eye
on her. One of her "nice boys," a young man she calls "a great
person," came back to school the same day (in 1961) she did.
At the age of six he described that return like this: "I didn't
even want to go to school, because my daddy told me you
can't learn with the colored all over the school. But they only
brought in three, and now that I'm back there's only one in
the room with the rest of us — the white kids. She's always
looking around at us; I guess she's worried we may not like
her. I don't think she's bad. I'd rather play with my own
friends, though. Sometimes I play with her, and she's good at
running after a ball, as good as the boys are. My daddy says
the colored can run fast.

"They won't stay long with us, I was told that. My uncle
told me it won't be long before we'll be all-white again, because colored kids don't stay in school. I said I don't want to
stay in school, either; we have a better time at the play-
ground, all of the kids do. But when you get bigger there's a
lot of homework to do; I know, because my cousin is in high
school and my aunt and uncle said I won't have to worry: No
colored boys will be on our baseball team or basketball,
either, when I'm fourteen, like my cousin, and in the ninth
grade, like he is. The colored wanted to try and get some of
their people into the high schools, too; but they didn't get
their way, like they did when the judge ordered our school to
let in those girls. One of them told me yesterday that she'd
probably leave school in a year or two, and maybe go back to
Mississippi, if her parents decide to leave New Orleans. She
said her parents are thinking of leaving because they're
scared. She says even now, with no more people shouting at
her, she can't make her brother believe she's doing OK in
school. He thinks she'll get killed. He's afraid she won't live
to grow up. But she says she will grow up, and I hope she
does."

She did grow up, as did he. When he was twelve he was far more comfortable with black children than he once dreamed possible. More of those children had been admitted to the school he attended, and though he never in the elementary grades became very friendly with his black classmates, he did take note of them — indeed, watched them more closely than his parents ever imagined. Just before his thirteenth birthday he took note of the coming milestone in his life, and made some interesting forecasts about his future: "I'll be a teenager next week. My dad reminded me my birthday wasn't just another birthday. He said I have a lot of common sense, and I'll study hard in high school next year. I told him yes, I will. My father wants me to go to college. He never finished high school, because when he was a boy growing up there wasn't any money around, and his father was sick in bed all the time and my dad had to go and get a job. He did everything. He swept floors. He unloaded the ships. He worked for a grocery market. He worked in a hotel, carrying suitcases up to rooms. He was glad to have a job, any kind of job. He says a lot of the jobs he once had, the Negroes now have them. The white people are moving up, and the colored are glad to have jobs. Before they picked cotton over in Mississippi and here in Louisiana. Now they've been coming into New Orleans. One of the colored boys sits in front of me, and he told me he expects to go right through high school, the same as I do. He said he might even be able to go to college. My dad says they are always pushing on us, trying to get everything the white man has — but a lot of them aren't willing to work too hard. Some of them are pretty dumb, but we have some real smart ones in my school. You can't figure them out; they talk different than we do, and they dress different and they bring different food to school. But I think they're people, like us, and the ones I know in school are mostly just trying to better themselves, and there's nothing wrong with that, our minister says.

I hope I can better myself, and I hope the Negro kids do. Mostly they seem a lot older than us, even if they're actually the same age. I can't explain why, but they do."

Three years later, at fifteen years and ten months, he could indeed explain why the black youths he knew "seem a lot older." He could explain to me that blacks are poorer, and are more on their guard, feel rather awkward in the presence of whites, hence become more "quiet" and more "grown up." He could insist that by and large "the races should still be separate," but go on to remind me that "times are changing," and because they are "you can't stand still, you have to go along." What held for his father does not hold for him: "The Negro people are entitled to be left alone. I wish they'd leave us alone, but they won't. So, the way I see it, the only thing to do is what we've gone ahead and done: let them go to school with us and try to be as fair and square with them as you can, but not do them any special favors. A black boy growing up should have every chance I do, but he should live with his own people and try to better them. It's all right for them to be at school with us, but that's as far as it should go. Even my dad says school integration is one thing, but when it comes to socializing, that's another.

"Anyway, the Negro kids of my age have a good time socializing among themselves. Those people, the colored, they are natural-born athletes and natural-born musicians. I believe they're made different from us. I'm on the track team and I play basketball, and I can't keep up with them. We're glad to have a few of them at school with us: They help us out in sports. They can be sharp dressers but they're kooky, you know: They put on wild, wild clothes, and they're always touching one another, bumping into one another, laughing with one another — when they figure we're not watching, when they're in the cafeteria by themselves. Sometimes I wish the white guys could be as loose as they are; my mother says it's because they're like children a lot, so they fool around. But I think they're more relaxed. They can laugh quicker than we can. I think it's easier for them to grow up and become men. For one thing, their bodies don't take the time ours do to get up to our full height, and besides that, a Negro kid who is fifteen or sixteen is probably going to be up against it: whether he studies and stays in school, or he's headed for the unemployed, which is where so many of them are. I'd be scared if I was a Negro.

"Of course, I get to worrying now myself. I hope I'll be able to get a good job one day. I'd like to go to college, but I doubt I will. I'd like to learn a trade. I'd like to be an electrician, I think; maybe a carpenter. It's hard to decide right now. Sometimes I forget about all that stuff — the future, the kind of job I'll have ten years from now, my grades, the summer work I'll be needing. All I want to do is run, or shoot the ball. All I want to do is turn on our hi-fi or watch the tube. Who cares what you'll be doing for work a long time from now! I mean, you've got to care, I know, but there's going to be plenty of time later to be worried sick over the size of your paycheck and the bills. I can go through the week and keep pretty relaxed. I can take each day by itself. That's what you ought to do — the best you can, and it's hard to expect more of yourself. My girl agrees."

His girl: she is his age, in his school; and she lives three blocks away. He has known her "off and on" for a long time, but now he is "really getting to know her" — though there are times when he concludes that "women are a strange bunch, and I don't think they even understand themselves, so how can a man hope to figure them out?" A Methodist, a believing Methodist from a devout Methodist home, he wants to "get close" to his girlfriend, "but only so close." He would not respect a girl who "wants to give in too much." He reads in the newspapers and hears on television that "there's a lot of drugs being used" and that "kids of my age are just going off and having sex, or something pretty close to it." And he needs no sociologist to explain *who* and *why*: "It's a lot of spoiled rich kids. Our minister says we're all lucky around this neighborhood to be sober and without too much money. (Not that my dad would mind having more cash!) If you've got nothing to worry about, if you've got thousands and thousands of dollars, then you take drugs and you lose your good judgment about what's right and what's wrong. I hear the poor are the same way, especially the Negro people. They've just given up. They don't have any ambition for themselves. That's a bad state to let yourself get in — not thinking of your future. I can't see how a fellow can let it happen. I don't think a day passes that I don't catch myself daydreaming: I picture the car I'll be driving a few years from now; or I'll picture myself in the army, or maybe the air force. I wouldn't mind flying a plane, I'll tell you — that would be a job for life. But they don't need too many pilots now, and I think you have to have a college degree. Besides, I like to work with my hands. I like to build things. I've built myself a small workshop, a chair and bench, so I can build other things. I never buy my kid brothers presents. I make them a toy boat or a small car, you know, with wooden wheels. I built them a small ladder, so they can climb up to the window and crawl into the house. I built a doghouse for us. I love our dog as much as anyone in this world. She's only a mongrel, but she won't let go of me. She's the most reliable, dependable one in the world — I was going to say the most dependable *person!* I'll get into a tiff with my girl — over nothing, nothing at all — and I'll think to myself I'd like to go get my mutt and take a walk and not hear all that dreamy talk, and big ideas, lots of big ideas. Women are full of big ideas — but it's the men who work and work and bring in the hard cash. You know, there can be a day when I agree with what my dad says: Men are the niggers of this world; it's up to them to be slaves, so the woman can go and buy her earrings and her fancy shoes, and always be worrying about how her hair is, her coiffure, you know. But I guess you want them looking pretty for you."

He goes on to observe what he says applies to blacks as well as whites; his black classmates are in that respect no different — the young men look for work after school or for summer jobs, and their girlfriends talk about "dream houses" and dresses and "how they look, all dolled up." And he is right, some of his black classmates talk very much like he does; and let it be known how serious they are or will be, how tough it will be for them to keep ahead of bill collectors, and not least, the appetites of their girlfriends, some of whom may be their wives in a not too distant span of time. Yet, the black youths feel by and large more hard-pressed, less confident about getting and keeping jobs; and at the same time more or less aware that the girls, the young women they think of as frivolous and self-centered, may well have better luck at finding work than their "men-folks." Consequently there are differences between the way black and white boys come to think of themselves as they "turn the corner and get going on the bigtime stretch," which was the way one black boy of eleven described for me the beginning of his manhood.

In fact, he had demonstrated himself to be a rather impressive young man two years before, at the age of nine, when he entered an all-white elementary school in New Orleans against substantial resistance — though not of the hysterical and violent kind the city had experienced several years earlier. "I'm one of thirteen in the school," he told me in 1964. "I'm doing okay. Yes, I am. We stick together. So long as we can spot each other one or two times a day, we're all in good shape. But if I had to be the only one in this school, with all the whites there — well, I'd still be willing to go. We've got to fight for our rights. I don't want to grow up and be like my

uncle. He says he's afraid to look at white people. He says
they're the devil, and they can snap their fingers and that's
the end of you. It's not just because he drinks — that's not
why he's so scared and talks like he does about the white man.
He's never even dared look at himself in the mirror, never
mind look at the white man; that's what I think. I hope that
when I'm a man I'm really a man. I hope I don't sit around
waiting for some bossman to smile down on me and pat me on
the head — or kick me in the pants. Some other kids, my own
cousins — they're too good: They say white people don't
mean us harm, and we should be nice to them, and they'll be
nice to us. I laugh out loud when I hear them talking like
that. They ask me why I go to the white school if I'm so
against the white man, and I tell them that I want to learn all
I can, and I want to see what they're like, kids who will be
wanting to boss us around in a few years when they're bigger.
Then maybe I'll be wise enough about them to fool them;
they've been tricking us ever since they brought us over here,
and it's about time we learned to get even with them. My big
brother says he wishes he had the chance; he wishes he could
have gone to school with whites. If he'd gone, he thinks he'd
be better off today. He'd be up to the whites. He'd know their
number. I hope in a few years I won't be sitting around feeling regrets, like he does now. I hope I'll be in the ring, fighting it out with the Man. Our minister always says life is a
boxing match, and he's right."

In 1970 he was fifteen and as tough as ever, though somewhat more philosophical. He still had no great love for white
people, but he had had ample time to become acquainted
with them and see their failings, their limitations, their blind
spots. They appeared less threatening, more approachable —
maybe because American society itself had changed in the
intervening six years, maybe because he had come to know
certain white children as individuals, and maybe because (in

addition) he himself was growing up to be a particularly
strong-minded and able man who could increasingly appreciate his own worth, and who would not easily be intimidated
by anyone, regardless of race. I asked him that year what he
saw ahead for himself and he replied by first looking back: "I
have to stop and think every once in a while, and when I do I
catch myself remembering the first few days — when I came
to that school and suddenly found myself surrounded by
white kids. I was scared, I guess. I didn't feel scared then, but
as I think back to those days, I was. The weather is changing
you know; I realize that now. There's a different climate now
between the races. The white people have to watch their step,
just like we've always had to watch our step. It used to be the
sun always shined on them, and it was raining on us. Now
we've got some of the sun and they have some rain. That's
what I believe. So far as I'm concerned, I'm pretty hopeful.
When I was a kid I used to fear growing up. I'd look at my big
brother and my uncle, and I'd think of how my daddy died —
in jail, because a white man hit him and then called the police and got them to arrest my daddy, and not the white man
— and I'd get low, real low. I'd think to myself: There's no
good life ahead for a colored boy like you.

"But I'm not a colored boy. I'm a black man. Not all my
people really grow up to be black men and black women. A
lot of us are still colored; we're still niggers, or if we have a
little money but no respect for ourselves, we're Negroes. To
be black you have to feel you're going to get somewhere, and
no one's going to stop you, no sir. A while back I used to have
a dream, a nightmare, that there was a tornado coming up,
like the kind that killed my granddaddy. I would be standing
there, a little colored boy, I guess, and soon I'd be gone. I'd
wake up thinking I was dead and gone, and expecting to see
my granddaddy who is in his grave, near where the tornado
killed him. I don't have the dream anymore. After studying

in school and playing basketball and studying some more and working and trying to hold on to my girl — well, no wonder I fall into bed and the next thing I know it's morning, and I've never had a thing to dream about. If I did dream I think there'd be no tornadoes. Since I've gotten older I believe I've become more optimistic: I think I'll be able to do all right. I think the weather ahead will be pretty good. Actually, the weather has been getting better and better the last few years, and I guess I picked the right time to be born and to grow up."

He elaborates. He talks about his prospects — the work he'd like to do (law or engineering), the kind of life he'd like to live — "comfortable but not spoiled-comfortable." He also talks about his fellow-man. Like others of his age from Louisiana I have talked with these past years (of both races) he can be at once cool, calculating, self-centered — and open, idealistic, compassionate and impressively dedicated. I have learned to respect the imagery he uses. When he talks about weather he talks about himself; he lets me know that he once felt afraid and vulnerable, but now feels more confident, less dependent, less at the mercy of life's arbitrary side, more intact and self-sufficient. The outside world does not threaten him as much as it once did; he is growing up, feeling his developing competence as a student, an athlete, a man. He has borne up against certain difficult challenges, survived his own anger and bitterness as well as his doubts and misgivings, and all in all weathered a time in this nation's history as well as a "period" in his own life.

Sometimes when I listen to the young men and women I have quoted in this essay I find myself taking note of the troubles they have, the contradictions within themselves (not to mention within our society) they struggle with, the inconsistencies and ambiguities they try to cover over one way or another. Yet, the more time I have spent with these youths, the less troubled they have struck me as being. Perhaps one can only know about a life by staying with the particular person in question long enough to get a sense of his or her history. What seems like a pathological moment out of a *case*-history can often enough be revealed (only in time, though) as part of someone's *life*-history — and maybe a necessary and valuable part, too. So, in a way, I have in the past decade been growing up myself — becoming a little less apprehensive about the various "things" I see and hear. I do not mean to whistle in the dark, or blindly dismiss the South's still very serious racial situation as "solved"; but I think the decade and more I spent with black and white children like those from Louisiana described here has been an important period of time for them as individuals as well as for the region, not to mention all the United States. The South has changed enormously and for the better, even as these youths who have just spoken have also changed. And who can separate (except those theory-minded ones who are determined to do so) the growth of a country from the growth of individuals like these young men and young women?

Again and again I hear the Louisiana children and youths I visit talk about their particular experiences as members of particular families; but I also hear them talk as Southerners, black or white Southerners, and Southerners who were six in 1960 (not 1940 or 1950) and sixteen in 1970 (not 1950 or 1960). Put differently, I hear them express the fears and hates and aspirations which their parents, as Southerners, are heir to — the latent populism of the region, the racism in the region, the passivity and obsequiousness characteristic of blacks some call Uncle Toms, the meanness and narrowness characteristic of whites some call red-necks. True, such youths have been "special," have been pioneers of sorts. They have led their race into white schools or been the first generation of whites to study with black children. Yet, they have also been thoroughly "ordinary" or "normal"; they have carried on over the years, fought with their mothers and fathers, brothers and sisters, friends and acquaintances — and also felt drawn to, close to those same people. They have "held the torch" of their people (the way one black youth of fifteen put it) or they have "helped move the South along to a better day" (the way a white youth the same age put it). I suppose, if I had to tidy it all up, collect my thoughts and put them into a sentence or two, I would say that I have found myself in 1971 looking back at the way certain young Americans have (in the last third of the twentieth century) managed to weather some important years in their lives and in the life of their region and their country. Especially in recent years, especially since 1965 or 1966 (after school desegregation began in New Orleans and Atlanta, after the Mississippi Summer Project took place, after Dr. King's efforts in Birmingham and Selma had their effect), the youths I have been privileged to know in states like Louisiana and Georgia have found it possible to have new ideas, new assumptions, new expectations. And how lucky for them and all of us that such was the case just as they were growing up, becoming men, becoming women, feeling suddenly stronger, more themselves and less children of their parents, more weathered as individuals as well as participants in the South's, in America's coming of age.

Daedalus, 1971

A Black Civil Rights Worker

The South has changed because federal laws have compelled change — as in the case of school desegregation. But the South has also changed because a tough breed of youthful activists have year after year taken on all sorts of "powers and principalities." Here, for instance, are year-by-year observations of a civil rights worker who has worked as an "organizer" in a community since 1962. He happens to be black and he happens to be working in the rural South, but I can vouch for the fact that the white youths I have come to know in the South and in Appalachia go through some of the "changes" or sequences of feeling and attitude his remarks indicate. Obviously these remarks are excerpted from much longer recorded conversations.

1962

"I'm here just for a few days. I mean, there's so much time a person can give. I have school to worry about. I want to graduate, and go on to law school. But I couldn't *not* come here. It's about time the Negroes of the South stood up and said: enough, enough of second-class citizenship, enough of

no voting and enough of segregation and enough of the treatment we get in this so-called democracy. Of course you can't
let your hopes go too high. You can't bet your life on what a
sit-in will do, or a protest march. You do all you can, then go
back to your regular life. That's how I see it. I've tried to
reason with myself. I've tried to figure out what is right to do.
You have to be practical. You have to remember that it takes
a lot of time to change things. Rome wasn't built in a day.
The South won't just suddenly be converted to a new way of
life. But we have to push things along — and that's why I'm
here."

1963

"I never thought I'd stay on so long — doing this kind of
work. I wonder when I'll go back to college. I wonder when
I'll become tired of organizing and tired of fighting all the
apathy and inertia in the Negro community. It's bad enough
knowing how dishonest white people are — only to find out
your own people are exploited by Negro undertakers and
Negro lawyers and Negro businessmen and Negro schoolteachers. They're the worst, our schoolteachers. They work
for the segregationist state governments, and they teach our
children to hate themselves, be ashamed of themselves —
apologize all the time for everything, for being alive! What
made me stay here and work was anger; that's right, anger. I
saw how corrupt the leaders of the Negro community are. I
always knew that whites lie to themselves and exploit us and
get self-righteous when they have to face the truth — that
they're active bigots or unwilling to take a stand against the
bigotry that American institutions breed and perpetuate.
(Why *should* they take a stand? Why *should* they stick out
their necks and risk trouble for *us?*) But when I saw Negroes
teaching Negro children to think little of themselves, and Negroes lying to other Negroes, and to themselves — that was

too much. Yes, you might say I stayed for negative reasons, though I also stayed because I have grown more and more attached to the people here. I like them. I love them. Oh, I hate them, too — a lot of the time I do. They drive me up the wall. They seem so indifferent to their own fate — until I stop and realize how brutal the police are and always have been, and how poor and vulnerable the Negro farm workers are, at the mercy of every bossman's whim, every sheriff's mood, every trigger-happy policeman's Ku Klux Klan mentality. I sound bitter, I know. I'm so bitter some days I don't want to go out and start talking with anyone. I have enough trouble keeping my anger inside myself. Hold your tongue, my mother used to say — and I'm sure learning."

1964 — at the end of the Mississippi Summer Project

"We're getting someplace, but there's so much to do. I'm going back to school, at least to finish my college education. I may come back here. I may not. I don't know. I need time to think. I need to get away from here. If I'm going to come back and stay, then I've got to get away for a while and stop and look into myself, you might say. I've turned into an introvert, or something like that, during the last two years. You can't do this kind of work and not ask yourself all kinds of questions. What is life all about? What is a person supposed to do — challenge the status quo or submit to it? How much can you take — of fear and danger and the threats we get every day? I ask myself questions all the time now — and they're not multiple choice questions. I can't come up with any answers at all some of the time. I'm mixed up — not in my mind, but about life. Maybe you shouldn't think too much. Maybe it's dangerous. Maybe the best thing to do is go along and live as comfortably as you can — with just enough political involvement to soothe your conscience, but not enough activity to get you in trouble and cause you to jeopardize yourself, take real risks — I mean risks that shake up your whole way of living."

1966

"I'm here, and I hope I can stay here. I don't know. I can't be sure. I can only try. I can only hope I've got the strength. Every day I pray — I guess to God. Who *can* you pray to? I was brought up to pray. My mother prays all the time. My dad does. But when I was sixteen or seventeen I stopped. I saw how they fooled themselves all the time with those promises of Heaven and God's presence and all the rest. There they were, being pushed all the time by a foreman, and getting practically no money for the privilege of raising crops for the white man — and they believed God wants it this way, and they're lucky to suffer, to be poor and have no rights, because they'll get into Heaven later on. How can you believe that in the sixties, once you're in college and able to start thinking for yourself? Well, I don't, not now any more than I did a few years ago. But I do pray. I pray to God that He see His brothers here, His sons and daughters here. They're suffering like He did, like His Son did. They are the poor and the meek — but they're fed up underneath, I'll tell you. Behind those obliging smiles is dynamite; it's taken me years to find that out. One, an old lady, who prays hard and long every morning instead of having breakfast — because there isn't any — asked me if I thought Jesus Christ ever wanted to curse at His enemies, and strike them down. I didn't know what to say. I told her that He wasn't an angry man; He was a forgiving man. But she was too smart for me — that ignorant, illiterate woman. She said I was wrong. She said that Jesus got angry at the priests and the big people, and the rich, important people, all of them who were out to hurt Him and deny Him and kill Him. She said He was unpopular and He was called a lot of bad things, and He didn't like it one bit, and at the end He wasn't even sure it was all worth it, His sacrifice, except that He knew it was, despite His doubts."

1968

"I'm still here. One day I think I might never leave; the next day I'm ready to say good-bye and take off. I go on my rounds. I talk with the families. I work at our co-op. I drive people to the one doctor we trust in the county. I teach the children in the evening — after they've wasted a whole day at school! It's slow work. I'm often not sure what I'm doing. I'm often not sure where I'm going. I get tired. I get depressed. I lose all my confidence and my nerve. I feel everything is hopeless. I wonder what I'm doing. I wonder what anyone could do. I toss and turn at night. I can't sleep. I get a head- ache. I'll be in bad shape, man, real bad shape. Then all of a sudden I feel better. I'm not hating everybody so much. I'm more easygoing with people. I can work for others — and not resent them afterwards for not doing everything I think they should do. I can feel real close to the families I visit — they're all my people, my family, and I'm one of them. I guess we have to live as best we can, and do all we can to live better. I guess we have to fight, but not become haters. I guess we have to have faith — in each other and in what is right, what has to be done."

1970

"Come around in 1980 — and I *think* I'll still be here. That's how I feel today. Tomorrow I may pack my bags and leave, but if I do it won't be because I want to, it'll be because I've failed, and I've come to realize I've failed. For me each day is hard and tough: I'm tempted to throw in the towel, but I also know I want to be here, I love being here, I love my friends. You read in the magazines about 'community.' Well, the people here have had that, a sense of shared suffering and

at times joy, for as far back as they can remember. They get
up. They look into each other's eyes. They touch each other
and laugh and become sad. They fight the hunger pangs.
They go out into those fields and do their work. They come
back and eat what there is to eat and get the rest they need.
They'll listen to me. They'll tell me to keep my spirits up.
They'll become sour and nasty sometimes — like I become almost all the time, it seems. But they 'keep the faith,' they'll
say to you. And I guess they've taught me to do so — pray as
they do and try to match in my mind their ability to talk with
God and 'gain some of His strength,' as they'll put it. I don't
really feel I'm *working* here anymore. I'm just here. I'm with
my people. I'm spending my time in this place — and I hope
I can use that time well. I don't know what I'll *accomplish*. I
don't think in terms like that. Sometimes I don't think much
at all — for days and days. I just *do* — do things. I work. I
give all I can, and receive a lot from people who don't mind
giving a lot of themselves, even if they are poor. And I pray
— for myself and them and the whole world. I pray one day
things will be better for the little children I've seen get born
since I've been living here in this county. Do you know the
oldest of them is now eight years old? Would you believe it? I
look at her and shake my head. I can't believe it's true, that
we're into the seventies and she's nearing ten. But every once
in a while I know it's true; I can see the lines on my face, and
I know it. I can feel the changes in my mind, and I know it. I
hope and pray it's all been of some use; I believe so — I believe I've done what I should have. The girl told me so when
she had her eighth birthday. She said I was her godfather, and
I'd kept her hoping and thinking all these years, and she was
glad I was here. It wasn't what she said that got to me. It was
the way she looked at me. It was the spirit in her eyes that
made my eyes fill up, yes sir — fill up and overflow real
bad."

We hear about those who have succumbed to despair and hate, those who in the name of "justice" or "progress" would turn an already troubled nation toward more bitterness, more violence. We hear from those who have given up, walked away, taken up yet another "cause" — and how faddish our "involvements" can sometimes be. We hear from those who never really became part of a particular struggle, yet feel able to talk and talk about what is right and what is wrong and what is needed and what is unacceptable, all told so unequivocally and confidently and often enough, stridently — especially if any demurrers come up, however honest. We hear from those who speak with slogans, who have a taste for publicity, who know how to get into the press and on television. We hear from self-appointed prophets and polemicists, not to mention their self-aggrandizing counterparts in "our" world, the world of colleges and universities.

Meanwhile this young man goes about his business. He has his doubts. He becomes moody. He worries that he is worthless and useless, utterly and completely so. He feels good, feels he is getting someplace, feels the people he lives with are getting someplace — only again to sense gloom coming over his mind. He wants to leave. He thinks he can never leave. He sees the strength and decency and tact and kindness in his neighbors. He sees their weaknesses, their hunger, their lack of money, the diseases that ail them (diseases which no doctor is around to treat). He admires them until they seem virtually flawless. He finds them tired and superstitious and at times almost inert. He calls himself "mixed up." He declares that he is sure of himself and his purposes, and glad at last he can know that and say that. Sometimes when I listen to him I want to shake him and tell him to stop being so unpredictable. But that is often the way people like me are: We want the "subject matter" we are studying to have a coherence to it, an intactness, a consistency — and sometimes we achieve for ourselves and our "impressions" (as they get told to readers) what in fact does not exist.

The particular young man whose words I have just drawn from is by no means as rare as we might believe. I know dozens and dozens not unlike him in many respects. He recognizes life's ambiguities and ironies, even as he often has two minds about himself and his friends and neighbors. Through all the hesitations and doubts and worries and fears, through all the despair (followed by moments of nervous self-assurance) he persisted; stood his ground, stayed the course.

Some men and women take themselves (whatever their assets and liabilities) into situations which demand from them the very best that is not only in them but in all men and women; and for all their mistakes, they somehow manage to meet the challenge, respond to the demanding occasion with what is needed. Such a man is the American youth just quoted — hard-working and decent, faithful to those he works with and to his own best instincts, unwilling to use his work and his sacrifices in order to bludgeon others, able to concentrate on the moment's demands without losing sight either of what has been won or what is being won or what needs to be won.

He needs no long-winded, heavily romanticized, insistently self-righteous "defense" from me — of the kind that all too often insults both him and those who hear about him. Nor does he need to have his mind and heart and soul "explained" by this or that "motivation" or psychodynamic formulation. He believes that his people — and yes, this country — are still worth fighting for. He believes that God is nearby and a constant source of strength. He believes that the greatest sin is to lose hope and succumb to despair.

Not that despair isn't always there — to be fought and fought, but never completely banished. Here is the long-time organizer once more talking (in 1971) and his words offer a listener or reader a grim "follow-up" indeed: "I hate to think back; I mean I hate to stop and ask myself what happened to this one and that one, to *him* and to *her*. It's frightening, the way people fall by the way; and I know it, some guy someplace is probably right now saying that *I* was a nice enough fellow, but poor soul, he's buried in some town in Georgia or Alabama or Mississippi and he has the *delusion* that he's doing something.

"It's hard to know who is really a survivor, and who is all washed up — ruined by the hate and bitterness and cynicism and plain old foolishness you run the risk of succumbing to if you work against the courthouse gang, the status quo. So many of my friends have come to hate white people the same way the Klan people hate us. So many of my friends have come to feel so low and pessimistic. And then there are some who get into their own private world — I mean, they get preoccupied with ideas the ordinary black man hasn't got the time or interest in hearing about: Africa, Swahili, a black nation within Mississippi, secession from America, Négritude and all the rest. I shouldn't talk like that, I know. I just have my own ax to grind, and I'm grinding it. But I think I know what's on the mind of the poor black people of the South — which means I think I know what's on the mind of a large percentage (still!) of the black people in America; and I'll tell you what it is: the next day's meal, the next day's work, where the next dollar is coming from, and on Sunday, church. Let anyone say what he wants, most black people are like most white people: They want the best they can get for their kids out of this country; they don't want to go anyplace else in the world; they want to join in, not walk away and be separate. Sure, they're full of suspicion and hate. Sure, they say a lot about white people that would make their ears ring if they could be within hearing distance. Sure, they don't believe what they're promised by white politicians, and they want to be left alone, and they may for a while think that going to church is a waste of time, and even going to school is a waste of time. But just watch my people; watch them here in the rural South and watch them in the cities. A lot of us are confused, and some of us in Harlem and places like that are addicts and thieves and all the rest, and some are as radical as you can be, ready to tear down 'racist America'; but every day, if you could look all over the country at the same time, you'd see millions of us getting up and going to work, or trying to. You'd see mothers trying to bring up their kids the best way possible, and fathers trying to work and bring in as much cash as they can, and kids going to school, and on Sunday our churches filled with people praying and believing God eventually, somehow, and hopefully one day soon, is going to 'do right' by us.

"Mind you, I'm not agreeing that it's right we just go along, go along. I've been trying for over ten years to get people around here *moving* — that's what we meant by 'the Movement'; we wanted to move people and we wanted changes in society and changes, as well, in the way people think about things. But it's dangerous when you start confusing what you as a person believe and want to see happen with what others, all those you visit and talk with and try to influence, believe and want to happen. And it's just as dangerous to say that you don't really *want* to influence 'the community' you're working in — just find out what *it* wants. People — plain, ordinary, mostly 'uneducated' people — are a lot smarter than 'we' think they are. They're not as taken in as we think by the lies of our big-time politicians; and they're not tricked by me and others like me, either. They know what I'm in favor of. A lot of them are in favor of the same things. (Some don't care one way or the other.) I find that I work best when I level with them — and with myself. I guess you could say it took me a long time to realize that — no longer, though, than it's taken the South to come to *its* senses. Not that the South has. And maybe I still have some learning to do; and so do the people I live with here. One mother told me the other day that she only hopes ten years from now she's smarter than she is today. That's the beginning of wisdom, I told her; too many people think they already know all there is to know."

Like the rest of us he can go on and on, not always with absolute consistency or logic. He is as troubled and torn as is the South he both hates and would never for a minute think of leaving. Often he has asked me what is happening to "the white folks." He knows that I am in no position to give him sweeping generalizations about millions of white Southerners; and anyway, he himself knows many of them, knows them as a fighter knows his enemies. Yes, many whites in the region have all along been open friends or secret sympathizers; and in recent years even the avowed segregationists have started talking differently, and more important, behaving differently. They take for granted what they once said never, never would be permitted to happen — blacks voting, blacks in formerly all-white libraries, restaurants, schools. Still, how far can they be trusted? How much do they "really" change? What would happen, were the federal government to let up its pressure on the South? In gloomy moments he asks if *any* white man, even his white co-workers in the "movement," are free of substantial "racist" inclinations. When he feels more confident he points out the gains achieved, mentions white men and women he truly respects — but goes on to mention "them," the many white people he sees every day but does not speak to, and wonders about, and still very much fears or resents, for all the progress he has seen, and for all the "understanding" he tries to mobilize within himself.

Harvard Today, 1971

A Young White Agitator

I now want to turn to another Southerner. When the children described in "The Weather of the Years," were going through the stresses and changes I happened to witness the man whose experiences are to follow, the youthful so-called "agitator," was already out of school and well along in college. Like the black civil rights worker he has also struggled to achieve "what is right, what has to be done," and like his compatriot in the South's civil rights struggle, he has never left the region for any long stretch of time, and has gone through his ups and downs: severe moments of doubt, periods of moderate satisfaction with himself and the work he does, times of real joy and celebration. As always, I have taken certain sentences out of much longer conversations we have had; and in this case I have wanted to emphasize not the particulars of his life, his background, and his various motives, but the fluctuations which, in turn, shed light on how a young man comes to terms with history's changes, and in his own way helps bring about those changes.

1961

"I'm no Yankee. No matter what the segregationists say about Negroes and the whites who send them help from the

North and the Yankees who come down here and start 'interfering,' they can't call me anything but one of their own; my dad and his dad and my great-grandfather were born in South Carolina, and we go all the way back to the early nineteenth century, when my people moved south to this state from Virginia. No one in my family has ever been up North, even to visit. And we're not descended from fancy Virginia types, tidewater aristocracy. My dad is a minister, and that's what his dad was. Further back there were teachers and carpenters and storekeepers. We're not white trash and we're not big, important people. We're in the middle, where all the newspaper editors think everyone should be. When I was a boy I would ask my mother a question about something controversial and she'd always say: Avoid the extremes. My daddy would say: Pray and don't decide what you think until you've thought carefully. Well, I thought carefully before I got involved in all this racial trouble.

"I never really *decided* to get involved. I just stumbled along. One thing led to another. I told some of my friends in college to stop calling Negroes niggers, and they called me a fool and a Communist and everything else (when they saw I meant what I said) and then I decided I'd better go and show them that I really *did* mean what I said, so I went over to the Negro side of town, and got to talking with one of their ministers, the only one who doesn't bow and scrape before every white face he sees coming — and that's how I got here, to where I am now. I don't know how long I'll be able to hold out. I mean, my family is after me. They heard I was living in Atlanta in a Negro neighborhood ('with the colored!') and they've been saying I'm 'doing something about civil rights.' My aunt writes to me and tells me what she's heard. I think my mother is afraid to write. She feels confused by what I've done. And my father, he's proud of me one minute and angry the next. They want me back in college. Maybe I'll be back

there faster than they think. It's hard being with colored people all day, and seeing only a few white people now and then,
mostly in cars driving by. Sometimes I look at myself in the
mirror and I say: There you are, a white man! But I'm trying
to do the best I can. I'm going from house to house with a
friend — he's a Negro from Morehouse College — and we
talk with people. We ask them if they're registered to vote,
and if not, why not. It's an education for them — seeing the
two of us together, and both of us believing the same thing."

1962

"We're making progress. I really think we are. People are
coming to the South now, lots of people. I mean, white students filter down here from New England and New York and
the Midwest and California — from everywhere. Some of
them turn me into a segregationist, I'll tell you. Good God,
they think they know everything. They're so full of themselves, and they have an *idea* about everything. You drive
with them and you pass a roadside stand, and they'll tell you
about 'social mobility.' You drive through a neighborhood,
and you get a lecture on the 'class structure' in the South, and
what a 'caste system' is, and what so-and-so has said about 'social change' and 'political change' and all the rest. I keep on
saying yes, yes. They've read all these books, and when they
asked me where I came from, and I told them South Carolina,
I didn't have a chance to add anything else; they told me
about the 'conservative eastern part of the state' and the 'populist western part of the state' and before I knew it I was
feeling like a small-town boy again. But they want to do
everything; they'd easily give their lives for the civil rights
movement, so I try to be as friendly as I can with them — and
after they relax a little and prove to you how smart they are,
and how much they've memorized, then they quiet down and
let themselves *learn* a few things.

"My granddaddy used to tell me that we're all storytellers, Southerners are. But I can't talk as fast as these Yankee kids can. You know what? I'll go with them to a meeting, and there will be the Negro kids and a few of us Southerners — white kids; and then there will be the kids from the North, most of them white. All of us from the South will stick together, and all of them from the North talk alike and have the same ideas. Oh, I'm exaggerating a little; but one of the Negro girls from Morris Brown here in Atlanta told me a week or two ago that she's tired of these northern kids coming down here. I said: You mean the white ones? She said: No, I mean the northern ones, period. I guess she's afraid they're going to take us over, just like they took over the South with their money. But I'm still glad they're here. We need bodies. We need bodies and wherever they come from makes no difference. We've got to knock on every Negro's door in the South and tell them that they are American citizens and they have the right to vote and they ought to start organizing and even marching. They should boycott stores where they can't have the same rights other customers have. They should walk into cafeterias and ask for coffee — and if they are refused, they should sit and sit and sit. Let the cafeterias close down. They'll lose money that way; and in this country money talks."

1963

"I may be leaving the Movement. My mother is sick. It's her nerves, I'm convinced of that. My father won't tell me, because he thinks I'll assume they're pressuring me and get angry. I went home two weeks ago and the whole family came together: my parents and grandparents and my uncles and aunts and cousins. I've never seen anything like it. We weren't there to celebrate Christmas or Easter. We were there to talk about race. They wanted me to stop what I was doing

and go back to college and become a lawyer. They came to see
me as if I'd been away on Mars or Venus or some planet like
that, and now I was home for a visit. Before long they started
in — and I listened to them. They're not bad people, you
know. I'm sick and tired of justifying my family to these
northern kids who come down here. The Negroes leave me
alone; they know what I've been through — the *southern* Negroes. We're getting more and more northern Negroes, and
they're different — at least some of them are. Some are Negroes who were born down here and talk about the South as
their home, a bad home, but home. But there are some Negroes we get who are white; that's right. They talk white and
act white. What I mean is, they're Yankees. They make *me*
feel like I'm colored. It's hard to tell you what I mean.

"I started out wanting to work with our Negro folks down
here. The best thing was in the beginning, when there
weren't too many of us, and we went from house to house
and talked — talked and talked with the folks. They were
scared of us. They didn't know what we wanted; or at least
they pretended they didn't know. They'd been pretending to
themselves so long that it was easy to pretend with us. One old
Negro man told me: 'Son, I used to tell my children that it
was a waste of time to vote, no matter if you're colored or
white, because all these politicians are no good and crooked
and full of lies that they tell people. But you know what — I
didn't believe my own words, and my children didn't believe
them either, because one of them asked me if it wouldn't be
different if some colored politicians got elected. After that I
stopped pretending.'

"I'll never forget that — listening to that man talk. I
swapped stories with him. I told him that my daddy used to
tell me that everyone is equal before God, and we are all His
creatures, and He loves us all equally. So, I asked my daddy
once about the colored. Did God create them, too? Yes, he

said. Did He like them as much as us? Yes, he said. Why don't
we follow His lead, I asked. My dad hesitated and came up
with a shrug of his shoulders and a little homily about how
the world is unfair, and that's the way it always will be. I
could see he didn't really have an answer for me. My mother
interrupted and said God wanted us all to be good to each
other, but He *did* make us different, and we should respect
His will by staying with our own kind. My dad wasn't too
happy about what she said, but they must have figured there
was no point in arguing in front of me. My mother said it was
suppertime, so we'd best go right to the table — and that was
that. Well, the old Negro laughed when I finished talking. He
said he could see how it was hard for the white people, just
like it is for the colored. And then we moved on to the next
house — and another spell of talking!

"But these days it's meetings and more meetings — to discuss our *strategy* and our *tactics* and our *long-range plans* and
all the rest. I can't for the life of me figure out why we have to
be so clever all the time. The more we talk and try to out-
smart the politicians and the segregationist organizations, the
weaker we become. We play their game — politics. We start
calling up those northern people: the rich liberals, the congressmen and senators, the government officials. They all say:
Yes, we're on your side. They tell us to go to the newspapers.
They tell us that if we can only get the *New York Times* to
write more and more about us and what we're trying to do,
and the *Washington Post*. I've never seen either of those papers, and I don't care if I ever do. I'm from the South and I
believe we can change ourselves. The fewer outsiders we have
come down here, the better. Oh, I don't mean that; at least I
don't always feel that way. Sometimes, though, I sure do. But
maybe in a month or so I'll be home and getting ready to go
to law school."

1964 — at the end of the Mississippi Summer Project

"We did pretty well this summer. I think I've finally realized why we need to become more *political*. I think I've finally lost some of my illusions about the South. After those three were killed in Neshoba County I went through a kind of religious crisis. I was ready to become a revolutionary, almost. I was so angry, so disgusted with the people who run the state of Mississippi, and my own state, too. Men like James Eastland and Strom Thurmond — I used to think they were pathetic, worth only my scorn. But in June and July of this year I suddenly began to realize that those men are incredibly powerful, and it is their power which holds thousands and thousands of people in the kind of slavery we still allow to exist here in the South. It is the Eastlands and Thurmonds who choose the federal judges we have down here, and decide who gets what from the federal government. Those people in Neshoba County, the *white* people, they may have killed Schwerner and Goodman and Cheney, or enjoyed learning that they were killed, but the white man down here, *most* of us, are cheated as much as the Negro is.

"Oh, I know there's nothing new in what I just said. But I'm from the South and I'm white and I grew up in a home where people try to think about things — and yet we never did stop and realize what was happening to us. We knew there was that 'race issue' — but the less said about it, the better. We knew there were some poor white people — the 'rednecks' or 'white trash' some black folks mention. But we never really looked closely at the facts — the hard, social and economic facts of life. In the North the rich, industrial and manufacturing and banking interests have at least had to give some ground; there is enough political democracy up there to force that to happen. Down here whole states are run by a few men; it's oligarchy not·democracy we have in the South. The unions have been kept out. The working people are divided conveniently by their racial fears: Whites are so busy looking down on the blacks, they don't notice what's going on *up there on the top,* where the bankers and utilities people and railroad people sit down and decide who is going to be in office and what the 'attitude' of the state will be toward just about anything important. Maybe that's too radical a view; maybe I'm carried away by all the bright kids I've met this summer from the North. I don't know. But they have the facts; they know who owns what, and they force you to stop and think. One minute I'm ready to join them, and the next I fall back on my old self and think they miss a lot about the world. I mean, you can't say that people only do what a few people tell them to do. This world is more complicated than that. I don't even believe a few men sit around and plan and plot and make decisions as if they are dictators. I'll bet the bankers would like to control people like George Wallace, but they can't. They're powerful, the rich are, everywhere; I don't know any country without rich, powerful people. But there's a lot here in the South that confuses the rich, too.

"You see, I'm all mixed up. That's what has happened to me this summer. I've never gone through a tougher time. I honestly don't know what I believe. I don't even know what I *think;* from minute to minute I change my mind and contradict myself and feel tied up in knots. I know how far I've got to go if I'm to be able to analyze what's happening here in the South like those people from Harvard and the University of Chicago and Berkeley do. They made me feel I was in nursery school — sometimes they did. But other times I thought they were the ones who belong in nursery school. They don't know how *people* live; they know how 'the system' functions and how the 'social structure' works. We'd sit up all night a lot of nights. They'd talk and talk. I'd mostly listen. First they had me hypnotized; then the next day I'd be walking by myself and I'd think this: They're not as smart as they think; there's a lot about the world they've never heard or seen, only read about in all their books. I don't mean to sound mean or ungrateful. But they talk and talk about the 'racist whites' here in the South and the 'slaves' our colored people still are. I agree; I'm sure even I have racist feelings, as someone white who grew up in South Carolina; and I'm sure most Negroes in the South *are* slaves if you want to use that word. But the white people of the South aren't *only* racists, and the Negroes of this region deserve better than to be called 'slaves' and 'exploited' and 'white man's chattel' and all the rest.

"More than anything else I hate the way the Northerners (white and Negro) come down here and call every Negro who disagrees with them 'Uncle Tom.' And I hate hearing them talk about the 'seggies' all the time; they use the word for every single white man they happen to meet. The fact is, they really don't meet any of the white people of Mississippi or other southern states; they see those people and may overhear them talking, but they don't know them. I know, how can they, when they're here to take on the whole 'social structure'? But they talk as if they've known all of us for years. They have these psychological words about us — and I guess I *do* start feeling that it *is* 'us' and not 'them' I'm hearing dissected. Maybe I should shut my mouth; maybe I'm being unfair. What have *I* done? Nothing, they say; and that's what I myself say a lot of the time. I get so low I can hardly stand it. I ask myself what I'm doing and why I'm fooling myself that I'm doing anything.

"I can't be colored; I can't be a Negro. The Negro in the civil rights movement knows what he has to do. A year ago, two years ago, I knew what I had to do. I didn't talk as much as I do now. I could go from one Negro home to another and sit there and listen. After a while the barriers seemed to drop. We loosened up and spoke honestly with each other. We

laughed a lot then; I suppose because we weren't sure we
were ever going to accomplish what we wanted to — the people I was visiting and me. But I was sure, I was *so* sure, that
we were starting something: We had people going to those
registrars, telling them they wanted to vote. They didn't always get to vote, but they surprised the registrars and surprised themselves, and neither they nor the white people have
ever been the same since. Now all that seems a little quaint;
the northern people tell us it will take a hundred years, at the
rate some of us work, to get a few thousand Negroes on the
voting lists. That's not fair to us, but it shows you the difference between someone like me and the Yankees: They want
to go to Washington and hold rallies all over the country and
boycott national companies up North to force them to hire
Negroes down here in their branches. They want to get *campuses* organized, get their classmates to come down here during holidays and vacations to picket or stage demonstrations.
They know how much Harvard owns of the Mississippi Power
and Gas Company, and they want to organize around that issue; I guess they want Harvard to pull out of the company.

"It's all too much for me; I feel like I'm inadequate. I want
to go on talking with Negroes, and I want to see them and my
own people, the white people of the South, get reconciled.
That's right, that's the word I used one evening when we
were having another of those all-night bull sessions. This guy
from Berkeley, California, asked me what my 'goal' was. I said
to help reconcile the Negro people of the South. *Reconcile,
reconcile;* he repeated the word two or three times and then
he laughed and he asked me what in the world I was talking
about. Did I want us all to be reconciled to the status quo, or
to some sugar-coated version of it? Well, he apologized; and I
make him even now sound worse than he actually was. He is a
good person — decent and kind; he really is. He didn't have
to spend the whole summer of 1964 in the hot, humid Delta,

being shot at by white hooligans hiding out on the side of the roads, aided by the sheriff and his deputies. He could have gone to Europe or gone someplace for a vacation. I have to keep that in mind when I become angry. I guess I make *him* angry — we're so different. It really matters, where you're born and grow up, even within a country. If I'd grown up in California I'm sure I'd be like some of the people who have come down here from there. I'd talk differently and think differently and have a different way of behaving — that's the best I can do to describe what separates a fellow like me from someone here in Mississippi for the summer from Berkeley. They don't look like us, speak like us, talk with people the way we do. By 'we' I mean Southerners, be they colored or white."

1965

"This has been the worst year of my life — the most confusing and wasted year I've ever lived through. Up until now I was working. I visited homes. I talked with people. I ran a mimeograph machine. I helped build a nursery school. I marched and picketed. I sat with my Negro friends in cafeterias and asked to be served, waited all day to be served. I said *yes,* I'm a Southerner, I'm from South Carolina — and no Yankee, like everyone says a white man is who takes the side of the Negroes in this war. It *is* a war; I know that now. But I'm beginning to think I'm a casualty. I'm beginning to think I should get out, leave the Movement and go to law school. And I'm beginning to realize that I belong with my own people; yes, that's what I should have thought about a long time ago — how much work there is to do with *whites.* It was so easy for me to come into a Negro neighborhood and take advantage of their fears and weakness. They couldn't tell me to go over to the white people and help change *them;* Negroes until recently have had to sit back and watch themselves

tricked and conned and abused by whites — and if they protested they were lynched. I'm not saying they were upset with
me in any way. It's not *me* I'm talking about. I'm trying to say
that the real problem Negroes have, obviously, is the white
man; and I'm a white man, so my job is to be with my own
kind and try to influence them.

"I guess it was last summer that turned me around; up until then I thought I was doing a pretty good job. Well, I'll be
honest and admit that I was proud of myself, real proud.
There's no use pretending to be so humble that you make
yourself sound like a fool. I liked what I was doing and I liked
forcing people I grew up with — my family, my friends and
neighbors — to stop and think, *really* stop and think. They
couldn't summon the convenient excuses the white people of
the South have used for generations — not when Sonny, *their*
Sonny, their own kin, their flesh and blood was 'out there living with the nigras.'

"I don't want to be mean about them. Actually, all last summer I wanted to defend my family (in my mind) against the
'damn Yankee' students who came down here from the North,
from New York and California and places like that. They
would be calling us all, every single white person in the
South, 'racists.' They would say we are all 'guilty,' and we all
profit from the way the 'white power structure' runs things.
I'd want to stand up and talk about my Aunt Sally. I'd want
to say that she's a kind and decent and generous person. I'd
want to say what I know the Negro people in the little South
Carolina town where she lives think about her — and say
about her, not to her face but behind her back. I mean, she
has befriended so many of them, and not just in a patronizing
way. She has gone out of her way to meddle — take a child to
the hospital, help another child through school, give money
and food and clothes to families. Oh, I know (as I speak now)
how awful it sounds, how condescending; that's why I never

said a word during those bull sessions. They would have torn me and old Aunt Sally to shreds — and maybe we both should be torn apart. Part of me says yes; but the other part knows that in the context of the South that *was,* that still *is* in many towns and even cities, my aunt was really (I don't exaggerate) a beacon of hope to dozens and dozens of Negro people. 'Go see Mrs. Wilson,' they would say. 'She'll plead for you,' they'd say. Now, it wasn't just pleading. She worked, spoke, acted for them. And they knew it.

"Still, I admit, she said those words about me, and I can't get them out of my mind: 'Our Sonny, out there living with the nigras.' She would say, if asked, that she was simply worrying about me. She always did worry about me and her other nephews, just as she worried about her own two daughters until they were grown and married. But I'm afraid I can't let either her or myself off the hook too quickly; the fact is that she felt I didn't belong among those who want to challenge the South's social and political system *all that much* — to the degree organizations like SNCC and CORE do. She's a great one for gradual change, for slowly moving along, for step-by-step 'educating' people. Once I told her that people are educated by *events,* by confrontations which bring out the brute force behind so many velvet gloves. She looked at me as if I'd gone and lost my poor mind. She told me that she didn't know what I was talking about. And she wasn't fooling. She wasn't pretending ignorance. She honestly believes she knows all the secrets in the county my family comes from in South Carolina. When I try to tell her about a 'power structure,' she thinks of Mr. So-and-so, with whom she grew up, who is a judge or a businessman or the district attorney or the editor (*and* publisher) of the local paper. Then she thinks to herself that those people don't *conceal* what they think or feel or do; they just go ahead and live out their lives — which means they do what they were brought up to do, what they believe is right and proper and all the rest. I know there's nothing very unusual in what I'm saying; but it's issues like this that are on my mind now. You see, I agree with the people who want to *expose* — tear into me and my aunt and all the white people of the South like us (and all the Negro people like us, too, I should add!); but I also am afraid that the people who do the exposing and the criticizing come and quickly go, like they did last summer. Meanwhile the rest of us, who are so hypocritical and blind and 'duped' and 'taken in' and 'used' have to go on and try to make this a better world, this poor old South we didn't choose in some other life or 'existence' as the ideal society, but happened to be born into.

"Look at last summer. All those nice, bright, analytical people came down here; some of them were friends of big, important people up North, even related to them. And us, the poor Southerners, we welcomed them. It's the old story of the South: We've always welcomed the Yankees, much as we fear and hate them. We have the idea that they'll save us, they'll bring us money or factories or some new piece of knowledge about ourselves that miraculously will turn us around and make us over. So, we sat there (us Southerners did, Negro and white both!) and said, yes sir, yes sir, pour it on, tell us what you know, don't spare us, give us the dope, the real strong medicine we need — and deserve! God, it was awful, now that I stop and think about it. I have to admit this to myself now: I never once spoke up and tried to argue with them. And I have to admit *this,* too: If I had a chance to do so now, I wouldn't. I'd be afraid; I'd feel inferior, that's right. They are so smart and articulate and they feel so sure of themselves. They've taken all these courses in sociology and psychology and political science, and they have learned how to express themselves. I mean, they make me feel like the village idiot or something. Then the next thing you know, they've left. It's not only that they have to go back to school.

Some of them *didn't* have to go back. Some of them stayed on
an extra month or two, into the autumn of 1964 — but they
were gone soon enough, just about all of them, ninety percent
I'd say, by the end of the year. And they were gone because
they'd seen all they believed there was to see. They'd made
their analysis, come to their conclusions, sized up the Delta
scene, the Mississippi scene, the southern scene, written their
quota of letters home, with the postmarks from Batesville and
Greenville and Greenwood and Yazoo City, received back the
letters telling them how brave and courageous and idealistic
they are, established in everybody's mind (their friends' and
relatives' and their own) that they were not only smart but
activist — so now they could go on to some other 'cause.' Already in late August of 1964 I saw them getting a little bored
with us. They'd confirmed for themselves what they knew in
the first place!

"I shouldn't talk like that, I know. I'm grateful to those
people; they've forced me to stop and think about my own
assumptions; I have to say that over and over to myself. I hear
myself thinking in a certain way, or I hear my parents or my
aunt or uncle talking in a certain way — and suddenly I'll
realize that they're right, those people from Harvard and
Berkeley; they're right sometimes, but wrong sometimes.
Maybe I should stop saying *anything* until I know what I do
believe; maybe I talk so much these days because I'm plain
mixed up. Stay in this business of 'agitating' long enough —
if you're white — and you'll surely get mixed up!"

1966

"I don't know where I'm going, but I'm not as confused as
I was last year. This is my last year with the Movement, full-
time at least. I'm going back to school. I want to be a lawyer; I
can say that now and believe it. I've *said* it before, but now
I'm sure. The vote is only one thing poor black people need;

they need lawyers — as do poor white people. I'm finding it harder and harder to talk about my future. I can't even talk about 'the Movement' any longer. Everything seems to be falling apart. We fight so much; even old friends do. We're always catching ourselves saying the wrong thing. We're always reminding ourselves that the word is *black*, not Negro. We're always apologizing, then having another argument. So, I'm ready to leave; I'm not made to fight over phrases and words and slogans. Maybe I'm not made to do the kind of fighting that needs to be done. We get into these terrible squabbles; the blacks call the whites racists and the whites call the blacks racists. We don't talk to each other the way we used to. We don't trust each other the way we used to. There are days when I honestly think all these years have been in vain. There is so much hate coming to the surface — among men and women who worked together so long. Sometimes I'll be sitting and reading or walking by a church — and all of a sudden I'll recall how it used to be: the singing and the arms locked together, black and white, black and white together. Now the blacks are fighting with each other and the few whites who have stayed on — well, we're all in pretty low spirits, I'll tell you. I never thought the day would come when I began to question the value of integration; but blacks in the Movement talk more and more about pulling away from all contact with whites and building what life they can for themselves — *alone*. It seems as if we've gone full circle around; it seems as if we're back where it all started, each of us keeping away from the other race. I don't know what more to say. Some things are too hard to put into words."

1967

 "I'm in law school. I can't stand a lot of the work; it's details about subjects that don't interest me. Some of the professors are crusty and pompous. Some would like to be more outspoken, but are afraid. I suppose I should have gone north to law school, but I want to stay here in the South — and frankly, after the Mississippi Summer of 1964 I'm not sure I could spend three years up in the North with high-powered northern students. They make me nervous. They make me angry. Sometimes they make me feel guilty — and at other times I think they ought to look at their own trouble and try solving it. The riots now are breaking out all over the North. Black people went there full of hope, and now they're disillusioned. Not that we aren't to blame; the South is where all the trouble started. But at least down here the people of both races get to spend time with each other; up there it's so crowded and the races have no contact with each other.

"I still do some civil rights work, even if I'm in school. I work in a black community. (The people there are proud to be known as *Negroes,* but I try to explain to them why *blacks* is better. They don't believe me.) I try to get people registered to vote, like before, and I do volunteer legal work. I also help teach some kids. I like the teaching best. I'm tired of politics. I'm tired of giving long speeches, or hearing others do so. I think it's up to us in the South to work with each other, community by community. If any students come down here now from the North, I'd join the segregationists in telling them to get out, fast. But there's no problem, because everyone has forgotten the South now. During my vacation I went over to Mississippi; I visited some of the people I knew and lived with there. They kept on asking me why no one comes to see them any more, why everyone has forgotten Mississippi. I was so ashamed I couldn't answer or look them in the eye. I wanted to talk about Vietnam and the ghettoes in our northern cities, but I couldn't. I myself don't really understand how we can be so irresponsible — I'm talking about all of us who stirred so many southern blacks up, gave them a vision of the future, then walked away. True, we've moved along; we have two good federal laws, and black people can register to vote all over the region, and if they want to go into a cafeteria and have the money, they can get served, *sometimes*. But in the Delta and in my home state of South Carolina they are so poor it's hard for outsiders to realize *how* poor, and a lot of them are confused and discouraged. They thought us students were bringing a new day to the South, and instead we've lost interest in the very communities we once lived in and worked in. Not all of us, but most of us.

"SNCC is falling apart. CORE is also falling apart. The 'Movement' is gone; there are only a few individuals left, and a few programs are going, supported by the government or foundations. But the days of real struggle by young people are over. Even Dr. King is looking up North, to Chicago and Cleveland and places like that, from what I read and hear. I know most American people live outside the South and have their own problems, though a majority of black people live inside the South, even now they do, for all the emigration of the last decades. What bothers me, though, is the moral commitment we made a few years ago. We came into these frightened, suspicious communities and promised them a better life, if only they would take risks and go along with us. They hesitated. They said no. They said maybe. Then, often because they grew to like us individually, they said yes. We could leave any day and be safe and go on to some other job; but they were here, and would stay here. We'll stay, too, we kept on repeating. We mean it; we're here for good — we must have said a thousand times. Well, we left, and they are still there, and they were right: They are being reminded every day by those sheriffs that 'your buddies are gone.' When I went back to Greenwood, Mississippi, I was told this by the sheriff's deputy: 'I'm glad to see you, boy. It's about time you came back and saw your nigger friends. They've been crying their hearts out for all you agitators, Communists and nigger lovers. You've gone and left them. You know who's stuck with them now, don't you — us! And we mean to take good care of them.'

"How do you think I felt? I suppose I could have tried to trick myself, make myself feel better by saying that at least *I* was there, and at least *I* have kept up some civil rights work here in the South. But I couldn't persuade myself even if I tried — not when I know how much we did let ourselves promise, and how quickly we did leave. An old black man in Greenwood put it to me: 'You came in '62 and left in '65, that's three years.' I wanted to quibble with him about dates and about how much we accomplished — little, he felt. But I nodded and tried to change the subject. Then he lowered his head and there was no point in talking any further."

1968

"I still don't know what to say or do. It's September, and both King and Kennedy are dead and gone, and we're listening to Hubert Humphrey and Richard Nixon, and we have to pinch ourselves and say yes, that's right, yes, that's right. Every black home I visit I see Dr. King looking at us and Robert Kennedy smiling at us. I've been trying to work with white people, my own people, like Stokely Carmichael and the others have said I should do; but it's not so easy. They don't want any part of me. I haven't figured out a good way to move into a white working-class neighborhood and help organize the people there. Maybe they don't want any part of people like me. Maybe — there's no *maybe* about it; they don't! I hear it said now that we 'exploited' the blacks, us white organizers. Well, I can't buy that, not all the way. I have some fine friends from my civil rights days; I go see them, the families I used to spend time with, a few times a year, more often than I go see my own family. I know, it had to end. History tells us that 'movements' appear, then disappear; and with Dr. King's death and Robert Kennedy's death the end has really come. I'll be sitting here, finishing up law school, thinking of what I'll be doing next, and all of a sudden I have to take out my handkerchief. I can't even talk about how I feel with anybody here in the law school; as for my family, I have little to say to them, either. They didn't really hate Dr. King or the Kennedys; they just didn't really listen to them, hear them, respond to their Christian message. I hate to sound so smug, but I honestly can't stop judging the white people I grew up with. They own their little world here in South Carolina, and they won't give it up without a fight. And if two men like King and Kennedy get cut down, they are not going to be mourned by their enemies — my family among them. Oh, I shouldn't talk like that. I should keep my mouth shut; after all, my own life is ahead of me, and who knows how I'll live it."

1970

"I'm glad I went to law school. I like being a lawyer. I like being able to *do* something for black people or white people — for the poor. I like being in a profession I can try to change — while at the same time I 'practice' it, use the law as a means of helping out people in real need. More and more of us young lawyers are staying away from the old-type firms — or joining only firms which let us do a substantial amount of 'public service law.' I work for people who haven't got money to hire lawyers. I work for blacks and for whites — yes, finally, I've been able to work with my own people, the way my black civil rights friends told me to do a few years ago. I couldn't go preach to poor whites, or talk 'social change' with them, or 'organize' them; but I can help them out when they're in a 'fix' and need a lawyer. And while I'm helping them out we can get talking about politics and race and all the other subjects they ordinarily don't want to discuss with some fast-talking outsider from some damn college or university! So, I've found my way, I guess — my 'thing' to do. And I can't say I'm ashamed of what I do; I'm proud of it, the work I do. I'll just say that right here and now, even if it's not being very modest to do so."

1971

"You asked me last year if I ever get tired or bored by this kind of law; I'm in the third year of doing it, and the answer is no. I'm getting old — over thirty. I'm lucky; unlike some others in the Movement I went back to school and finished up all my education and have a profession — a useful profession which can be 'turned to good account,' as my grandmother would put it, so far as helping poor people goes. If I were black maybe I wouldn't have needed to go to law school; maybe I could have stayed in a community — in the Delta, in South Georgia — and kept at 'organizing' and 'working with the people.' But for a white guy it had to be different. Of course, I could have just quit altogether, like a lot of people did — I mean, they moved on to the 'peace movement' · or they forgot about politics completely, or they remained interested, but only from a distance. I think I've done the best I could; I've tried to remain truthful to my beliefs, and I've tried to find a way to be effective. Back in the early sixties we all wanted to *do right;* now we want to *be effective.* But that doesn't mean the two don't go together. Maybe I'm getting older, but I believe you can keep your ideals and still accomplish something — a lot, really — for others. At least I try to do that; and I think I'm getting somewhere. I even wake up some mornings and think the South is getting somewhere."

A Klansman

In the first volume of *Children of Crisis* I described the fluctuations of mood and attitude I encountered among the white people of the South — some of them last-ditch defenders of "white supremacy" and some of them "lookers-on," ready to follow the shifts of sentiment they are adept at sensing in those "others" — who, in fact (so it turns out, ironically) are up to the very same game. I would now like to set down some remarks that have been made to me at various points in the sixties and early seventies by a man who considers himself above such wishy-washy fluctuations. He has been a member of the Ku Klux Klan. He has been (during its heyday) a member of the White Citizens Council. He has fervently followed the lead of Governor George C. Wallace of Alabama and former Governor Lester Maddox of Georgia, to name two of his heroes. He knows what it is to say "never" to integration; and he knows what it is to frighten and intimidate those black people who "get ideas in their heads." Nor is he crazy, or any of the other things someone like me might be tempted to call him. He works. He has his family, which now includes grandchildren. He can be a kind and thoughtful person one time, another time sarcastic and angry and full of rage. I suppose I could call him frustrated and embittered and ignorant. Maybe he is all that and more; but I know he did not spend so much time talking with me, give so much of himself to me in the course of our talks, merely in order to be called a series of categorical names in a book which I later wrote up North in my study. He feels, anyway, betrayed enough by people from a "class" I suppose I belong to — as he many times has told me.

Here, for instance, is what he had to say in 1967, a year of race riots and increasing slaughter in Vietnam, a year when "black power" began to meet up with a "backlash," a year which would turn out to be the last one Dr. Martin Luther King and Robert Kennedy would know, at least on this earth — and none of those issues or slogans or individuals did he fail to mention: "I think this country is getting into real trouble. Remember a few years ago when you and I talked? You seemed to think it was going to get better and better for the nigger, and I said no. Well, you were right: They did get to win a few rounds. But you know what? I think the South is going to be rescued by the North. I never would have dreamed that we had so many friends up there, but we do. It's in the white man's blood to stay clear of the nigger. I believe that. It's only natural. Hell, I like colored people. I have to tell you that all the time, because a lot of people up North (and a lot of people down here, too) don't want to see the truth; they want to make us into dragons and monsters like the ones kids look at on the television. The Ku Klux Klan was founded so that white people could keep together and the colored could keep together. They're beginning to find out up North that it's the only way — because God had His own good reasons to make some of us white and some dark, and who is anyone to go disagreeing. Lately the colored themselves are speaking up; they don't want any part of us, and good for them. They want to be by themselves. It's that Dr.

King and the Kennedys and all the others who want race-mixing, but there's only so long the American people will listen to people like them. Look at those Asiatics, they're trying to beat this country. The President has got their number. It's about time he stopped trying to invade us here in the South, and force all that integration stuff down our throats — and instead took after the Communists over there in Asia. The way I see it, the whole world envies this country, and inside the country, the colored envy the white. Now, is the white man supposed to give up all he's worked for, and is America supposed to turn over all its wealth — lock, stock and barrel — to Russia and China and those little countries in Asia and Africa?"

In 1968 — late in that year, actually — he was even more hopeful; and hopeful for reasons that had little to do with the day-to-day realities he was then encountering in the South, where school desegregation was increasing, where blacks were voting in larger and larger numbers, and where blacks and whites were seen side-by-side in restaurants and movie houses, a development he had five short years before told me would be resisted with a ferocity I could scarcely imagine, "being a Yankee." When I asked him why he felt so optimistic, in the face of the deplorable trends he constantly told me about in his native Louisiana, not to mention what he called the "nigger-crazy South," which meant cities like Atlanta or Charlotte, he lectured me and gently scolded me like this: "The South has fought for the right things all its life, ever since the country was started. Now, we've been beaten many times. We've lost a lot of battles and wars, not just the Civil War but a lot of smaller ones; I mean, each time the North has tried to push something on us, they've succeeded for a while, I believe. But what you keep on forgetting is this: It's not the South that we have to worry about, it's the whole country. I truly am convinced that the white race in this country is not going to let itself disappear. Right now people all over are waking up and asking themselves if they want America to be taken over by niggers and nigger lovers — by hippies and college radicals who are Communists and drug addicts and all the rest of them, people of the gutter they are.

"I am convinced that our minister is right: the Lord in His righteousness is striking down His enemies. That's why King and Kennedy were shot. That's why Nixon won. That's why our George Wallace got all those votes — from people in every state, millions of people, not just here in the South. You smile. You don't see what's happening to this country. I think the plain, average Mister Citizen is fed up with welfare programs to help out those lazy niggers, and little nigger kids robbing and stealing all the time, and the beatniks and hippies with their long hair and crazy clothes, and those college kids, who love everyone except their own people, and swear at everyone who's law-abiding. That's why my spirits are up; it's just so long you can fool people. Right now there's a tremendous wave of common sense spreading over the minds of people, that's how I've heard it described. The ordinary white American man has said he's had enough of being pushed around. The South isn't being looked down on anymore. Today everyone's from the South, you could say; that's because everything we've been fighting for all along, the plain white people from down here, is what everything the people like us in other sections of the country are fighting for. And it's self-respect, that's what we're fighting for, our self-respect. A man needs self-respect. He needs to know he's as important as the next guy. The people who want to destroy the South, they've wanted to make a man like me think he's no one; think he's just like the nigger or anyone else; think he's got nothing he can fall back on and say that he was born with it, and by God, he'll die with it, and he's never going to have it taken away. If you haven't got your race, you haven't got what God made you to be. We knew that a long time ago down here; and the good news is spreading to Chicago and Los Angeles, and let me tell you, to Washington, D.C."

Yet, in 1970 he was no longer so cheerful and confident. At least momentarily he felt the same old doubts and misgivings he would so angrily (and also plaintively) express to me in the middle sixties. Once he spoke with a touch of poignant resignation I found remarkable: "I don't know; I'll wake up some mornings and I'll begin to wonder whether the United States of America isn't coming to an end — I mean the country I was born into and grew up to love. We're giving up there in Vietnam. We're losing a war. Can you imagine that? It's hard to believe, but it's true. I don't trust that Nixon; I never really did. If George Wallace had won, we wouldn't be pulling out and surrendering. We'd be winning. Nixon is a tool of Wall Street. The Republicans bring in a depression every time they get elected. All they care for is the rich. They've been playing with the South, using us, that's what. That worked for a year or two, but we're catching on, I'll tell you. Why should I trust Nixon? Why should I trust most politicians, even our own brand that we have down here? I'm beginning to see that a man's a fool if he places too much faith in people he doesn't know. The people I can rely upon are my neighbors and friends, not Nixon and all the supporters he has.

"Here in Louisiana it's changing, even with Washington, D.C., telling us they are sympathetic to us. I mean, it's changing for the bad. To tell the truth, I don't feel the old fight in me, that I used to have. Time was, I would shout and say we'll fight the niggers and nigger-loving white kids and beat them, drive them north. We got rid of the Yankees once, after the Civil War, and we can do it again. But what's the use? You can't fight and beat the inevitable. And I'll tell you this: I believe it's inevitable that the South is going to die. That's right: The South isn't going to be anymore. We're going the way of the rest of the country. And the country is going the way of the rest of the world. That's how I see it. Today people don't think they're different from other people: The white man forgets he's white, and the colored man doesn't know his place anymore. The colored are becoming white — the way they dress and carry themselves and talk. The white people are mingling all the time with the colored, and so they forget themselves; they don't pay attention to who they are.

"I was going to work yesterday, and I saw some white kids and some colored kids playing in a school yard, and I've never seen anything like it. They were eight or ten, not four or five, and so old enough to know better. But they didn't, and the teachers there, standing around talking to each other, didn't seem to care at all about what was taking place right under their eyes. I stopped my car. I parked and got out and stood there, leaning on my fender and thinking to myself. All I could hear in my head was something I used to hear from my granddaddy when I was about as old as those kids playing in that school yard. He used to tell us: 'The South is dying; she is.' He used to say, even then he did, that the whole world was going to get mixed up, and the United States wouldn't be able to keep itself from being absorbed. That's the way he said it, *absorbed*. Well, isn't that what is happening? I was going to go and tell those white kids and those little nigger kids that they're killing the state of Louisiana by what they're doing, but they'd look at me as if I was out of my head if I talked like that, and I guess I can't blame them. It's not their fault all this has come about. It's not their fault there isn't hardly any South left. By the time they're all grown, they'll be seeing kids as old as they are now playing with Orientals (the Chinese and people like that) as well as the colored. At the rate we're going a boy who comes from the South — well, he won't really think of himself like that anymore. He won't say

I'm white and I come from Louisiana, and that's one of the most important southern states, and I'm an American and I'll take on anyone who's out to bother my country and take away all we've got. Remember all that talk back during the Second World War about One World? Well, I pretty well have given up thinking we'll be able to stop it; I think we're headed that way, to a big, mixed population, you could put it, of all the races and nations. And here in the South it won't be the same, not any longer. Our children will be worrying about everyone, not just their own kin. Don't ask me how they'll fit all those worries into their heads, but they will. I believe they will. That's how it goes, you see, once these changes get started. There's no stopping them. I said that ten years ago, and I say it now; except now I don't just say it, I *know* it."

Thus does an individual talk about "social change," describe the way a nation's political evolution affects his sense of his own "self," and foretell (as well as reflect upon) historical developments. By the same token, he shows more than his limitations, his terrible fears and resentments. He shows what he can do to move along, to extend the range of his own mind and heart. I find it hard to justify what I have just said by the words just offered in quotation. For one thing, I know the same man might (later on, he did) fall back upon his old rhetoric, his old near-hysterical denunciations and recriminations and forebodings of evil and recitals of woe. But for a moment his mood even more than his words revealed him not only to be tired of the progress his "enemies" were making, but tired of his own, stubborn struggle against those "enemies." I will not say he was glad that the South he grew up to know is now disappearing, but I did sense in him the kind of relief a fighter feels when he at last and for real is ready to quit. And I found the man's portrayal of the future world his grandchildren (well, maybe his great-grandchildren) will live in a genuinely impressive statement. So often I have heard him talk about himself and others like him all over the South in *negative* ways: The region was beaten and plundered by northern soldiers, northern businessmen; the region's beauty, its hills and lakes, its warm sun and fine beaches, its polite, hospitable, giving people, are taken advantage of by tourists and other intruders; white people are not black, not lazy, not dumb, not spendthrifts, not animals or near animals. Now, for an eloquent moment he was still coming up with negatives, but somehow they were canceling one another out, even as he was no longer talking himself into a narrow, regional corner, but extricating himself, however reluctantly and sadly, from all the important things that corner had meant to him — familiarity, security, a sense of self-definition. Like others, he in his own way was saying good-bye to the old South, maybe even to all the old Souths this nation and other nations have kept in their souls for so long. It was, I thought, a courageous moment for him; and I wondered if I really had any right to think I was capable of doing any more than he was then and there doing.

The Observer
and the Observed

I mentioned in the introduction to this book that I very much want to "follow up" the observations I made in the first volume of *Children of Crisis* with some further comments, based on an added five years of visits with those children and youths and older people. In *Not by the Color of Their Skin*, written by a Cleveland psychoanalyst, Dr. Marjorie MacDonald, words of praise for what I have tried to do are correctly qualified by an insistence that a psychiatrist like me, involved in the studies I have committed myself to, at some point has the obligation to be more forthcoming about his own way of working — that is to say, the manner in which (and the reasons for which) he came to see the range of men and women and children he later describes in his articles and books. And no doubt about it, I have been working with an especially wide "range" of individuals: They have been members of the Ku Klux Klan; they have been civil rights activists; they have been proudly "neutral" or "moderate" or (in essence) committed only to what the prevailing political winds (of the day, of the year) urge; and too, they have been rather obviously old and young and in between, and black and white, and residents of cities, suburbs or rural areas.

I believe it is only recently I have asked myself at any great length *how* or *why* I came to see the people I did; and so this discussion quite properly belongs here, as part of the "follow-up" clinicians are always anxious to have. For one thing, I rather stumbled into the "study" that now has become my life-work. I have already in the first chapter of the first volume of *Children of Crisis* described at least that: how I happened upon a "swim-in" while I was living in Mississippi; how I was moved by what I saw to start looking around at things more carefully, and looking as well at my own assumptions and values; and how eventually I began to spend time with both black and white children in Louisiana (and later, other states) as they went through the crises that invariably took place when the South's public schools first began to desegregate. It is true, I did toward the beginning of that book go into considerable detail about the substance of my work, the numbers of people I saw, the frequency, the style of our "relationship," as a continuing meeting of two human beings is referred to these days. But I did not at any length talk about my own responses as an observer who was getting to see such different (and so often mutually antagonistic) groups of people. Nor did I answer Dr. MacDonald's question; I described what I saw and felt to be true, but did not discuss the difficulties and tensions and hazards I met up with — to the point that, as my wife well knows, I often despaired, became thoroughly confused, and on more than one occasion very definitely gave up doing what I was doing, only to be pulled back on course by her unwillingness to let me do anything else but (her way of putting it) "go on, just go on with the visits, from day to day."

To reach the black children I had to convince their parents (and most significantly, certain black leaders in cities like

New Orleans, Atlanta, Little Rock, Asheville) that I came as a friend. Those leaders had no interest in giving their approval to one more "research project"; even in 1960 blacks had grown doubtful (to say the least) of the value such projects have — for anyone but those who do them. I first spoke with Dr. Kenneth Clark in New York City — as he and I have had more than one occasion to remember. He helped me to get in contact with the leaders of the black community in New Orleans, as did Thurgood Marshall, then with the NAACP Legal Defense Fund. Over the years I have noticed that many people are quite ready to imagine and understand the difficulties a white northern observer like me had as he came into daily contact with the South's black families, but less willing even to speculate about what moved me to start working with white families, too — some of them strongly, even violently (quite literally so) segregationist. Of course I can rather quickly summon the reasons; they are the obvious ones anyone doing "research" lists: to learn more, to understand "both sides" involved in a struggle, to study the way social change influences not only *these* children, or *those* children, but *all* the children in question — that is to say, black children whom white children see and begin playing with (after not doing so for such and such a period of time) as well as white children whom black children stay away from, then (again, it takes time) feel able to speak with and respond to with increasing comfort. Yet, I did not "plan" my "study" in an evenhanded and farsighted way. (I think it is fair to say I never really planned the study in any scrupulously "methodological" way.) Dr. MacDonald is right when she implies that something more than intellectual curiosity must have prompted me to seek out such a range of people — and do so in a manner that conveyed to all of them (I believe) my real desire to speak with them, share time and relaxation and food with them, *be* with them, really.

There came a point (and I was not then all that far along in my work) when I felt deeply the difficulties I was having as a white doctor who was not only struggling with racial issues but with his sense of himself as a professional man who was "trained" to work under certain circumstances and behave in certain ways — and to expect that others do their share, respond to his ministrations with a kind of obsequious willingness if not eagerness. I was unnerved by the silence and suspiciousness I met from the black parents (more so than from the children), and I was also unnerved because as a physician I was doubly a threat to them. They had every reason to fear doctors: Either they had never really talked with one, or they had been insulted again and again in those hospital clinics they go to as a last resort. So, when I saw a white woman shout obscenities at a black child I was trying to know (and felt I did know — somewhat) my mind went out to her and others like her. Again, I wanted to hear her viewpoint, learn about her beliefs and passions; but I now am willing to acknowledge that I saw in the embattled white people of New Orleans (most of them blue-collar and white-collar workers) a chance for a return to a constituency of sorts, a return to a kind of people medical students often get to know and find to be their "favorite patients"; and yes, a return to the values and ideals one like me is more tied to than he often dares realize, let alone talk about with others. Rather obviously I am not now talking about the overtly segregationist viewpoint which so many white Southerners have rallied around these past years; perhaps it is another collection of attitudes I have in mind, the attitudes of the American workingman — who is as proud as he (often enough) is apprehensive, or at the very least, uncertain.

In any event, I should right now put before the reader the remarks of a white man I have known for a decade. He is the father of a white girl who eventually did go back to a school once completely boycotted. He is the husband of a woman who shouted and shouted at a black child, only to give up in despair and disgust and (it took time to develop) boredom. He is a worker, a carpenter, an electrician, "a man of all trades" he has often called himself. In 1961 I began talking with him and his wife and their children. I met his wife and her sister when I watched them (with hundreds of others) heckle the first black child to enter "their" neighborhood school. I went up to his wife and started talking with her, and she and her husband agreed to see me at home later in the week. After about a month had passed, after we had begun to trust one another — we spoke far more easily than was the case in the black homes I was at the same time visiting — I spent a particularly long and eventful evening with the man, who by then had several times characterized himself to me as "an average American guy," or "just a plain fellow, like most other people in the state of Louisiana." We confronted one another, so to speak; we shared our views, and since they differed in many respects, we disagreed — not argued, be- cause he was (and is) quite polite, and I had my "role" to protect, as someone "objective" or "interested in learning" or "doing research." To pull together some things he said at var- ious moments that evening and in the course of the weeks immediately following: "I'm prepared to admit that the white man has a better deal than the colored. I didn't make this world, though. I read the editorials in *Look* and *Life,* and they say we should change here down South and become different in the way we think — and how we treat the colored. No one is delivering sermons to the people up North. They're the ones who are in the majority; they're the ones who own this country. If they really wanted us to change, I'll bet they would have made us do it, one way or the other, a

long time ago. But I'll tell you something. They're hypo-
crites; and what's more, I do believe they know it themselves.
They don't need me calling them any bad names.

"I didn't choose where I was born, and I grew up like everyone else here in Louisiana — to have a belief that the races
just don't mix with each other. These days you hear that mixing is coming; people say it's coming in the schools and I believe that's true, and people say it's coming in jobs, and
maybe so. But I'd like to make a prediction. I'd like to tell
you something here and now, in the spring of 1961; and by
God, if we're both lucky enough to be alive ten years from
now, then you come back here and talk to me, and we'll see
how far wrong I am for thinking like I do. I predict that it
won't be long before the South is let off the hook. I was in the
army, you know; I was stationed up there in New Jersey, so I
know the North. I'd sooner be one of our niggers down here
on a plantation in the northern part of Louisiana than one of
those poor *Negroes* (they're called) who live in Harlem or in
Newark, New Jersey. Before long the white people of this
country will begin to realize that they're never going to win a
popularity contest with the colored or the Indians, with all
those kinds of people. Let's face it, they don't like us any
more than we like them. I admit, there are white people who
are real nigger lovers, and they don't really bother me too
much. I figure that a man is entitled to think as he pleases —
so long as he doesn't try to tell *me* what to think. If he has so
little pride in himself that he has to go chasing after the colored, then that's his problem.

"I myself feel sorry for the colored, sometimes I do.
They're not too smart, and they're not really suited to the
kind of living we have in our cities. I mean, they're slow, and
they lack ambition, and they're lazy, more lazy than a lot of
their white friends will ever admit. The rich whites, the liberals from over there in the Garden District and near Tulane

(the college types live there) are all in favor of giving the colored more and more — and you know at whose expense. They have *us* start school desegregation; and they want them to work beside *us* in our jobs. They want to move the niggers on top of us — and hell, with the number of kids they have, they'll drown us out of our homes. Meanwhile the rich lawyers and doctors and professors send their children to private schools, and they live in neighborhoods that no damn nigger is ever going to live in, except if she's a maid or a cook — so even if the kids of those people *do* go to the public school, they don't have to worry about desegregation. No judge is going to order some little colored kids to be moved into the school where the rich go, not when they can push the little darkies on *us*.

"Let me tell you something. I'll admit to it: I once went to some Klan meetings. I wouldn't join, but I have friends who used to belong. They told me to come, and I did. I think they've quit now. The White Citizens Council are better, because they're more respectable, you know. Some in the Klan are crazy. They've let those niggers go to their heads. They're as crazy in their own way as the rich, liberal types, who come slumming over to our neighborhood, to see if we're treating that poor little colored girl OK. Well, we're not going to hurt her. She doesn't know that, but let me tell you: It's true — we're just not going to put a bad hand on her.

"Now, you're a doctor. You must know people. Isn't that your job? So, don't you think that we know better than to go harm a little six-year-old child? Sure, we've been telling her to get out of here. Sure, we've been letting her and those federal marshals with her (they're beside her all the time) know what we feel. But let me explain something to you about human nature. I mean, I know you're the doctor, and I have the greatest respect in the world for doctors. They've kept my daddy alive. They're so good to him — to all of us. We go over to Charity Hospital, and they treat us like kings. They'll ask after every one of Daddy's children, and his grandchildren, too. And they've been very good to my wife and me. Of course, my wife and I, we have our own doctor; and he's ours, he belongs to us. I'd rather pay a man a good price and call him *my* doctor. But my dad doesn't have the money, after all the illness he's suffered through. Even so, they treat him well over there at the hospital. Anyway, if you'll just put up with me, I'll tell you what I think. I think that child is just being used by a lot of white people. The only people who are really open and aboveboard with her, *honest* with her, are us, the ordinary, average, working people who live around here. Her own people are trying to grab all they can; thousands of them are pouring into our cities down here in the South, and now people like me, who work hard all day and half the night — well, it's going to be us who will be docked for keeping them fed, through the taxes we have to pay so they can be on welfare. And a lot of the colored leaders, they're trying to develop a new attitude in their people. They're trying to make them pushy and cocky. They're trying to give them the idea that they're entitled to anything they can scare us into giving them. A little girl like that one, coming into our school like she is — that's just a first drop in a big bucket.

"Then, there are the white people who are causing the trouble, too. I believe a lot of us Americans have lost faith in ourselves. We don't believe in this country anymore. The rich kids want to go to South America and Europe and Africa; they don't know their own country. Now this new President we have, Kennedy, he's talking about the government *paying* them — imagine that, my taxes going to pay for a rich college kid to go spend his time with some natives halfway around the world. No college kids are coming over here to find out how we live, and offer their help to us. Mind you, I don't want their help. I'm not looking for the easy way out. This is a tough world, and if you're going to get by you have to work. But some of our white people are becoming like the colored. A lot of the college kids these days don't believe in this country; they're only interested in foreign countries, or here at home they only want to look at the trouble we have, not the good things about America, only the trouble.

"I think we're headed for a real bad spell. You may see a lot of school desegregation take place here in the South, but it won't be long before both the colored and the white people find a way to keep their distance, no matter what the federal government wants. We're losing a lot of our colored to the North, thank God, so up there the white people are going to discover what a problem they have on their hands, and then they'll be more sympathetic to us. But the real danger ahead, as I see it, is that there's a type of rich white people — well, they're well-off if not rich — who look down on their own kind, and want to hold hands with the niggers. Before long you'll see the white people of this country fall to fighting: A lot of us aren't going to work all day and half the night and then see our tax money go to supporting all these colored women and the ten children they have by five or six men. Something has to be done about that. Don't ask me what, but I'll tell you: If the politicians don't come up with an answer, we'll vote them out and get a new batch in. The ordinary white man, not the college professors and that kind, but the ordinary white man isn't going to be pushed around forever by his rich bosses and their radical children who love niggers and want to spend five years visiting foreign countries — any more than we're going to be pushed around by a lot of people who would like to sit around and fornicate and have one baby after another, and be paid, be *paid* for living like that by the working people of this country whose taxes pay for everything, I guess.

"That's why I say there may be changes ahead, a lot of mixing in the bus terminals and school desegregation and all the rest, but you watch, there will be a reaction, a big reaction to this push from the colored and their white friends — and when that day comes we'll see who's in the majority in this country. There's just so far you can go, pushing people and pushing them. There's just so much a man will take. There's a limit to how long people like me are going to let themselves be looked down on by college professors and college kids and the politicians who are always listening to them — but not to us, no, because we're not complaining, and we're not doing a lot of fancy talking. And while the rich invent clever schemes to get out of paying taxes, and while the colored come running into a city like this one, expecting money from the city every week, the rest of us have big deductions taken out every week from our paychecks, and there isn't a thing we can do about it. We can't hire clever lawyers to help us trick the government. We can't figure out all sorts of dodges and schemes. And we don't go shouting, either. We don't ask for pity, and say that we've been getting a raw deal. We don't ask for the college professors to feel sorry for us and write books saying we are in bad shape, and we need the federal government to step in and give us everything we want, while we sit around and complain some more, and get more attention from the newspapers."

Who can call his ideas "right" or "wrong," "correct" or "incorrect"? For a long while I did; I silently was the "college professor" he so often railed against in our talks. That is, I concluded in my mind that he was "prejudiced," that he was a "bigot," a "racist"; and I felt myself at times only half-listening to him, because after all I really did know what he was going to say. "He and his wife are so predictable," I once said to my wife as we left their house — after they had been thoroughly kind and courteous to us, fed us even; fed us delicious fried chicken and okra and cooked tomatoes and mashed

potatoes and beans and home-baked bread and pecan pie
topped with ice cream. If I was annoyed, my wife was annoyed with me. She sensed my irritation and impatience and
at times outrage. She, too, felt dismayed and saddened by
what she heard. But she also felt something else; she felt that
in such a home we were in the presence of more than odd or
idiosyncratic or unusual people. Nor was she prepared to go
in the other direction — think of the particular family we
were visiting as representative of this or that "class" or
"group." True, the carpenter and his wife were white Southerners, and they can also be called working-class people. But
they considered themselves other things, too. They called
themselves Americans and Christians. They constantly emphasized how law-abiding they were, how hard they worked,
how carefully they saved their pennies, how ambitious they
were for their children, how far into the future they looked as
they went about their daily tasks. For my wife "they" were in
many respects "us" — if not all of us, then most of us. When I
heard that being urged on me I found myself again and again
saying no. And I found myself on those occasions becoming
rather smug and pompous and self-important. I would list my
academic credentials, or I would remind myself that my parents do not talk like that carpenter and his wife, have different values, are far more "open-minded," do not speak about
black people with such scorn or contempt, consider themselves reasonably well-off and well-read and in general feel
satisfied with their lot. Yes, my wife would agree, and the
same could be said for her life and her family's background;
she, too, went to college and came from a home in which the
kind of raw, bitter remarks I have just presented were never
made. So, *we* were not like "them"; nor were our friends like
"them."

After a while, though, my wife made me stop and think.
She simply would not stop pointing out that if there were

differences between us and some of the white hecklers we had met on the street, some of the white people we were getting to know, there were also so many things that we shared — again, as white people, as Americans, as men and women alive in the second half of the twentieth century. Nor would she let me get away with the idea that my job was only to find out how the black children, the black families were getting along. They were getting along all the time with white people, with *us*, she kept on insisting. For one thing we were both visiting them at home — the first time for any of them that whites had come as regular guests; and, of course, at school there were white children and white teachers to be reckoned with every day. As I look back, though, I realize that my wife had in mind more than perhaps either of us could fully acknowledge to ourselves in the early sixties. She saw, she felt, how difficult it was for us to earn the trust of the poor and frightened and embattled black families we were visiting; and she also saw how isolated those families and their supporters were from the school officials and others in New Orleans who were constantly making decisions that affected the little children we knew. I believe she sensed that we, too, were becoming cut off — and maybe made more nervous and fearful than we had any reason to be.

Moreover, she knew that even though we were not coming to those black families as "therapists," or whatever, we were certainly not *only* friends, even if we were declared so with increasing frequency. And in fact one day toward the end of 1961 we heard this from a black mother: "I tell my husband when he comes home that it's a good thing you two come here and talk with us, because we learn from you what's going on in the city. I don't read the newspapers, because I never did get the schooling I should have got, and our television set broke down, and there's not the money to fix it, not with my husband fired from his good job after we sent our child to that white school. His boss told him: You keep your girl in that building, and you can leave *this* building and never come back. So, he left, and he's got small jobs he does part of each day, and of course we get help from the neighbors, because they say we're all in this together. Still, it hurts, because we don't have the regular money coming in every week.

"I tell my children that if they listen to you, they'll understand that there are all kinds of white people. We can never figure out what is going to happen next, even after we go next door and hear the news, and the minister tells us what to expect. I was taught never to rely upon a white man's word. They can change so easily, don't you see. That's why I'm afraid to go to that school and talk with that teacher and that principal. I wouldn't want to look in their eyes. I'd be scared by what I'd see, to tell the truth. Maybe I'd be scared that they would see how I regard them. I try to be nice and obliging with white people when I talk with them, but honestly, they have been so bad to us that I just don't like them at all. You're the exception. Yes, I do believe we've been so very lucky to know you two. It takes time to feel easy with a white man. We never have before. Yes, you're right, we still may be a little nervous.

"When you drive up, some of the kids still hide. There's a child who thinks you come here to throw bombs, but we change your mind each time. She's only four, and she has a big imagination! But I can understand why a colored child can think that way about a white man. I remember how I used to think; I remember I'd see that foreman, that big red face of his, and I'd run for cover. That was when we lived in Mississippi and we worked in the fields. He'd be coming toward us, and we'd all 'fix our faces' — that's right, we said it to each other: Fix your face, the mister is coming. He wanted to be called the bossman, but he had a bossman over *him,* and we just called him mister. Here in New Orleans I hear the

NAACP wants us to be called mister and missus, like they do
with the whites when they go shopping. I heard a saleslady
tell her friend she was never in her life going to call a nigger
mister or missus; she'd quit first. That's how white people
think. I sometimes wonder if there's any use pushing ourselves on them. They're so mighty sure of themselves. And
there's no way of telling what they'll do from day to day.
They get one idea in their heads, and then another. My
granddaddy told me a white man's head is all full of bad
blood, with a little sweet milk on the side. He said when they
talk nice to you, don't forget that they could as soon turn
about and try to get you lynched. When they're being bad,
the sweet milk will rise up, but there's not much of it to rise,
so don't depend on it.

"What do you think? My sister and I will be talking, and
she'll tell me to go talk with you. I tell her I do, of course.
Then she says we're lucky to have you, because now we can
find out what they're thinking and what they're going to do. I
guess it's like that with any people, you have to be from them,
if you're going to know what they're thinking. For us to figure out what's on the mind of white people is like trying to fly
around the world in one of those jets; I hear tell it costs more
than most of us colored from Mississippi and Louisiana
make in a year, maybe two years."

Perhaps when I wrote the first volume of *Children of Crisis*
I ought have included such comments; but I did that writing
in 1966, and now it is 1971, and as I have already indicated, in
five years a lot has happened to make me more willing to discuss candidly and at some length the difficulties that go on
between an observer like me and those he hears and watches
and hopefully, learns from. True, I have not completely re-
frained from mentioning those difficulties in each of the volumes of *Children of Crisis;* but I have also avoided going into
details, probably because remarks like the ones I have just

recorded unsettled me more than I knew at the time and stirred in me a whole range of (sometimes contradictory) responses. Besides the tension and fear and distrust which come across in almost every sentence the mother speaks, there are other "attitudes," and yes, requests: She is grateful; she has a stubborn, canny side which takes the elements of tragedy and makes light of them; she wants some help, needs not what one hears referred to at psychiatric conferences as "support" or "reassurance" or an occasional "clarification" but rather a friend's willingness to call the shots as he sees them — he being an umpire of sorts who knows the game, the white man's game, and is willing (*apparently*, though one can't be too sure, of course) to translate it, so to speak, for some black people. I call myself an "umpire" because over the years I was called that by several black mothers. They may not have been accurate, but they were indeed telling me something; they needed someone to "read the white folks" for them. And I think it is many hundreds, maybe a thousand times that I have heard that last expression directed my way.

As I write this I find it embarrassingly self-centered; and yet it is a fact that I had to go back and forth between two worlds not only because I stood to learn something by doing so, and not only because I was asked to do so by the black families I was visiting — but also because I needed to do so for what I suppose people like me often call "subjective" reasons or "emotional" reasons. As my wife felt at the time, we were in danger — as whites going exclusively to black homes — of getting so preoccupied with the worries and hopes of one set of people that we in fact would not be able to help them with precisely the problem they believed us able to do something about. To call upon a black father this time: "It helps talking about white people with white people. I know that there are all kinds of white people and all kinds of us colored, but it still helps if we can talk with a friendly white

before we have to face the unfriendly ones. Of course, maybe
after white people spend time with us, they'll begin to feel
friendlier. That's why integration should help in the long
run. But right now we have to go slow; I think white people
are so used to each other, it'll take them time to discover
they're a minority in this world, and the majority doesn't look
like them."

He was speaking generally, but maybe he was speaking of
me as well. He was acknowledging help, but maybe he was
also giving me a little advice. He was a kind and soft-spoken
man, but maybe he had his angry side, and maybe he all along
wanted to warn me about something: It *does* take time; one
cannot leave one world and go into another without misgivings, regrets, confusion; and when the point is to find out how
those two worlds are coming together (at least a little bit, if
ever so tentatively) then one ought indeed go back and forth.

In writing about my work I have tried primarily to convey
or evoke the thoughts and feelings of others; I have tried to
describe the circumstances, the conditions of life, that they as
particular individuals must come to terms with and (such is
their fate) try somewhat desperately to overcome. I still feel
no inclination to go on an ego trip, as some of my students
now put it; nor do I wish to go on and on about the hang-ups
my work causes — a kind of monologue which can ever so
coyly and disarmingly become self-congratulatory. But legitimate modesty (not to mention self-protectiveness) can be at
times misleading. Once the black father I just quoted gave me
a compliment, but it was also a warning: "I hope there will be
others like you, going from colored people to white people
and back again and back again. There has to be more. There
has to be." If "there has to be," we owe it to each other to
share our experiences, to speak openly and even a little pe-
dantically about the hazards and temptations, the dangers and
opportunities such visits, such *work,* can provide.

In that spirit let me come up with some warnings I have heard directed at myself by myself as well as by others. For one thing, at times I found myself (and my wife or indeed some of the people I was speaking with found me) too taken up with one rather than another part of the particular person or "problem" I was spending time with. I would forget other things, other "factors" at work, other sentiments held or ideals believed in. I would in many senses of the word "overidentify" with a person, a people, a situation. That is to say, I would take on the viewpoint of others to the point that I was losing my own; and I would take on some *part* of that viewpoint. When people are engaged in a social struggle they fall back upon, draw from, certain qualities of mind and heart they happen to possess. On other occasions they may be quite different people, may express quite other thoughts, than one like me is apt to hear. I recall in 1962 hearing a rather cynical and bored ten-year-old girl remind me of what she called "something." At the time I thought she was annoyed with her sister, who as a black child going to a white school, was getting so much attention from everybody, me included. But psychological sophistication can often turn out to have *its* hazards, even as social observation presents the kind of risk implied in the following statement: "I'm tired of all this school desegregation business. I'm tired of hearing about the colored people and the white people and what they think about this and what they think about that. I listen to my mother talking, and my father, and my grandmother, and my aunts, and my brother and even my little sister now, and all those neighbors, and I tell myself they've gone and lost their heads. All they say — well, it's only *part* of what is true. A lot of the time they don't go repeating that they're colored, they're Negroes, that they think this about the whites and think something else about the whites. My mother admitted to me last week that she has more on her mind than worrying about which race is the good one and which race is the bad one. It's just that with one of us in the family going into that white school we have to think about all this business more than we ever did before. I hope we'll get through the trouble. I hope one of these days we can go back to being *ourselves*."

I do not believe she meant by that last wish a return to some kind of apathy or social and political indifference. She realized (long before I did, I fear) that there is a larger context to the lives observers like me encounter at a certain moment of "crisis." She realized that I was in danger of feeling so "involved" that I was overlooking significant "areas" of their lives, of the lives black people *as human beings* live. Psychiatrists these days warn one another about becoming "overinvolved" with their patients — lest the doctor lose his "objectivity" and become unable to provide the men and women who come to see him the kind of emotional distance on themselves they so urgently need. I was obviously in such a danger when I started talking with black families in the rural and urban South — and was so warned by particular children and grown-ups. By the same token, I have felt a similar chain of events take place as I go from one home to another on the white side of the tracks. One hears doubt and fear and a sense of betrayal expressed. One hears confusion and anger. One cannot but feel that here, too, are people who have been victimized by a historical chain of events which for them is not something abstract, something studied in a textbook (or written about by a writer) but something intense and immediate and concrete and personally experienced.

Yet, now that I mention my work with white families who have also been caught up in the South's (and the North's) social struggles I have to say that in the case of those families, too, I often would dwell too exclusively on the "negatives" as it were. If in time I was romanticizing the blacks, I also began dwelling upon the terrible price whites must pay as the op-

pressor — to the point that the white people whom I actually
knew fairly well, were becoming caricatures in my mind. The
two developments went hand in hand; it was as if I were
needed as a psycho*pathologist,* to find serious and almost un-
remitting "trouble" in *some* of the individuals I was getting to
know. Originally the "trouble" would be found (I speculated
before I ever started the work) among the black children who
were to face such awesome obstacles for the sake of obtaining
an education with other American citizens, or among those
black youths who met threats and violence and had to face jail
sentences simply because they insisted on registering to vote,
or eating in public restaurants or watching movies alongside
everyone else. When all those southern boys and girls and
young men and young women showed themselves to be far
sturdier than I had imagined, I suppose I turned out of habit
to others; and yes, turned out of impatience and frustration,
too. Surely those who hate must be "sick." Surely those who
are "prejudiced" are also in some kind of psychiatric jeopardy.

I have at some length explained how simpleminded and
dangerous I believe that "approach" can be. The South's long-
standing social and political system can be justifiably and
strongly criticized, but to describe every white Southerner
(every white American) who harbors a kind of senseless and
morally objectionable ill will toward black people with a host
of psychiatric words is at the very least a useless venture. Certainly there is something sad and even at times crippling
about hate — self-hate or hate for others. Certainly many of
the South's white people, many of America's people, many of
the world's people, have all too much of that hate in them.
And as a number of black people have kept on reminding me,
many of their own people are also "sick" with anger and resentment and hate of a blanket kind that tolerates little if any
modification — even in the face of the most honest and decent overtures from white people. Are they, is everyone,

"sick"? Maybe so. But if so there is no point in saying *that* over and over again — not when those same people show various other sides to them, sides one would call "healthy" if the same psychiatric yardstick were being used. All of which means that we are back to human beings, because each of us (it is almost too obvious to say) has his grim and sulky and petulant and mean side, and his more sensible and kind and thoughtful side — including, I might add, those who are lumped together by me at times as "segregationists" or members of the White Citizens Council or the Klan, let alone "white Southerners."

Another danger I faced grew like this: I found myself so critical of certain individuals I called segregationists that I missed seeing a lot of their particular, human and often enough attractive qualities. I was becoming conveniently categorical, a tendency I fear too many "well-educated" people learn. Put still differently, I was becoming condescending, and in addition I was *using* people, using the South's blacks and using the South's whites, and here I use the word "use" in its utterly negative sense. There is a difference between on the one hand gaining information from people or working out one's various "needs" or "drives" "with" people, and on the other hand singling out one aspect or another of an individual's frame of mind in order to denigrate (or for that matter indiscriminately ennoble) him or her or everyone "like" him or her. Thus do blacks become beautiful and wonderful and infinitely good and patient beyond description and possessed of virtues no one else (certainly not anyone the white person doing the describing) has ever known before. Thus do southern whites become cruel and narrow and hateful and vicious beyond the power of words to convey. I suppose for me in either case I could only win; if I was unhappy with certain developments in the North, I could strike back with my heavily romanticized "observations" of southern blacks.

By the same token if I was looking for evidence of this nation's shortcomings I could take the many segregationists I was meeting and stand them up in my mind as proof. No doubt everyone has his axes to grind. Yet, it does seem wise that *we* grind them — rather than using others to do the job for us. If I want to criticize or denounce this country or any section of it I had best do so on my own — without misrepresenting the white and the black people of the South by turning them into wooden caricatures of themselves.

For me, a white doctor trying to fathom the complicated racial experience of the South, it was absolutely necessary to see and spend time with a broad range of Southerners. My wife, and the black families I knew first in the course of my study, realized this before I did. In addition to any academic or intellectual reasons, in a psychiatric study the investigator's state of mind is, of course, the "instrument" of the research. An outsider, a newcomer, a witness to unprecedented social change, I had to resist my constant desire to cast my lot, completely and unreservedly, with the black children I had come there to see — pioneers that they were, leaders of a region and maybe a nation, too. Instead I realized that I would be of more help to them if I maintained a certain distance. Since then, however, I have come to understand that I never had as much choice as even now I seem to indicate. There is a streak of rational skepticism in me, and as well an aversion to ideology, *all* ideology, which together made my decision to seek out many, many individuals of various and different backgrounds a virtual certainty.

On dozens of occasions at psychiatric and psychoanalytic meetings or conferences I have been asked what I "did" for the children or youths I worked with; less often, but still somewhat repeatedly, I have been asked what they "did" for or to me, how they "affected" me. As I have said on a number of occasions, it is rather obvious that "they" managed to educate me, to teach me a very great deal. But the colleagues of mine who asked the questions I just mentioned had what they call "subjective factors" in mind. I am not sure one can so easily distinguish between what one learns and how one feels. What one learns has a lot to do with how one feels. But I would have to say that as I continued working with black families in rural Mississippi and in the "industrial canal" section of New Orleans and, eventually, all over the South I found myself feeling admiration and at times awe that "they" could have survived, and can keep on surviving so very much! I also felt in myself stirrings of fear and resentment. I was being tested and at times teased, though I did my level best to push out of my mind the anger I felt, even as on more than one occasion I successfully managed not to notice such anger toward me, in those I was speaking with — not until much later, when I could "afford" to do so, when I was home again, walking and talking with my wife and sifting over what we had gone through and were in the middle of going through. If my wife and I often had difficulty acknowledging our fears and moments of anger, there were also unforgettable moments — when we recognized all too clearly the thinly veiled sarcasm, the scorn we were meant to hear, the envy, the wry humor that can express so very much: "I'll be thinking that you two are coming over for another visit, and I'll be glad. But I'll catch myself smiling. I'll catch myself chuckling and saying: My oh my, those two nice people from Boston, Massachusetts, are way down here in New Orleans, Louisiana, trying to find out how the world goes around. I sure hope they do; and when they do, I sure hope they come and let me know. I believe I do know already, but it would be nice to hear from a doctor, you know, what he's found out."

Psychiatrists use words like "transference" and "countertransference" when they attempt to indicate the various responses their patients make to them, and they to their patients.

Old expectations and desires, old spells of pain or indignation or affection (directed at, say, a parent or brother or sister) become newly evoked in our offices — and not only in the minds of those who come to us for "help." We, too, find awakened in us irrational responses to the irrationalities we are asked to comprehend and if possible banish. And of course some quite rational or "real" things get going between us and our patients; the past with its vexing, unsolved grievances presses upon the two individuals in the doctor's office, but they bring as well their present-day wishes and hopes to that meeting-place. The patient wants a kind of willing ear, wants for a few minutes respite, reassurance, the advice of someone not caught up in his or her network of human associations and involvements. The doctor wants to listen, to observe, to discern; he wants to affirm the meaning and value of his knowledge, his training — and yes, his very life. It is a complicated and from time to time a tortuous mix of emotions that come together in those offices and clinics; and an anthropologist or social observer or journalist has to struggle with the various motives and satisfactions and dissatisfactions he and his "subjects" confront each other with. I exclude the psychiatric fieldworker because I recognize that there is a special dimension added when for years a psychologically and socially harassed family (such as those, black and white, I worked with in the South) are visited quite regularly by a man who is a physician, a child psychiatrist. Maybe the issue is only one of degree — the intensity of relatedness may increase. Personal and emotional issues are being brought up again and again and are often discussed over long stretches of time. Maybe there is a qualitative difference, also; quite special anticipations and worries are aroused on both sides, the visitor's and that of the visited. Will he find out our secrets — secrets that only a person like him ever would want to, ever *could*, find out? Can he help us solve any number of personal or medical

or psychological problems we have hanging over us? And
from the doctor: What will I learn about their thoughts and
dreams and unacknowledged yearnings and unknown (to
them) rages or lusts or obsessions? And can I, over time, *do*
anything about what I catch sight of and hear spoken?

To get pedantic again, I am more certain now than when I
wrote the first volume of *Children of Crisis*, five years ago that
from the very start I was constantly seen as (and responded to
as) one who knows about the body's illnesses and the mind's
various ways of behaving. For all my intense and persistent
curiosity about the ways social customs and cultural traditions
(and a particular moment of history) affect the mind, I was
also trying to make sense of various complaints I was hearing
— personal complaints; and I was trying to say a word here, a
sentence or two there, which might clarify, interpret, enable
one or another person to exercise some measure of psychological control over his or her destiny.

In 1970, I was told this by a youth I had known for ten
years: "You talk about coming back to see us; we ought to
come North every once in a while and ask you 'How's it going?' I used to hear you ask that and I'd wonder what you
meant. Then I figured it was your way to get me or some of
the kids you see talking. Later I realized that you really did
want to know how it's going — the way a doctor does when he
asks you what seems like an innocent question, but then fixes
his eyes and ears on you! I know, I know; it's true, a good
reporter does the same thing. But some of those remarks you
would make, and the kind of questions you'd ask — well, reporters don't go asking about what my brother is doing, and
how he reacts to the civil rights struggle, or how he and I
handle our mother's need to go to church two or three times a
week, and be taken in by our minister, who's getting rich on
his poor flock! You've been zeroing in on the psychology,

brother, that's what; and once you start that, a guy gets to doing it himself. He'll go away from a talk, and he'll be driving up some dusty road in Butler County, Alabama — and the next thing he knows he's talking to himself, he's musing, he's asking himself: Well, what about *that?* What *about* that? And once you've begun asking the questions you can't so quickly stop. It's not that I never before had my moods and doubts. It's not that I'm accusing you of anything. It's just that when you talk with a doctor you end up knowing it, even if it takes you a while to catch on."

For a long time, several years, I was all taken up with that man's *deeds;* it was hard enough keeping track of them, and obtaining some idea how he managed psychologically to endure their consequences — countless arrests, episodes of confinement to a county jail or a state prison. He had to put up with setbacks, with progress that could in a flash be revealed as only a smallest step indeed forward. I always knew that it was of some help for him to sit and talk about all that with me, but I never quite knew at the time the significance of that help (and maybe I shouldn't have, because if things had become too self-conscious, he may well have said good-bye for keeps). I hope I am clear on this. I hope I make no excessive (or outrageous) claims — that such a person needed "treatment," and might have suffered God knows what fate had he not had the chance to talk with me. A fine thing it would be if I were to start parading one southern child or youth or parent after another before the reader, and in each case let slip how anxious or afraid or down in the dumps or overly sure of himself or herself (hence full of self-doubt) the person was — until, of course, the full benefit of our ever-so-important talks (I could even call them "sessions") was finally realized. No, I hardly believe we need thousands of psychiatrists "on the scene," there where the action is, manning the barricades alongside various social activists, or for that matter, at hand when those who resist change themselves take to the streets.

I am trying to get across the nature and tone of the "relationship" I have had with various Southerners for over a decade — and I am having trouble *defining* that nature or tone,
spelling it out exactly, formulating it in sentences that make
clear and pointed sense. Maybe I shouldn't be trying. Maybe
some events in this world defy wordy social scientists or psychiatrists, who all too often, anyway, go rushing to define
things, classify them, come up with statements about their
meaning. Still, one tries. One does what one was trained to
do — and of course (to some extent) wants to do. One keeps
on sifting experiences, turning around and around in the
mind memories of various conversations — the questions
asked over the years, the answers given, the outbursts, the acts
of kindness, the moments of tension. And in so doing one
comes back to certain exchanges which seemed then suddenly
luminous and later enormously instructive — and more important, sustaining: "We're glad you've been coming to see
us. There are so many of these damn Yankee Communist
types arriving in our state these days. They want to put their
noses into everyone's business — and meanwhile up in their
states (New York and places like that) there's all that crime
and violence, and the white people and the black people stay
clear of each other. We were raised with the colored. We
know them and they know us. You've heard that a hundred
times from us, but I finally do believe you're getting to *know*
it!

"It's meant a lot to us for you to talk with the children,
especially Jimmie. He's always wanted to go further. He's
told us since he started school that he wanted to go to college.
He broke his arm and he had to stay in the hospital, and after
that he wanted to be a doctor. I'm not sure we'll be able to
afford the cost of educating him; like I keep on telling you,
the white man isn't so fortunate. All you hear these days is

'the poor nigger, the poor nigger.' It's getting so the ordinary white man is beginning to believe that bellyaching talk from the radicals. But I do think this country would be better off if they let a boy like mine, bright as he is, rise as high as he wants to rise. Then, let a colored boy like him rise, too. It takes money to rise. The South is poor, you know. We don't have those big, rich, fancy schools you people do. Our minister told us that the whole country kicks us around, so they won't have to look at themselves right in the eye. My wife and I have decided we like speaking with you, just as the kids do — because with all the trouble we're having in this state now, you don't know what to think from day to day, and it begins to get on your nerves, all the changes and the uncertainty, you know. One day I wouldn't mind traveling through the country and seeing the whole of America. I've never been out of the South. Even when I was in the army I was stationed in Georgia and that's friendly territory — except for Atlanta, where all the northern left-wingers have been coming to settle. I think you've helped us see the country as others do, people who aren't living down here in Mississippi and Louisiana. I've not changed my mind about the colored — I always will feel they're *not us,* and that's that; but I agree with my boy that we shouldn't let them be bothering us all the time. I'll forget about them if only they'll leave the white man alone. If I had another life I wouldn't mind being one of you doctors. I guess you get to hear all kinds, don't you?"

There have been so many other moments with him — times when he really did rant and rave, times when he himself said he was losing his temper because he was so enraged at what he saw happening before him in his beloved South. He is proud, patriotic, military-minded, against all foreign countries, convinced "the white race is better than all other races and the Christian religion is better than all other religions," suspicious of strangers from the North or the West or even the upper South, where "they've been bought out by the race-mixers and the federal government in Washington, D.C.," a loving father and husband, a hard-working factory worker, a conscientious reader of Scripture, as he refers to the New Testament. He all along sensed my mixed feelings to him, even as I often tried to figure out how he could be so contradictory at times and not be bothered by that state of affairs. Needless to say, we always see the inconsistencies in others more easily than we keep in mind our own.

At the end of the talks I have just quoted from he delivered to me his surprise punch — at once his reminder of something and his fiercely self-assured statement about something and his plea for something: "I know you haven't liked all we've said to you these past ten years. My wife and I can tell. We never finished school, either of us, and I never once dreamed I could go to college, like my boy does, but we're not dumb, no sir. Too many people up there in the North think we're dumb. I can tell, listening to them talk, talk, talk on television. They look down on us. They think too highly of themselves; then they wonder why we don't like them any more than they like us. You held your tongue, though; and I guess we've grown to respect each other's opinions. I know you've never told me what you believe, but I'm sure you're for the colored. You must be. I guess if I were higher up on the ladder in this world I'd be looking on the poor colored and feeling sorry for them. A man like me, he has all he can do to look after himself, though. But I don't want you ever to forget this, please: We grew up with colored kids, my wife and I did, and we never have been mean to the good colored people. It's the lazy, no-good ones, the ones that push their way all over everyone — those are the people we're against. I'd feel the same way if a white man was elbowing into my rights and property, my life. The white man who wants to rise up, he just *does;* he leaves the rest of us alone and goes on to make himself a success. But the colored man always starts complaining about how bad the whites are, and how much money he wants from us, and everything else.

"I wish more people up North would come down here and talk with us. The last few years they've been coming down to our cities and towns and rushing over to the colored sections. My sister lives in Hattiesburg, Mississippi. She's pretty easy-going, much more so than I am. She's always been partial to the colored. She doesn't love them, but she feels sorry for them. She says she's been turned against the colored by the Yankees who come down here. They won't talk with us. A few years ago when those college students invaded this state, my sister saw some of them in the post office, and she tried to go and talk with them, but they turned up their noses at her. She told them she just wanted to hear their side of the argument, but they told her the state was bad, full of racists, that's what they called us. We're racists. Well, I don't believe my sister is that. She's been supporting two colored families for fifteen years. The women helped her out, and the next thing they got sick, and my sister paid for them to see the doctor, and she visits them and brings them money every other week. Do you know what her husband does? He's an auto mechanic. He's no rich plantation owner. I saw on television that the only white people of the South who are supposed to be nice to the colored are the plantation owners, and they're supposed to pat them on the heads, but not give them any money for the work they do out in the cotton fields. My sister has no cotton field, I'll tell you that. She works herself. That's right. She goes to an insurance company and types half a day, so her kids can go on with their schooling. And her husband all day is under those cars; he comes home so dirty that we joke with him and tell him he could pass for a real black nigger. I've been arguing with them for years; they tell me the colored deserve more. She's no believer in race-mixing. She doesn't like this school integration business. But she's not against the colored. She's not a racist. And those Yankee kids who came down here for the summer with their heads full of ideas, and so sure of themselves, and so preachy, and so sure they know everything and no one can tell them anything, because they've read all their books — well, I think they owe it to us (hell, they owe it to *themselves!*) to go speak with the white man in the South as well as the colored. And I'll tell you this: You can't separate the two, the two races, the two people — not down here you can't. Up North, yes; but not down here you can't."

If I needed what social scientists call a "methodological" justification for my visits to him and others like him, he provided me with one then. But I have to emphasize again that I came into his home in the first place for a complicated variety of reasons — and that complexity perhaps reflected the complexity of the social and political reality I was trying to learn about. I came to see him and his neighbors because they had chosen to become part of the lives of the black children whose predicament I initially wanted to study; by heckling those children, attempting to dissuade them from their chosen course (of entry into once all-white schools) such opponents in their own way became teachers, figures of prominence, people who matter — as this black girl's remarks indicate: "I don't think I'd know what to do if they all suddenly stopped coming one morning. I've got used to them. I don't mind them. I mean, I do; but after a while you can feel sorry for them. There are a few I think know better; they just can't help themselves. It's too bad. Our minister told us all to pray for them, but I keep on forgetting. I guess I'm finding out about the white people. I don't think all white people are the same. I think some white people are good and some bad. Going to school with them means you find out which are which, the good and the bad. I'd rather have the bad ones on the outside, shouting at me, and the good ones on the inside, trying to be as polite to me as I am to them. I told my uncle the other day that I really don't mind them standing out there and calling me names. You know why? I think to myself every morning that the worst of the day will be over, once I get myself into that building. If they weren't there, I might be nervous about what would happen once I got inside the building; but now I feel I'm past the really bad trouble, after I've stepped inside the school door, so I should turn around and smile at them and thank them for helping me out. But I never do."

Then she went on to tell me, as so many other blacks have told me, what to say when I talk with such people. Her advice was especially terse, ironically so in view of the longer, more drawn out, statements she could make at other times: "Maybe you could tell them I don't mind them being around." She was only fooling, of course. She was teasing me a little, of course. And since she knew I was talking with some of "them," she was in her own way trying to send a message. I also think she genuinely wanted to know why those people felt as they so obviously did, because often she would remind me that they do not know *her*. Moreover, her curiosity became mine, even as eventually I did just what she slyly suggested I do, tell some of the white families I was getting to know about the *particular* black families I was also getting to know — and vice versa.

Was I, then, running some kind of part-time college — in which I went back and forth, to and fro, furnishing one set of individuals information about another set? To be less grandiose, was I a messenger, maybe — or a mediator? I doubt any of those ways of putting things would strike either the blacks or whites I am describing or quoting in this section as very accurate or helpful. Unquestionably they all had many things in mind, including what I have just suggested. Yet, they were talking with *me*. They asked me constantly what

else I was doing, who else I was visiting, where else I might
one day go. They worried about me, even as they sensed my
own anxieties, my own self-questioning. What *was* I doing? I
believe I am not stretching things when I say that many of the
blacks and the whites I was spending time with wanted me to
"cross over" (as one black put it) and see "the other side" (as
he also put it) because they all knew in their bones that I was
in so many respects ignorant, and wanted and needed to be
educated. After all, how can one presume to write about people caught up in an extraordinarily difficult situation until he
knows that situation, knows by seeing and hearing all its elements? That is why I was told by one black youth to "go see
them," and by a white mother to "keep on talking with them,
so you can find out why they're not happy anymore, like they
used to be." Certainly I was often quite unable to appreciate
how much I needed to know that I didn't know, and how
clearly that state of affairs was appreciated by those I was
"studying," and how persistently in their own way they were
trying to educate me, broaden my horizons, make me more
aware.

Meanwhile, I was worrying about how "they" felt because I
also saw whites or *also* saw blacks. Was I suspect, a spy or a
double spy? What did I plan to do with what I heard and saw?
Those were the questions I asked myself, because I expected
to hear them asked of me — maybe awkwardly, maybe indirectly, but in time unmistakably. Indeed I was surprised, dis-
armed I think, by the open-mindedness (as I then looked
upon it) of the various individuals I was talking with. So, I
began to hear other questions in my mind. Were they "denying" the annoyance or anger or distrust they felt toward me?
Were they really "indifferent" — and was that why they
cared very little about what they (or anyone else) told me?
Were they simply not being candid? That is, did they object
strenuously to my apparent lack of complete identification

with their "side" or cause or whatever? Did they, rather, suspect (as I was beginning to suspect) that I was really at loose
ends, torn by conflicting purposes and ideals? I was a professional man who was trying to be "objective" and scrupulously
even-handed. I was a man with certain political views. I was a
man who had been brought up to have certain beliefs and
ethical standards. Any "participant observer" struggles with
all these things; yet, I wonder how often we give those we
"study" credit for sensing our struggles, wanting to help *us*,
and indeed having in mind some of the same conflicting interests or aims we do.

I knew in 1961 or 1962 that I needed the "balanced" viewpoint, the more complete or broader or many-sided viewpoint
I have just been talking about. I knew during those years that
at times it was painfully awkward or unnerving for me in certain black homes — and later for altogether different reasons
or for similar reasons I would experience discomfort or nervousness in a white home. Meanwhile I was hearing, but not
quite taking in for all its significance, advice like this: "You'll
find it hard to talk with a lot of the people here on this street.
I believe you will. In Mississippi we never saw white people
inside our houses; they would be friendly if we knew them,
though we had to get out of their way when they were walking down the street and they had a bad mood stirring inside
them, and you could see it on their faces. Here there will be
the white salesman who comes to see you. I guess they think
we have some money, now that we've come to the city. But
before you there was nobody white sitting in one of our
chairs. Now, do you think there are some white people in this
part of the country, in the South, who would ever let a colored man (be he a doctor, or a lawyer, you know) come over
and sit and talk? I guess not. It's not a two-way street, America; and I guess that's always going to hold. So, you're a lucky
man. You can go in one direction to the colored people, then

you can go and speak with the whites. I won't call them your own people. I was going to, but I know better. Maybe I shouldn't even talk like I'm talking now. Maybe it's not right to speak so. My wife told me the other day I should, though. She said you'd catch what we mean. She said you were trying to find out all you could, and she thought you felt ashamed of yourself for being with the white people, for going over and taking their coffee, like you do ours. I told her if you could take it — listening to them and hearing all that's going through their heads — then you were entitled to more than coffee from us, yes sir. I wouldn't want to sit in their living rooms and hear that talk. But there's no chance I ever will.

"Don't you go and apologize to us. Don't tell us about your work, how you have to see all the people you can. I know you do. You told us that the first time we met, and afterwards my wife said you sure were worried that you'd hurt our feelings or that we wouldn't see what you were up to. Well, we do. I told my wife after you first came here: He'd be the most help to us if he went over to them, to the white folks. Lord, white folks can be mean; and if I was that mean, I'd sure be down on my hands and knees praying to the Almighty God up in Heaven, asking Him: Why is it, why do I feel so mean toward those poor colored folks over there? Maybe you can find out; then you can come and tell us. Then we'll know. Maybe it won't make any difference in the way we live, but we'll know. Our minister says every Sunday: If you can see ahead, even if it's a tough road, you're not in such bad shape. It's when you can't see that you're in trouble. So, you go ahead and visit with them; and don't be thinking we're going to turn on you because a lot of the time you're hearing bad things about us and sipping their coffee. You can't know us if you don't hear for yourself what we hear. Oh, do we!"

From another father I would hear blacks called all sorts of names. I would hear President Kennedy and his brother the

Attorney General called all sorts of names. I would hear the Jews and the Catholics consigned to Hell, whence they supposedly have escaped to plague the South. I would hear rich people called "nigger lovers," and universities called "centers of Communism." And if I was disgusted and if I wondered why indeed I was there, "sipping their coffee," I was upon occasion stopped short in my tracks. I was told in no uncertain terms to stop and wait and not take anyone's ideas for granted; and important for this particular part of this particular book, I was told *why* I shouldn't do so: "It's a funny world. My granddaddy used to tell me that scratch a white man and you'll find a nigger, and scratch a nigger and you'll find a white man. He said the white people of the South have been keeping the niggers going, and it's the same with us; the niggers keep us going. He didn't mean the money or the work; he meant that we're all in the same boat here, and the real enemy is those Yankee bankers. They own us. I tell you they do — and a lot of people don't want to know that. We're each of us too busy trying to get through one day and then the next day, so we say to ourselves that we're just not going to worry about spilt milk; they beat us, the Yankees did, and then they plundered us, and what can you do but shrug your shoulders and go on. That's why I like the Klan. That's why I think they're doing a good job; they scare them up North. The Yankees may own us, but they're sure scared, a lot of them, to come down here and push us around. They just pull their strings up in New York City and places like that.

"No one is fooled, though; not us and not the nigger, either. I feel sorry for the poor nigger. Do you think a white man can understand them? I've wondered sometimes. I grew up with them and played with them all the time when I was a kid. I go home to my daddy's place upstate and I'll go fishing again with Old Joe. They call him Old Joe, but he's my age, thirty-seven. He's not old. His hair turned white, fast, when he was twenty-five, maybe. The next thing I knew he was Old Joe. I don't think anyone would call me Old Charlie if my hair turned. But they have a cheerful mentality, I've always noticed. I read in the paper, I hear on television, that they're marching all over, and they will keep on marching. I think it's a small minority of them that marches. You know better, you've been taught how to look into their minds. Do you think you'll find much? I mean, will they trust you? Today you hear they don't trust any white man. Today they try to tell you, the experts, that if the nigger smiles at you and tries to be obliging, he's really wanting to cut your throat, only he's afraid he'll end up in prison for the rest of his life or be killed. I know different. I know the talks I've had with Old Joe. He'd tell me what was on his mind — everything. I'd go and help him. It wasn't just money; I'd hear him out and he'd hear me out.

"When my mother died, it was him I first cried in front of. He went and got me a towel. He asked me if I wanted something to drink. I told him no. I was afraid I'd cry out every single bit of water I took in, or beer, too. When he lost his boy in an accident (he drowned) I was there visiting his family, and I helped him out. He turned to me and he recalled all the good times he'd had with his boy — and with me when we were kids. But maybe I've figured out everything wrong. Maybe there's a big fence between us, the white and the colored. That's not what I think. That's not what I grew up to know. But it may be changing down here. In the city it's different, even in the South, even in New Orleans. (You can't go further South than New Orleans and be in the United States.) So, you go and talk with them and find out. Find out what they want from us. If they're going to be getting mad at us all the time, we'd better get ready for them."

It is not difficult to dismiss him with words: He is bitter, hateful, arrogant and at times laughably (if it all weren't so tragic) parochial. Yet, he urged me to see his version of "them" even as "they" urged me to see the likes of him. As I have indicated, I had good "objective" reasons to do so; and I also had my own limitations as a human being to overcome. There were just so many harassed black families I could visit without feeling overwhelmed with sadness and shame and despair; and there were just so many white families I could visit without feeling quite similar emotions. Yet, because I went back and forth the whole effort seemed somewhat easier. Maybe I managed to achieve temporary distance on one kind of difficulty by plunging into another. I do not deny that I met up with common assumptions, too; anyone who knows the region knows what the two races share. Perhaps the two negatives in this case amounted to a positive of sorts — in that at least I was able to keep going, keep visiting, keep listening and looking and gaining some sense of the richness in the lives of those supposedly "average" or "poor" people — "niggers" the whites call some, and "red-necks" the blacks call others.

So, it was not as hard and trying as it sometimes most assuredly seemed — or at least I can say that now. I was in fact refreshed (yes, somehow) by moving from one section of a city to another, and from one group of people to another. The crucial word, obviously, is "refreshed"; I could go on and on spelling out the psychological implications that word has for me. It was serious and upon occasion painful "business," the talks we had in the early and middle sixties. Still, there were good and satisfying moments — times when we enjoyed a meal together, a laugh together, a bit of simple, direct, everyday talk, unburdened by the weighty national and regional issues of the day, not to mention a lot of high-strung self-consciousness. One man's mind, up against the quite definite limitations of his own history and experiences, found in variability, in motion, in the intricacies and subtleties of the South's society, a certain workable challenge — that is, something (in spite of stretches of discouragement) provocative and stimulating and again, *refreshing*.

Index

Abernathy, Tom, 98, 99, 103
Activists, civil rights, 5, 10, 67, 78–79, 132, 146, 181–199, 363; black student, 181–199, 323–333; background of, 187–189; life style, in South, 189–190, 192–193; field secretaries, 190, 193; notoriety received by, 191, 244, 268; white student, 199–204, 334–354; living with danger, 204–212; evaluation of, 213–218; despair and weariness of, 221–241, 251–252; clinical symptoms of, 226–229, 231–233, 249, 253–254; sense of betrayal in, 227–228; war language of, 231, 251, 253, 344; suspicion and aloofness of, 231, 242; rejection of Negro stereotype, 233–234; guilt and self-doubt, 234–239, 244–245; level of psychological development, 236–238; vulnerability of, 238–239; and Mississippi Summer Project of 1964, 243–256; optimism of veteran, 255; psychological adjustment of those who return to school, 255; accomplishments of, 255–256; thinly disguised slandering of, 285–293; attitudinal changes in, 323–333, 337–354. See also Civil rights movement
Adams County, Mississippi, 54, 55
Adolescents, 152–158; attitudes of, 153; their evaluation of social changes, 298–322
Agee, James, 274, 276; his *Let Us Now Praise Famous Men* (with Evans), 6, 47–48
"Agitation," 54, 104, 129
Agriculture, U.S. Department of, 96, 97, 117
Alabama, 5, 6, 12, 23, 30, 113; sit-in movement in, 78; welfare payments in, 117; freedom rides, 188
Albany, Georgia, 83
Alcoholism, 41, 189
Allen, Ivan, 67

Ambivalence, 390–392, 397–398; toward the Yankee visitor in South, 347–348; of black child, 392–393
Anderson, Margaret, 164, 165; her *Children of the South*, 145, 166–169
Anger, 186–187; Negro, 25, 43–44, 56, 57; student protester, 227
Anthony, Paul, 17
Anxiety, 148–150, 154, 204–212, 221; in student activist, 227–228, 231–234, 249
Apathy, Negro, 25, 41–42, 56, 324; and student activist, 190, 226
Appalachia, 4, 86, 98, 285; children's health in, 170–171
Arizona, 98
Arkansas Gazette, 131
Arnall, Ellis, 69, 70
Arrests, of activists, 188–189, 191, 234
Asheville, North Carolina, 188, 365
Atlanta, 4, 25, 28, 43, 49, 145, 182, 322, 365; and Maddox, 67, 68; Negro leadership in, 80; school desegregation crisis, 152–156, 242; teachers of, 158; changing attitudes in, 161; demonstrations in, 188; "northern left-wingers" in, 389
Atlanta Constitution, 70
Atlanta Journal, 81
Attitudes, 14, 147, 151–152, 366, 370; of adolescents, 153; of teachers, 158–159; changes in, 159–162; of student activist, 246, 249–250; of black civil rights workers, 323–333; of white civil rights worker, 334–354; of Klansman, 355–362; toward the author, 374–378, 388–389
Auden, W. H., 271, 272, 273
Austin, Texas, 113

Backlash, 264, 356, 371–372, 388–389
Baldwin, James, 21, 37–46
Barnett, Ross, 53
Batesville, Mississippi, 12, 348

Humanities, relevance of, 271–284
Humphrey, Hubert H., 352
Humphreys County, Mississippi, 96, 103, 172
Hunger, 81, 86, 87, 145; in Mississippi, 95, 99, 103, 173–174; in Texas, 107–108, 115–116
"Hunger in America," CBS documentary, 97
Hunger, USA, Citizen's Board of Inquiry into Hunger and Malnutrition in America, 97
"Hungry Children," Southern Regional Council report, 96, 145–146
Hypocrisy, 178–179, 182; of the North, 367–368

Identity: Negro, 44, 45; regional, 48–49; racial, 151; of civil rights activist, 234
Income, 55, 89, 102, 103; for Mexican-Americans, 109–111; Texas, 109, 114, 117
Indianola, Mississippi, 99
Indians, American, 98, 262, 368
Industry, 7, 69, 134
Infant mortality, 87–89, 93, 102; in Texas, 109–110, 117; in Mississippi, 175
Intimidation, 148–149, 155

Jackson, Mississippi, 255
Jacksonville, Florida, 83
James, Henry, 277, 278
Jasper, Georgia, 69
Jasper County, South Carolina, 85, 87
Job Corps, 100
Johnson, Lyndon, 69, 86, 290
Johnson, Paul, 95
Johnston, Isabelle, 17
Johnston, Paul, 17

Kasper, John, 165
Keesler Air Force Base, Biloxi, Mississippi, 3, 23
Kennedy, John F., 28, 45, 69, 79, 370, 396; and voter registration projects, 80
Kennedy, Robert F., 28, 44, 97, 301, 357, 397; death of, 352, 353, 356, 358
Key, V. O., Jr., 76, 77, 131
King, Dr. Martin Luther, Jr., 17, 129, 257, 258, 301, 322, 351, 357; death of, 352, 353, 356, 358
Knoxville, Tennessee, 164
Ku Klux Klan, 5, 7, 11, 128, 363, 369, 382, 397; in Natchez, 54; attitudinal changes, 355–362
Kwashiorkor, 95

Laing, R. D., 291
"Law and order," 27, 57, 61, 78, 178

Laws, 31. *See also* Civil rights legislation
Lay My Burden Down (documentary), 61
Leadership, Negro, 79–80, 364–365
Leflore County, Mississippi, 96, 103, 172
Legislation, civil rights, *see* Civil rights legislation
Lexington Advertiser, 132
"Liberty House," 65
Libraries, 54, 78, 188
Limestone County, Texas, 108, 115; income statistics, 117
Literacy, 41, 89, 112, 226
Little Rock, 67, 83, 145, 164, 365
Long, Margaret, 6, 7, 9, 11, 13, 17, 145
Los Angeles, 113
Louisiana, 5, 8–9, 11–12, 32, 146, 364, 367, 368; southern mentality, 49; sit-in movement, 78; and voter registration projects, 80; school desegregation in, 178 (*see also* New Orleans); adolescents' reactions to social change in, 298–322; a Klansman's view, 359–361
Lowndes County, Alabama, 170

McCarthy, Cormac, 119–126
McComb, Mississippi, 49
McComb Enterprise-Journal, 132
McCullers, Carson, 277
MacDonald, Dr. Marjorie, 363, 364, 365
McGill, Ralph, 17
McLennan County, Texas, 108, 116, 117
Maddox, Lester Garfield, 66–75, 81, 129, 355; Pickrick restaurant, 67–68, 72; gubernatorial campaign, 68–70; post-election behavior, 70–72; and patronage, 72; his "selling" of Georgia, 73–75
Mailer, Norman, 44
Malnutrition, 81, 86, 88–89; in Mississippi, 95–105, 172–174; in Texas, 107–108, 115; and pregnancy, 171
Marasmus, 95
Marshall, Thurgood, 365
Meade, Edward, 17
Medical care, 95–96, 171–177; in South Carolina, 85–94 *passim*; in Mississippi, 100–102, 171–177; for Mexican-Americans, 110; and pregnancy, 171
Medical facilities, 27, 96, 176
Medical personnel, Negro, 176–177
Meredith, James, 44
Mermann, Dr. Alan, 170n
Metcalfe, George, 54
Methodology, author's, 3–17, 21–22,

145–147, 297, 363–400; justification, 13–14, 363, 392; and use of
psychiatric jargon, 15
Mexican-Americans, 108–111; and Bilingual Education Bill, 111–112;
unemployment among, 112; and
La Raza, 112–113
Miami News, 131
Miami University, Oxford, Ohio, 266
Middle class, black, 25, 42
Migrants, 4, 5, 27, 170
Migration, Negro to North, 60, 63, 100,
371; and southern "way of life,"
130
Milam County, Texas, 108
Mississippi, 3, 5, 12, 21, 23, 48, 76,
113, 132–133, 364; school desegregation, 24; southern mentality in,
49; and film *Black Natchez,* 53–
59; Negro migration from, 60–61;
and sit-in movement, 78; and civil
rights movement, 83; disease and
malnutrition in, 95–105, 145; University of, 99, 104; welfare system,
117, 171, 175–176; newspapers on,
131–132; health of children in,
170–177; Negro population, 175;
freedom rides, 188; Head Start
program in, 254; progress in desegregation, 254–255; Negro education in, 279–283
Mississippi Delta, 12, 95
Mississippi Freedom Democratic Party,
57
Mississippi Summer Project of 1964, 5,
12, 54, 81, 146, 243, 322, 350;
orientation period for, 219–220,
243–244, 246–249, 254, 266–270;
recruitment for, 243; testing of
participants' motivation, 244, 245;
deaths of participants, 244, 267–
269, 340; medical and psychiatric
evaluation of participants, 246–
248, 268; unity of participants,
248–250, 270–274, 349; and participants' accommodation to poverty, 250–251; and participants'
accommodation to their role, 251–
253; historical significance of,
267; relevance of humanities to,
274–276; "slander" of participants,
285
Mobs, 83, 299, 301
Model Cities program, 116
Montgomery, Alabama, 113
Moore, William, 30
Moses, Bob, 80
Mountaineers, 4, 5, 27, 120
Mount Olive Baptist Church, Georgia,
79
Movie houses, 181, 184, 188, 357
Music, 130, 271, 278; and Negro, 280
Myths, racial, 160. *See also* Stereotypes

NAACP, 25, 365, 375–376; Natchez, 54,
55
Nashville, Tennessee, 188
Natchez, Mississippi, 53–59; violence
in, 53, 54, 57; population and
income statistics, 55
Natchez Democrat, 54
Natchez Free Trader, 54
National Academy of Sciences, 40
National Guard, Mississippi, 55, 57
Nationalism, black, 259–260, 264
Needmore, North Carolina, 120
Neely, Alvin, Jr., 17
Negro, southern, 7; and the white
man, 10, 11; and black power, 38–
39, 46, 58, 147, 257–265, 356;
white man's hatred and abuse of,
25–26; in South Carolina popula-
tion, 84; in Texas, 113; and the
Movement, 181–199, 223–224; stereotype, 233–234, 262, 368; Carmi-
chael's view, 259–260; as presence
in society, 260–262. *See also*
White-Negro relationship
Neshoba County, Mississippi, 172, 274,
340
Neuman, David, 53
New Mexico, 113
New Orleans, 4, 25, 83, 145, 298, 302,
322, 375, 398; school desegregation crisis in, 11, 26, 39–40, 43, 49,
148–152, 164, 178–180, 298–299,
301; riots, 67; and the author,
365, 366–367, 374
New Republic, 21, 145
New South, Southern Regional Council
quarterly, 6, 9, 81, 257
New World Foundation, 17
New York, 12, 60
New York Times, 64, 339
Nixon, Richard M., 86, 93–94, 99, 290,
352, 358, 359
Nonviolence, 181–218, 222; defined,
185–186
North, 12, 24, 49, 356; Negro migration
to, 60, 63; race riots in, 350;
hypocrisy of, 367–368
North Carolina, 28, 30, 83; University
of, 131
"Nostalgia," 10, 12–13, 50
Novel, southern, 13, 21–22, 37
Nutrition, 171–172. *See also* Malnutri-
tion

O'Connor, Flannery, 21, 22, 136, 276
Odum, Howard, 130–131
Office of Economic Opportunity, 100
Oklahoma, 103
Olmstead, Frederick, 54
O'Neal, John, 80
Operation Head Start, *see* Head Start
program
Orwell, George, 276
Oxford, Ohio, 219–220, 243–244, 246–

Vitamin deficiency, 41, 88–89, 172–173, 189
Vote, 23, 24, 26, 28, 54, 60, 184, 259–261, 337, 338, 348, 357; registration projects, 32, 41, 78–81, 181, 243, 336, 343, 350, 351 (*see also* Mississippi Summer Project); and the Government, 100
Voter Education Project, Southern Regional Council, 80–81
Voting rights bill, 79

Waco, Texas, 107, 108, 116, 117
Walker, Alice, 21, 137–141
Wallace, George C., 31, 129, 290, 341, 355, 359; in election of 1968, 358
Walwyn, Dr. Cyril, 170n
Warren, Robert Penn, 21, 134, 276
Washington, D.C., 62, 64; Lafayette Square, 62; Rayburn Building, 64
Washington Post, 64–65, 339
Watson, Tom, 66, 67, 75
Watters, Pat, 17, 76–77, 79, 81–82, 127–136
Watts, 58
Waycross, Georgia, 69
Wayne County, Mississippi, 172
Weather, 298–299; in black's imagery, 319–320
Weber, Max, 278
Weil, Simone, 276
Welfare, 7, 60, 63, 87, 358, 370; in Texas, 110, 111, 112, 114, 117; in Mississippi, 117, 171, 175–176
Welty, Eudora, 276
Western College for Women, Oxford, Ohio, 244, 266. *See also* Mississippi Summer Project, orientation
Wheeler, Dr. Raymond, 171n
White Citizens Council, 7, 11, 355, 369, 382
White-Negro relationship, 11, 27, 34–36, 49, 187, 343, 388; in Grau's

novel, 32–36; in Baldwin's novel, 37; intimacy in, 45, 49; in the North, 49; and student activists, 181–185; adolescents' views, 302–322; Klansman's view, 355–362; ambivalence in, 390–392, 397–398
"White power," 55. *See also* Power structure
Whites: as oppressors, 10; love of Negro, 11; historic relationship with Negro, 27; in the Movement, 199–204; ambivalence toward Negro, 390–392, 397–398
Whitten, Jamie L., 85–86, 96–105, 115
Wilkins, Roy, 259
William Faulkner Foundation Award, *see* Faulkner, William
Williams, "Big Joe," 283
Williams, W. C., 272
Wilson, Woodrow, 24
Wisdom, John Minor, 131
Women, southern, 166–167
Woodall Mountain, 99
Woodward, C. Vann, 164; his *Tom Watson: Agrarian Rebel*, 66, 128–129; *The Burden of Southern History*, 131
Wright, Richard, 276
Writers, southern, 76. *See also* Novel, southern
Wyckoff, Elizabeth, 80

Yalobusha County, Mississippi, 99
Yankees, in South, 7, 9, 335–338, 341–342, 345, 388, 391–392, 397; southern ambivalence toward, 347–348
Yarborough, Ralph, 111
Yazoo City, Mississippi, 348
Yeoman, southern, 47, 128; of Appalachia, 120
Young, Whitney, 259
Youth, nonviolent, 181–218